The Aircraft Commander in International Air Transportation

The Aircraft Commander in International Air Transportation

Legal Powers, Duties and Decision Making

Dick van het Kaar

In memory of Dr. Menno Sjoerd Kamminga and Dr. Aart Adriaan van Wijk

eleven

Published, sold and distributed by Eleven
P.O. Box 85576
2508 CG The Hague
The Netherlands
Tel.: +31 70 33 070 33
Fax: +31 70 33 070 30
e-mail: sales@elevenpub.nl
www.elevenpub.com

Sold and distributed in USA and Canada
Independent Publishers Group
814 N. Franklin Street
Chicago, IL 60610, USA
Order Placement: +1 800 888 4741
Fax: +1 312 337 5985
orders@ipgbook.com
www.ipgbook.com

Eleven is an imprint of Boom (Den Haag).

ISBN 978-90-4730-179-0
ISBN 978-94-0011-345-9 (E-book)

© 2024 Dick van het Kaar | Eleven

TABLE OF CONTENTS

INTRODUCTION

Unparalleled advancements in technology followed the first historic flight attempts of the Wright Brothers on 17 December 1903 at Kill Devil Hills near Kitty Hawk, North Carolina, with the overwhelming result that the entire aviation industry has evolved into a factor affecting virtually every area of world society.

The international aviation industry undoubtedly plays an important role in the global economic system and remains one of the fastest-growing sectors in that field. Indeed, the complex mechanism of the modern aviation system can only function through dedication, willpower and combined efforts, as well as the teamwork of countless individuals. Among those who are part of these joint efforts, the aircraft commander occupies a rather exceptional place.

> If one regards an aircraft in flight – together with all the persons and goods on board – as a small community temporarily cut off from the rest of society, it is clear that this community needs to have some rule of law. In view of the international character of civil aviation, it is desirable that such a rule of law should apply all over the world.[1]

During flight time, the aircraft commander, as the lead person in charge of its airline operator, has full authority and responsibility over the entire operation and safety of the aircraft and maintains good order and discipline towards all persons on board. In the time frame of emerging international air transportation, the aircraft commander was considered an individual, a man with a dominant appearance, guts and competence, giving him a sort of seemingly heroic image with greying hair and a calm reassuring voice, occasionally approachable during cruise flight through the open cockpit door.[2] However, times have changed.

---

1 Kamminga, M.S., *The Aircraft Commander in Commercial Air Transportation, Proefschrift ter Verkrijging van de Graad van Doctor in de Rechtsgeleerdheid aan de Universiteit te Leiden, op Gezag van de Rector Magnificus Dr. J.J.L. Duyvendak, Hoogleraar in de Faculteit der Letteren en Wijsbegeerte, Tegen de Bedenkingen van de Faculteit der Rechtsgeleerdheid te Verdedigen op Woensdag 1 April 1953 te 16 Uur* (The Hague: Martinus Nijhoff, 1953), p. 169.

2 Air transportation refers to the movement of people, goods and materials through the third dimension, usually in heavier-than-air vehicles such as commercial air transport (unmanned) aircraft that can sustain controlled flight. As air transportation and air transport are related terms, there is a slight difference in meaning. Air transportation is a broader term than air transport because air transportation encompasses all of the systems, infrastructure and services to move people, goods and materials. In this book both terms are used accordingly.

Rapid advances in technology, especially in the aviation industry, and changing global social behaviour such as, for example, hijacking and unruly and disruptive passengers, have turned today's aircraft commander into a virtually undetermined aircraft flight management system operator, hidden behind a closed key-coded, reinforced cockpit door. However, heroism is sometimes present in the cockpit when it comes to solving extremely complicated problems and then to make the right decisions to be able to execute a safe landing.

In international aviation, the aircraft commander is undoubtedly regarded as an interesting authoritative personality. Travelling by air in a relatively short period of time through many different sectors of airspace over the territories of sovereign States with their own distinct yet diverse national jurisdictions can have serious consequences with regard to criminal offences and other unlawful acts committed on board aircraft.[3]

In the past, this determination ensured that the position of the aircraft commander required a legal basis for his or her legal status in the discharge of his or her duties. At the international level, after a long time of studies and deliberations, the aircraft commander has been vested with certain powers as laid down in the provisions of the 1963 Tokyo Convention on Offences and Certain Other Acts Committed on Board Aircraft (hereinafter referred to as the Tokyo Convention).

As an aircraft commander, he or she is the most highly trained, experienced, qualified and certified person on board an aircraft, driven by the knowledge of procedures and practical experiences. The aircraft commander is able to analyse multiple data input and make decisions in a challenging environment by managing resources like flight instruments, aircraft systems, team spirit, coherent information and common sense, often in a short period of time. However, multiple human factors and external conditions may influence decision making in an aeronautical environment, albeit rarely resulting in pilot error, which in itself can jeopardize flight safety for which the pilot may be held legally liable for any consequences.

Modern aircraft increasingly rely on automation, basically the technology-oriented approach to automatic flight. But this does not prevent human error, possibly, on the contrary! Hence, automation must remain subordinate to the human supervisor. Nevertheless, single-pilot operations (SiPO) or even fully autonomous unmanned passenger carrying aircraft are typical future concepts which, however, raise new questions.

This book is about the legal status of the aircraft commander or pilot-in-command as defined by the International Civil Aviation Organization (ICAO, in the text also referred

---

3   The term 'jurisdiction' refers to the power of States to subject persons or property to their national laws, judicial institutions or enforcement capacity.

to as the Organization). After the Introduction, Chapter 1 emphasizes the historical course of events regarding the origin of the aircraft commander's powers.

Chapter 2 deals with the characteristics of international legal instruments and documentation on the legal status of the aircraft commander.

Chapter 3 provides information about human factors potentially affecting flight operations, especially human decision making. It is also dedicated to the issue of unmanned aircraft systems (UAS), whether they are remotely piloted or fully autonomously operated. In the future, these state-of-the-art unmanned aircraft lack, however, an onboard authority equivalent to the ultimate skilled specialist who, in this case, is the aircraft commander vested with appropriate powers.

In the editorial context of this book, the observation will also relate to the use of pronouns since in the texts of ancient but still prevailing aviation conventions and documentations, reports and minutes of meetings of the legal commissions of ICAO as well as the *Comité International Technique d'Experts Juridiques Aériens* (CITEJA) and a number of air law conferences the designation 'he' is used in all relevant formal texts and had prevailed until long after World War II even when both male and female were equally addressed. Even in the 2006 Ninth Edition of the Convention on International Civil Aviation (hereinafter referred to as the Chicago Convention), some articles have been still using 'he' and 'his' for a person in the text, which may be based on the one hand on non-gender-specific language use.[4] The same applies for other subject-relevant convention texts. On the other hand, ICAO has made a switch to the 'he/she' and 'his/her' designations in some Annexes and other documentation.[5]

In consequence, this book retains the designation 'he' in order to remain consistent with relevant ancient authentic texts and uses 'he/she' and 'his/her' if applicable based on contemporary, modern formal texts from different sources with regard to the aircraft commander's legal status, powers, duties and decision making.

Also, thereby the author firmly supports the pursuit of gender equality in the global aviation industry.

---

4   Art. 39 Endorsment of certificates and licenses, under (b) states: Any person holding a license who does not satisfy in full the conditions laid down in the international standard relating to the class of license or certificate which he holds shall have endorsed on or attached to his license a complete enumeration of the particulars in which he does not satisfy such conditions.

5   *See* ICAO Annex 1 – *Personnel Licensing,* Fourteenth Edition, July 2022, Chapter 2, Para. 2.12.3, ICAO Annex 2 – *Rules of the Air,* Tenth Edition, July 2005, Attachment B, Para. 2.1, ICAO Annex 6 – *Operation of Aircraft* Part I – *International Commercial Air Transport – Aeroplanes,* Twelfth Edition, July 2022, Chapter 1, Definitions, Flight duty period, ICAO Annex 16 – *Environmental Protection* Volume II – *Aircraft Engine Emissions,* Fourth Edition, July 2017, Appendix 6, Para. 3.1 and ICAO 17 – *Aviation Safety – Safeguarding Civil Aviation against Acts of Unlawful Interference,* Twelfth Edition, July 2022, Attachment B, Para. 2 Procedures.

Abbreviations

AAM	Advanced Air Mobility
ACAS	Aircraft Collision Avoidance System
ACI	Airport Council International
ACMI	Aircraft, Crew, Maintenance and Insurance (Wet Lease)
ADF	Automatic Direction Finding
ADM	Aeronautical Decision Making
ADREP	Accident/Incident Data Reporting
ADS-B	Automatic Dependent Surveillance-Broadcast
AGL	Above Ground Level
AI/ML	Artificial Intelligence/Machine Learning
AIREP	Air Report
ANC	Air Navigation Commission
ANNs	Artificial Neural Networks
AOM	Aircraft Operating Manual
ASR	Automatic Speech Recognition
ATC	Air Traffic Control
ATFM	Air Traffic Flow Management
ATIS	Automatic Terminal Information Service
ATM	Air Traffic Management
ATS	Air Traffic Services
ATTOL	Autonomous Taxi, Take-Off and Landing (Project)
CAA	United Kingdom Civil Aviation Authority
CAR	United States Civil Air Regulations
CFR	United States Code of Federal Regulations
CHM	Common Heritage of Mankind
CIDPA	Conférence Internationale de Droit Privé Aérien
CINA	Commission Internationale de Navigation Aérienne
CITEJA	Comité International Technique d'Experts Juridiques Aériens
CofA	Certificate of Airworthiness
CONOPS	Concept of Operations
CRM	Crew Resource Management
CUI	Committee on Unlawful Interference (ICAO)
DL	Deep Learning

DLNN	Deep Learning Neural Network
EASA	European Union Aviation Safety Agency
ECAC	European Civil Aviation Conference
EFB	Electronic Flight Bag
EFIS	Electronic Flight Instrument System
EGPWS	Enhanced Ground Proximity Warning System
EICAS	Engine Indicating and Crew Alerting System
eMCO	extended Minimum Crew Operation
eVTOL	electric Vertical Take-Off and Landing
FAA	United States Federal Aviation Administration
FAI	Fédération Aéronautique Internationale
FCOM	Flight Crew Operating Manual
FITAP	Fédération Internationale des Transports Aériens Privés
FLIR	Forward-Looking Infrared Sensor
FMA	Flight Mode Annunciator
FMC	Flight Management Computer
FPFM	Flight Planning and Fuel Management
GBAS	Ground-Based Augmentation System
GenDec	General Declaration
GLS	GBAS Landing System
GNSS	Global Navigation Satellite System
GPS	Global Positioning System
HIC	Human in Command
HITL	Human in the Loop
IATA	International Air Transport Association
ICAN	International Commission for Air Navigation
ICAO	International Civil Aviation Organization
IDSS	Intelligent Decision Support System
IFALPA	International Federation of Air Line Pilots' Associations
IFR	Instrument Flight Rules
IFSO	In-Flight Security Officer
ILA	International Law Association
ILS	Instrument Landing System
IoT	Internet of Things
ITCZ	Inter-Tropical Convergence Zone
LIDAR	Laser Imaging Detection and Ranging
LOSA	Line Operations Safety Audit

MFD	Multifunction Flight Display
MSL	Mean Sea Level
NASA	National Aeronautics and Space Administration
NDM	Naturalistic Decision Making
NLP	Natural Language Processing
NOTAM	Notice to Airmen
NTSB	National Transportation Safety Board
OGHFA	Operators Guide to Human Factors in Aviation
PANS	Procedures for Air Navigation Services
PF	Pilot Flying
PICAO	Provisional International Civil Aviation Organization
PLO	Palestinian Liberation Organization
PM	Pilot Monitoring
PMS	Performance Management System
RA	Resolution Advisory
RCO	Reduced Crew Operation
RPA	Remotely Piloted Aircraft
RPAS	Remotely Piloted Aircraft System
SAR	Search and Rescue
SARPs	ICAO's Standards and Recommended Practices
SIGMET	Significant Meteorological Information
SiPO	Single-Pilot Operation
SMM	Safety Management Manual
SOFA	Status of Forces Agreement
SOP	Standard Operating Procedure
SSB	Solid-State Battery
SSR	Secondary Surveillance Radar
SUPPs	Regional Supplementary Procedures
TA	Traffic Advisory
TCAS	Traffic Alert and Collision Avoidance System
TEM	Threat and Error Management
UA	Unmanned Aircraft
UAM	Urban Air Mobility
UAS	Unmanned Aircraft System
UAV	Unmanned Aerial Vehicle
ULR	Ultra-Long-Range
UN	United Nations
USOAP	Universal Safety Oversight Audit Programme
USSR	Union of Soviet Socialist Republics

UTC	Universal Time Coordinated
UTM	Unmanned Aircraft Systems Traffic Management
VLL	Very Low Level (Airspace)
VOR	Very High Frequency Omni-Directional Range
VPA	Virtual Pilot Assistant

1 HISTORICAL APPROACH TO THE LEGAL STATUS OF THE AIRCRAFT COMMANDER

1.1 THE NEED FOR A LEGAL STATUS OF THE AIRCRAFT COMMANDER IN INTERNATIONAL LAW

If one considers a commercial aircraft in flight as a small community temporarily separated from planet Earth, it is clear that this community needs a legal regulation to maintain law and order on board the aircraft. The international characteristic of civil aviation makes it desirable to apply such a legal regulation worldwide. From an exclusively academic aspect, the aircraft commander is undoubtedly an interesting authoritative personality. On the other hand, it may be worthwhile to examine his or her authority and legal status for more practical reasons in an international context.

After all, the aircraft commander occupies a key position in air transportation and rights, responsibilities and duties under both national public and private law. Under private law, the position of the aircraft commander regarding liability is, however, less clear.

Unfortunately, a conclusion has to be drawn that although a large number of national aviation laws and regulations contain provisions related to the powers and duties of the aircraft commander, for example, to maintain order and discipline on board, these laws and regulations are characterized by a great variety of structure and content.

No matter how substantively applicable national legislation is, in principle, its effect ends at the national border, and if regulations on the legal position of the aircraft commander should have any practical value, they must be effective on an international scale. This precondition makes it intelligible that they have to be uniform and functional on that scale. The main focus is on public international law. This observation is, in short, the starting point of this chapter and the next.

Uniform law in international aviation actually became successful partly because of its complex environment, generating transnational factual situations of unprecedented multitude and variety, and for the other part, the incipient international unification of contemporary private law in general, within a time frame of about three decades.[1]

---

1   Sand, P.H., "The International Unification of Air Law," (Spring, 1965) 30 *L. Contemp. Prob.* 2, pp. 401-402, Durham, NC: University School of Law. Essential private international law treaties related to aviation are, among other things: the 1929 Warsaw Convention for the Unification of Certain Rules Relating to International Carriage by Air, the 1933 Rome Convention for the Unification of Certain Rules Relating to the Precautionary Attachment of Aircraft, the 1933 Rome Convention for the Unification of Certain Rules

As the aircraft commander cannot make any beneficial use of the powers conferred by his or her national laws while operating under other jurisdictions, international regulations are deemed necessary to overcome these shortcomings. For this reason, an international convention determining the legal status of the aircraft commander, proportional to the important and responsible role he or she fulfils in international air transportation, would seemingly be an obvious solution.

It must be said that in the early years of aviation, preliminary studies with respect to the status of aviators were largely based on maritime law. The lack of precedents in air law led to the position of the aircraft commander being compared to that of a ship's captain, as well as other professional vehicle operators.

However, with regard to these apparent similarities, it should be noted that the typical isolation aspect for persons on board aircraft is considerably less in trains, buses and even on inland waterway vessels. Since these modes of transport will mainly operate within the territory of States or just across the borders, generally along fixed routes but never in stateless regions, States are at all times capable of asserting their authority within their territory to intervene in the jurisdiction on board.[2]

For these very reasons, it seems desirable, when formulating a proper international document regarding the legal status of the aircraft commander, not to easily assume apparent similarities with other modes of transport, but to consider the aircraft as a vehicle *sui generis* in accordance with the particularities of aviation.

In 1919, following World War I, some legal attention was drawn to the subject of the legal status of the aircraft commander. In that year, the first commercial airline companies were founded and the first international aviation agreement, the 1919 Paris Convention (Convention Relating to the Regulation of Aerial Navigation), signed at Paris on 13 October 1919, was concluded after preparatory work done by a special Paris Peace Conference Aeronautical Commission, which had its origin in the Inter-Allied Aviation

---

Relating to the Damage Caused by Foreign Aircraft to Third Parties on the Surface, the 1948 Geneva Convention on the International Recognition of Rights in Aircraft, the 1952 Rome Convention on Damage Caused by Foreign Aircraft to Third Parties on the Surface, the 1955 The Hague Protocol to Amend the Warsaw Convention, the 1961 Guadalajara Convention Supplementary to the Warsaw Convention for the Unification of Certain Rules Relating to International Carriage by Air Performed by a Person other than the Contracting Carrier, and the 2009 Montreal Convention on Compensation for Damage Caused by Aircraft to Third Parties.

2   Subjective territorial jurisdiction is asserted by those States in which criminal conduct commences on their territory or in their airspace, although the crime is ultimately consummated, or produces effects, in the territory or airspace of a third State. The State in the territory of which the effect was consummated has a legitimate interest in prosecuting the offenders. The interest will be exercised on the basis of objective territorial jurisdiction (Source: Bantekas, I., "Criminal Jurisdiction of States under International Law," (2011) *Max Planck Encyclopedias of Public International Law* [MPEPIL], Introduction, Territorial Criminal Jurisdiction).

Committee created in 1917. The 1919 Paris Convention instituted a commission called the International Commission for Air Navigation (ICAN), an international governing body under the direction of the League of Nations.[3]

ICAN was in fact the precursor of ICAO, and dealt exclusively with the regulation of international air navigation and was particularly working in the field of public international air law. Until the 1944 Chicago Convention came into force in 1947, the 1919 Paris Convention has been widely regarded as the principal international convention governing air navigation.

No doubt, the year 1919 was a significant milestone in the history of aviation and international air law. What seemed to be a futuristic idea just a few years earlier, was now transformed into reality. Aircraft, derived from post-war military surplus, carrying passengers and goods for remuneration were flying, albeit rather irregular, from one State to another, giving birth to international air transportation *avant la lettre*. Soon after, factors as increased airspeed, longer flight distances and more capacity of newly designed passenger aircraft intensified the commercial aspects of the civil aviation industry.

As expressed in the 1919 Paris Convention, a commanding officer on board of an aircraft carrying passengers was a leading requirement. The articles and annexes to this Convention, especially Annex E, incidentally referred to this special function.[4]

However, the text gave no comprehensive indication of its meaning, such as a legal description, nor the powers and duties regarding the key attributes of the aircraft commander. At last, the 1928 Havana Convention (the Pan-American Convention on Commercial Aviation, signed on 20 February 1928) provided in Article 25 the following description of the powers of the aircraft commander:

> *Articulo XXV: Siempre que un estado contratante no haya establecido reglas adecuadas, el commandante de una aeronave tendrá derechos y deberes análogos a los del capitán de un buque mercante, según las leyes respectivas de cada estado* [So long as a Contracting State shall not have established appropriate regulations, the commander of an aircraft shall have rights and duties analogous to those of the captain of a merchant steamer, according to the respective laws of each State].

A meaningful precursor of the 1919 Paris Peace Conference, in particular, the treatment of aviation matters by its Aeronautical Commission, was the 1910 Paris International Air Navigation Conference (Conférence Internationale de Navigation Aérienne), held at Paris

---

3   ICAN or CINA (*Commission Internationale de Navigation Aérienne*) consisted of representatives of the Contracting States and was provided with a permanent secretariat at Paris until 1946.
4   The articles concerned are: Arts. 12, 19(c) and 31.

from 8 May to 20 June 1910, which was finally adjourned leaving an incomplete but rather influential draft convention.[5]

The 1910 Paris Conference did not reconvene because of difference of opinion, international political tension and, above all, the real prospect of war in Europe and beyond, at the time. Most of the agreed-upon principles of this draft would reappear, but in the 1919 Paris Convention, drafted by the Aeronautical Commission, which, in turn, influenced the provisions of the Chicago Convention.

Whatever the exact role of the aircraft commander in international civil aviation may have been in the past, generally speaking, his legal status (at that time, only a male was considered aircraft commander) in private and public international air law, and, to some extent, in national legislations, has largely been neglected until the late 1920s. In that time period, the position of the aircraft commander was increasingly becoming involved in legal issues such as requiring an exact definition of his status with regard to the discharge of his duties.

1.2 THE STUDIES OF CITEJA

The official delegates from 44 participating States and, in addition, observers from the United States, Japan and Hungary, who attended the First International Conference on Private Air Law, held from 27 October to 6 November 1925 at Paris at the initiative of the French Government, adopted a resolution concerning general questions on private air law and the liability of the carrier in international air transportation that formed the legal basis for the creation and existence of CITEJA for the purpose of continuing the work of the 1925 Conference.[6] CITEJA was the first permanent international legal body consisting of essentially private air law specialists to deal with problems relating to private international air law.

The following motion was adopted by the Conference:

---

5   The Aeronautical Commission of the Peace Conference was formed as a result of a written invitation made by M. Clemenceau, President of the Preliminary Peace Conference to the principal Allied and Associated Powers. After considerable correspondence between the Heads of Governments, they authorized the proposal for such a body to be created (Source: Cooper, J.C., "United States Participation in Drafting Paris Convention 1919," (1951) 18 *J. Air L. Com.* 266, pp. 266-267.

6   CITEJA. *See Ministère des Affaires Étrangères – Conférence Internationale de Droit Prive Aérien* (27 Octobre-6 Novembre 1925), Paris Imprimerie Nationale, 1926, p. 45. *Questions à étudier par la Première Commission (Droit Aérien Privé) de CIDPA, parmi d'autres: Condition Juridique du Commandant de l'Aéronef. See also Revue de Droit International Troisième Anneé Premier Semestre,* J. Brown Scott, Paris les Editions Intenationales 1929, L'Allemagne et la Convention Internationale portant Réglementation de la Navigation Aérienne du 13 Octobre 1919, Dr. A. Wegerdt, pp. 154-155.

4

After having drawn up, as an example, a list of questions the study of which should immediately follow the examination of the problem of the liability of carrier by aircraft, the Conference, considering the importance, urgency, complicated nature and the legal technicalities of these questions, passes the resolution that a special Committee of experts be formed as soon as possible charged with preparing the continuation of the work of the Conference.

This Committee would be composed of a limited number of members. Its regular headquarters would be at Paris.

The Conference therefore invites the French Government to enter into relations with the governments invited to this Conference in order that this recommendation may take effect.

The Conference passes the resolution that the first questions for study by this Committee should be:

Damages caused by aircraft to goods and persons on the ground
Compulsory insurance
Establishment of aeronautical registers: ownership of aircraft, vested rights and mortgages
Seizure
Renting of aircraft
Aerial collisions
Legal status of commanding officers of aircraft
Bill of lading (air consignment note)
Uniform rules for the determination of the nationality of aircraft.[7]

The name of CITEJA in the French language was translated in the United States into the International Technical Committee of Aerial Legal Experts.

When CITEJA was organized, it adopted the following three principles to guide it in its activities:

1. Establishment of a programme covering various subjects pertaining to private air law to be studied by commissions of experts.
2. Preparation of texts of international conventions on legal subjects for consideration at periodic international conferences.
3. Maintenance of the principle of the progressive elaboration of a single international code of private air law.

---

7   *See* Report of 1925 Private Air Law Conference, pp. 82-83.

CITEJA, which prepared preliminary drafts of conventions on private air law, was virtually an autonomous body consisting of essentially private air law specialists. It was not under the administrative control of any other international organization. The Committee of Legal Experts acted on their own responsibility and their respective governments were free to approve or reject their conclusions at periodic international conferences, called for the purpose of considering the drafts. The 1925 Conference passed a resolution that contained questions for study by CITEJA, one of which was about the legal status of the aircraft commander.[8]

The State representatives to the periodic international conferences on private air law (diplomatic conferences) usually adopted resolutions calling upon CITEJA to undertake air law-related studies on several subjects. The ultimate purpose of the expert studies and consideration on particular subjects, such as the legal status of the aircraft commander, for reference to the Four International Conferences on Private Air Law, was adopting and signing international conventions based on CITEJA's drafts. The legal experts, nominated by participating States made a considerable contribution to the codification of private air law and went on with their work between the general conferences.[9]

Four International Conferences on Private Air Law were held until World War II interrupted the work of CITEJA and further unification of private air law. From 1926, four commissions of CITEJA, which in fact were subcommittees, would study various aspects for the purpose of preparing a full aviation code. However, during the plenary session of 19 May 1926, the view prevailed that the drafting of a complete *Code Général de l'Air* or full aviation code was considered a task beyond the legislative capacity due to the slow deliberation procedure of the international conferences of CITEJA and the extensive work and final revision with respect to a draft convention on the liability of the carrier in international air transportation. Moreover, another reason was that a full aviation code was considered not acceptable to non-Continental lawyers, who preferred to regulate only certain well-defined jurisdictions.

During the first session of CITEJA from 17 to 21 May 1926 at Paris, attended by representatives of 28 States, a resolution on the Work Programme was introduced containing a proposal for a compromise between the two directions CITEJA could take: the full aviation code vs. certain essential legal areas. The Work Programme, as adopted, contained all areas which were thought to be of paramount interest for an aviation code.

---

8   The aircraft commander, originally referred to as the *capitaine*, was often described by enumerating some of his powers: "*Le commandant de l' aéronef est la personne investie de pouvoirs d'autorité et de discipline à bord d'un aéronef et représentant le propriétaire et les chargeurs.*" The definition proposed by CITEJA *rapporteur* Garnault was: "*le commandant de bord est le chef de l' équipage à bord de l' aéronef en vol.*" See Kamminga, M.S. (1953), pp. 130-131.

9   Draper, R.A., "Transition from CITEJA to the Legal Committee of ICAO," (1948) 42 *AM. J. INT'L L.* 1, pp. 155-157. The CITEJA international conferences on private air law were held in 1925, 1929, 1933 and 1938.

Each of the four commissions was recommended to early study as the most urgent items essential for the development of a code of private international law through the preparation of draft international conventions to be finally adopted at periodic private international air law conferences.[10]

The matters to be investigated assigned to the Fourth Commission were:

1. *Condition juridique du commandant et du personnel.* Legal status of commanding officer and crew (the most urgent item).
2. *Accidents du personnel et assurances.* Accidents to the crew and insurance.
3. *Régime des passagers.* Status of passengers.
4. *Loi applicable aux actes et aux faits à bord de l'aéronef.* Law governing acts committed on board the aircraft.[11]

At the first session, CITEJA indicated the Fourth Commission, according to the general method of operation, to start a comprehensive study on the legal status of the aircraft commander. Subsequently, the Fourth Commission instructed its appointed *rapporteur* to prepare an analysis of the subject and then to send a Questionnaire to the members of the Commission to provide him with replies. Thereafter, according to the method, the *rapporteur* would draw up a preliminary draft text based on the replies for additional processing by CITEJA. If the text was found to be satisfactory by CITEJA, then it was submitted to the French Government for distribution to all interested States for the purpose of calling a Diplomatic Conference at which the draft text should be converted into a convention through consent and signature by the representatives of the States convened.

Mr. Edmond Thieffry, a Belgian World War I air ace, aviation pioneer and lawyer (hence his nickname 'The Flying Judge'), a *Université Catholique de Louvain Saint-Louis-Bruxelles* graduate, became the first *rapporteur* of the Fourth Commission. However, while Thieffry finally prepared an initial draft containing nine articles, reporting on the subject matter was postponed for some time because of special circumstances and prolonged discussions.

---

10   Van Wijk, A.A., "The Legal Status of the Aircraft Commander – Ups and Downs of a Controversial Personality in International Law" in Kean, A. (Ed.), *Essays in Air Law* (The Hague: Martinus Nijhoff Publishers, 1982), pp. 314-315.

11   Ide, J.J., "The History and Accomplishment of the International Technical Committee of Aerial Legal Experts (CITEJA)," (1932) 3 *J. Air L. & Com.* 27, pp. 30-33. First Commission: 1. Nationality of aircraft. 2. Aeronautical register. 3. Ownership, co-ownership, construction and transfer. 4. Vested rights, mortgages, privileges and seizure. Second Commission: 1. Category of aircraft (commercial transport, touring, etc.). 2. Bill of lading (air consignment note). 3. Liability of carrier towards consignors of goods and toward passengers. 4. Jettison of cargo and general damage. 5. Renting of aircraft. Third Commission: 1. Damage and liability towards third parties (landing, collision and jettison). 2. Limits of liability (contractual limitation, abandonment).

Unfortunately, in Africa on 11 April 1929, on a second test flight to set up a domestic air service in Congo, Thieffry was killed in a tragic fatal crash close to Lake Tanganyika. In regulating the powers of the commander under private law, Thieffry indicated in his preliminary report that it was left entirely to the operator to state the extent of the commander's powers in the letter of appointment.

Thieffry's work was continued by Mr. Leon Babiński, a lawyer and permanent delegate of the Polish government to CITEJA since 1928. It should be clear that this position change caused some delay due to familiarization with the subject. Moreover, CITEJA was in a quite difficult position, because, officially. it could only deal with questions of private law, and yet it was soon found that the status of the aircraft commander was also a matter of public law. Since 1930, CITEJA has been working on the draft relating to the status of the aircraft commander, originally consisting of 16 articles but, over time, firmly reduced to only 10 articles due to discussions, amendments and revisions.[12]

In February 1930, Babiński submitted a draft convention on the subject to the Fourth Commission for subsequent processing. Following discussions on the subject, another draft convention concerning navigating personnel (also referred to as air personnel or crew) was prepared and made available for discussions at the fifth plenary session of CITEJA from 6 to 8 October 1930 at Budapest, however, without a definite decision on the subject.[13]

In 1931, Babiński presented, with great passion and expertise, a supplementary report and a modified draft convention concerning the legal status of the aircraft commander, contained in CITEJA Doc. 127, which was agreed upon by the Fourth Commission. Babiński explained the background of the articles and the reasons why he had reduced the original number of articles. In addition, he introduced, unlike Thieffry, an intermediate draft structure, listing a number of statutory powers. These powers could, however, be restricted or extended by the aircraft operator. At the sixth meeting of CITEJA, the draft convention was provisionally adopted.[14]

The reason for this reservation had nothing to do with the material content of the draft; however, it was deemed desirable to initially contact the ILO, interested in the project, before submitting the draft convention to the French Government. Moreover,

---

12 Kamminga, M.S. (1953), p. 123.
13 *See also* CITEJA Report, 1936, Appendix G Preliminary Draft Convention Relative to Legal Status of Air Personnel (submitted by Leon Babiński, Reporter, and embodied in CITEJA Doc. 283). Art. 1. By navigating personnel, in the meaning of this convention, shall be meant any person employed or engaged in any capacity whatsoever, in the service of an aircraft in flight, with the exception of such persons as are on board under a special contract. (The quest as to whether the commander of the aircraft should not be excluded from this definition has been deferred. It will depend upon the ultimate decision as to the independent character or the possible merger of the draft convention on the legal status of the aircraft commander with this draft.) 1936 U.S. Aviation Reports, p. 574.
14 Van Wijk A.A. (1982), p. 315.

there was another point of discussion within CITEJA, namely the decision to combine the legal status of the aircraft commander with the regulations concerning the crew. In the meantime, the Fourth Commission had started a study on the legal status of navigating personnel, almost at the same time the ILO was dealing with this issue as well.

A historical impression about the composition and the order of succession in command of the navigating personnel was displayed in Article 1 of the 1947 draft version of the intended convention:

1. Every aircraft performing an international flight shall carry one person vested with the powers of a Commander.
2. The right to designate the Commander belongs to the operator of the aircraft.
3. In the absence of any Commander so designated, or in case the latter is prevented from performing his duties, and if no successor has been designated by the operator, the Commander's duties will be carried out by the other members of the crew in the following order: pilots, navigators, engineers, radio operators and stewards. The order of succession within each category shall be determined in accordance with the rank assigned by the operator.

The draft convention covering provisions on the legal status of the navigating personnel other than the aircraft commander defined certain principles governing the making of the contracts of employment of the navigating personnel of aircraft, the jurisdiction of the commander of the aircraft over the crew while in foreign States, the rights of the crew as far as their welfare during their stay in such States was concerned, and the obligation of the employers to repatriate members of the crew upon termination of their services. However, the US delegates were not in favour of such a draft convention on the legal rights of the crew of an aircraft in international service in connection with their national labour commitments. This controversy would possibly imply that the provisions of the draft convention should be modified.

> Difficulties are therefore only anticipated when in the perhaps rather distant future a considerable number of international aviation enterprises come into operation, or when there may be financial embarrassments of air lines resulting in employees being stranded without funds or means of travel in distant parts of the world.[15]

---

15 1936 U.S. Aviation Reports, Washington D.C., 15 June 1936 – CITEJA Report of the American Delegates, Paris meeting, February 1936, Appendix H. Fourth Commission – American Observations on the Legal Status of Air Personnel (CITEJA Doc. 292), p. 578.

At the 13th plenary session at Brussels on 28 September 1938 held at the end of the Fourth International Diplomatic Conference on Private Air Law, an ultimate decision to combine the two drafts was not reached despite the preliminary draft studies on the legal status of navigating personnel being nearly completed. The CITEJA Resolution No. 97 adjourned the consideration of the draft convention on the status of navigating personnel to the 14th session, planned in the following year, which in the end could not take place due to hostilities that marked the beginning of World War II (1939-1945) in Europe.[16]

Babiński fulfilled the position of *rapporteur* until the moment that his homeland, Poland was overwhelmed by the war. The war interrupted the activities of CITEJA and further development of the international unification of private air law. In 1946, the French *rapporteur* Mr. André Garnault succeeded Babiński, and it was decided that the draft convention relating to the status of the aircraft commander should anyway be revised in light of the recent technical developments and that this draft should be combined with the draft relating to the aircraft crew (contract of employment and labour conditions of the navigating personnel), which would make it a matter of private and public international air law as well as labour law.

Pursuant to the recommendation made by the delegates to the International Civil Aviation Conference (1944 Chicago Conference) with regard to the resumption of the work of CITEJA and the desirability of coordinating the activities of CITEJA with those organizations within the domain of public international law, the 14th plenary session, the first session since the outbreak of the war, was convened in Paris from 22 to 29 January 1946.

As regards the relationship with PICAO, Resolution No. 1 (Doc. 1567 A.15) was adopted by CITEJA by which it resolved to place under immediate consideration its liaison with the permanent agencies of PICAO (that had only advisory powers) the conditions under which CITEJA might assume a position with ICAO in order to fulfil the functions assigned to it by its traditional jurisdiction in its existence.[17]

As directed by CITEJA, *rapporteur* Garnault prepared a single text, dealing with both the crew and the commander, for discussion by the Fourth Commission during its meeting in July 1946. The draft submitted by Garnault, so far as it related to the crew, contained the basic principles regarding the form and effect of the contract of employment of the crew and the conditions under which they would be entitled to repatriation, which had appeared in previous CITEJA drafts.

The parts of the concept submitted to the July sessions that dealt with the aircraft commander contained certain basic principles of the CITEJA 1931 draft with certain powers of safety, discipline and authority on board the aircraft. The Fourth Commission

---

16 Knauth, A.W., "The Citeja Meeting in Paris in January, 1939," (1939) 10 *J. Air L. & Com.* 167, p. 167.
17 *See* PICAO Doc. 1699, LE/7, 24 May 1946, Commission No. 4 – Legal Questions, Memorandum of the Netherlands delegation regarding the relationship between PICAO and CITEJA.

had under consideration a draft convention prepared by Garnault, dealing with The Legal Status of the Aircraft crew (navigating personnel) and of the aircraft commander.

The draft convention covered ten concepts:

1. Every aircraft must have a Commander, and a method for appointment and a succession in case of injury, incapacity, etc.
2. The Commander must have authority to command and control persons on board.
3. He must be able, as Commander, to do what is necessary to expedite the voyage – procure supplies and repairs necessary for the voyage, and if a crew member drops out, hire a suitable man to complete the voyage. It is debatable whether his authority may be specially limited.
4. There should be public notice that he cannot, as Commander, do certain things: sell or pledge or mortgage the aircraft, perform marriages or act as notary.
5. His command of the crew begins at a certain point: as when they embark, and continues until the formalities of arrival are completed, or until he is relieved by another Commander. As to the aircraft passengers and cargo, his control begins when these are placed in his charge and continues until he turns them over to some other qualified authority.
6. He may go to the Consul of any nation whose nationals are interested in the aircraft, its managers, cargo or passengers; what the consuls may do depends on their consular laws and instructions.
7. Births and deaths on board must be suitably recorded and reported.
8. The Convention states that it does not attempt to prescribe any competency tests for commanders; that is a matter for home legislation, or for CINA, PICAO (the precursor of ICAO) and ICAO.[18]
9. The Convention will apply to international flight of aircraft registered in a State which ratifies or adheres, or registered by an owner who is a national of such a State.
10. It does not apply to military, customs or police aircraft.

There are the usual concluding clauses concerning ratification, denunciation, etc.[19]

---

18   PICAO was a temporary and coordinating body established through the 1944 Interim Agreement on International Civil Aviation. On 4 April 1947, upon the 26th ratification to the 1944 Convention on International Civil Aviation, the provisions of PICAO were no longer relevant and it became officially known as the International Civil Aviation Organization.

19   Knauth, A.W., "The Aircraft Commander in International Law," (1947) 14 *J. Air L. & Com.* 157, pp. 157-159. Note: the original text of the draft Convention was in the French language. Several articles were adopted in the English text as drafted by the US delegation to the Cairo meeting of CITEJA. PICAO presented three official texts: French, English and Spanish. Translations, however, require the most careful evaluation.

However, at this time, the US delegates, supported by the delegates of the United Kingdom, were in favour of developing two separate drafts dealing with the legal status of respectively the aircraft commander and the other crew members because of the fact that the 1946 proposed combined draft contained provisions with respect to the contract of employment that might interfere with the freedom of contract between the members of the crew and the operators of aircraft.

The argument in favour of this split up was to facilitate the freedom of choice of interested governments in becoming party to only one of the conventions, subject to their well-considered wish. After the July meeting, the US delegates began to take a very active part in the deliberations of CITEJA on the subject of the combined drafts. The reason was that they did not want to discuss part of the proposed combined convention because in their country, labour agreements with air crew were regulated by the 1936 Railway Labour Act. In the end, Garnault presented a revised draft convention at the Fourth Commission meeting held from 6 to 7 November 1946.

At this November meeting at Paris, it was found that the American and British delegates had serious objections against the combination of the two drafts. Around the same time, a PICAO representative suggested the Fourth Commission to defer discussions about the combination because of emerging differences in defining the drafts which would restrict further preparation.

Quite soon after the meeting of the Fourth Commission, CITEJA, including the four commissions, convened its 15th session at Cairo from 14 to 17 November. At this meeting, CITEJA agreed on various amendments to the draft convention presented by Garnault, resulting in the approval of the full text consisting of ten articles. The draft convention (CITEJA Cairo Doc. C-30), together with a general explanatory memorandum and an annotation on the draft articles together with a resolution (No. 161), including a recommendation of diplomatic action for adoption was submitted to PICAO. The PICAO Secretariat prepared a provisional revised draft by incorporating the CITEJA amendments, agreed upon at the Cairo meeting, in order to adequately inform the PICAO Legal Committee of the official text.[20]

The authentic ICAO document is called the Provisional text prepared by the CITEJA Secretariat (the PICAO version of the draft, 21 March 1947).

---

20 Van Wijk, A.A. (1982), p. 318. The PICAO Legal Committee was an interim body which at that time was composed of a small number of Council members. Its formal status was established only during the First Session of the ICAO Assembly on 23 May 1947.

Article 1.

Any aircraft engaged in international transport shall carry a person invested with the powers of a commander.

The choice of the commander is entrusted to the aircraft operator.

In the absence of the said commander or in case he is prevented from performing his duties, and if the operator has failed to appoint his successor, the commander's duties will be assumed by another member of the crew in the following order: pilot, navigator, engineer, radio operator and steward. The choice shall be determined according to the rank assigned by the operator to the members of a same category.

Article 2.

Within the periods as specified in Article 5 below, the aircraft commander:

a. is responsible for the aircraft, the crew, the passengers, and the cargo;

b. has the right and it is his duty to control and direct the crew and the passengers inasmuch as the order aboard the aircraft and the safety of the operations require;

c. the right to disembark any crew member or passenger at an intermediate stop, whenever he judges necessary;

d. has control over the crew members within the scope of their duties; in case of an emergency the gravity of which it is up to him to appreciate, he may temporarily assign any member of the crew to duties others than those he usually performs;

e. may take any other measures in order to secure that orders or instructions given under the present article are complied with by any member of the crew or passengers.

Article 3.

The aircraft commander is entitled, even without any special assignment:

a. to buy the items which are necessary for the performing of the undertaken trip;

b. to see that the necessary repairs, enabling the aircraft to carry on rapidly its trip, are made;

c. to make any arrangements and to undertake any expenditure which may be necessary for securing the safety of the passengers and crew and the safeguard of the cargo;

d. to borrow the sums required for the accomplishment of the measures afore mentioned by items (a), (b), (c) of the present article;

e.   to enlist, for the duration of the current trip, the staff necessary for carrying on to the end the undertaken trip in order to fill any vacancy in case of failure of crew members.

Article 4.

The commander, unless specially instructed, is not entitled, either to sell or by arrangement, mortgage or submit the aircraft to any securities of the same kind.

Article 5.

The beginning and the end of the period during which the commander maintains a disciplinary control on the crew may be settled by the operator. This control, in any case, is entrusted to him as soon as the crew embarks. It ceases at stops at the earliest date the arrival procedures are over or whenever the command is entrusted to another commander.

The powers of the commander upon the aircraft, the passengers and the cargo on board come into force as soon as the aircraft, with passengers and cargo, are handed over to him at the beginning of the trip. They expire at the end of the trip when the aircraft, the passengers and the cargo have been respectively handed over to the operator's representative or any other qualified authority. The very moment when the handing over of the aircraft, the passengers and the cargo takes place is determined according to the operator's uses and practices.

Article 6.

Whatever the country and circumstances, the commander is entitled to approach:

a.   the consul of the State under the jurisdiction of which is any person on board;

b.   the consul of the State in which the aircraft is registered;

c.   the consuls of the States under the jurisdiction of which are the charterers or the ship owners.

Once they have heard the commander, the consuls may take any measure incumbent to them, according to the laws and consular orders of their respective States.

If the commander first calls on the consul of a State other than the State in which the aircraft is registered, the former should notify this action as soon as possible to the nearest consul of the State by which the aircraft is registered.

Article 7.

Births and deaths occurred on board the aircraft shall be registered on the log-book by the commander, who shall issue certificates of them to the parties interested. He shall as soon as possible forward true copies of these certificates to the competent authority of the place of first landing, if requested by the local authorities.

Article 8.

The provisions of the present Convention do not encroach upon the international conventions nor upon the national legislations of the Contracting States, by which the competency requirements of the aircraft commander are specified.

Article 9.

The present Convention shall be applied in the case of an aircraft engaged in international transport, whether this aircraft is registered in any of the Contracting States, or is operated by an operator belonging to any of these States.

Article 10.

The present Convention does not apply to the commander on duty on board of military, customs, or police aircraft.[21]

Please note that Articles 11 to 18 of this document contain formal provisions relating to the ratification, adherence and denunciation of the ultimate Convention. Therefore, these articles are not of immediate importance for the legal status of the aircraft commander and, consequently, not listed.

Earlier, at the First Interim Assembly of PICAO held at Montreal from 21 May to 7 June 1946, Assembly Resolution No. 31 was adopted foreseeing the establishment of a Committee on International Air Law (the Legal Committee) after the creation of ICAO.[22] CITEJA, in the last phase of its existence, fully agreed with the view of the PICAO Assembly at the 15th plenary session at Cairo in November 1946 where it recommended, *obiter dicta*, that a permanent Legal Committee on International Air Law be established within

---

21   ICAO Doc. 4011, A1-LE/8, 21 March 1947 First Assembly Commission IV – Legal Questions, Appendix I, Draft Convention concerning the Legal Status of the Aircraft Commander. *See also* ICAO Doc. 4006, A1-LE/9, 18 March 1947 Draft Convention on the Legal Status of the Aircraft Commander (as revised by the Paris Legal *ad hoc* Committee) (February 1947) with a somewhat different text.

22   *See also* ICAO Doc. 4007, A1-LE/1, 21 March 1947, pp. 1-2.

ICAO. At the 16th and final session of CITEJA, which was held at Montreal in May 1947, the Comité was dismantled and the archives were handed over to the ICAO Legal Committee. Unlike the pre-war CITEJA, the Legal Committee and the permanent Legal Bureau of ICAO are also officially involved in public international air law.[23]

1.3   THE TRANSITION FROM CITEJA TO THE ICAO LEGAL COMMITTEE

> The commander's status is today quite undefined. Surely a man employed to exercise some sort of control over a half million dollar machine, with a crew of 5 to 10 persons, with 30 to 80 passengers, cargo and mails of high value, and travelling over and to many jurisdictions should certainly have his status, rights and powers carefully and clearly stated in every language. The public interest demands it.[24]

The PICAO version of the draft (Doc. 2417) was transmitted to its Legal Committee by the President of the Interim Council on 7 January 1947. On 10 January 1947, the Legal Committee was convened, having at its disposal not only the Draft Convention on the Legal Status of the Aircraft Commander, but also the Working Draft No. 20 concerning the recommendations of CITEJA as regards the definitions of the terms 'operator' and 'international carriage' and the Working Draft No. 19 concerning the final provisions to be inserted in the draft before sending it by PICAO to States in order to receive their response. However, time pressure forced the Legal Committee to develop at that time a draft convention concerning 'recording of title to aircraft and aircraft mortgages'. Nevertheless, to reach a final agreement on a text of a convention regarding the legal status of the aircraft commander and to open it for signature at the forthcoming Assembly was considered by the Legal Committee as an essential condition.

In order to permit a careful consideration of such a text by the Contracting States before the ICAO Assembly, it would be necessary to circulate, well ahead of 1 March 1947, a revised draft taking into account the answers received from governments and organizations. In order to prepare such a revised draft, the Legal Committee agreed to propose to the Council the appointment of an *ad hoc* Committee, as contemplated in Resolution No. 32 of the PICAO First Assembly.[25]

This *ad hoc* Committee began its deliberations at the PICAO Regional Office at Paris on 17 February 1947. Remarkably, the *ad hoc* Committee first adopted a draft convention concerning 'the recording of rights *in rem* in aircraft'. However, more conscientious work

---

23   *See also* Constitution of the Legal Committee (As approved by the First Assembly, 23 May 1947).
24   Knauth, A.W. (1947), p. 160. Please note that further on an authentic text will be displayed.
25   Van Wijk, A.A. (1982), p. 319.

had to be done in view of the fact that, just a week ago, the Secretary General of CITEJA had forwarded the final French text and a provisional English text of the draft convention concerning the legal status of the aircraft commander to the Paris Regional Office.[26]

The assistance of Garnault, also a member of the *ad hoc* Committee, was invoked for a final revision of both the English and French texts and the addition of final provisions from the governments and organizations. In order to avoid any delay in the transmission from Montreal to the governments and organizations of the drafts which should be considered at the next ICAO Assembly, assistance of this expert was very much needed.

The *ad hoc* Committee thoroughly examined the revised draft convention in both languages and made some minor modifications mainly for the purpose of having it in conformity with the decisions reached at Cairo and to clarify certain provisions without any amendment in substance being made. Paragraph (e) of Article 2 was considered useless and was deleted. A preamble and final provisions were added along the very same lines as in the case of the draft convention concerning 'the recording of rights *in rem* in aircraft' just completed at Paris. The issue of inserting definitions received a great deal of attention; however, in the end, the draft did not contain any definitions since the terms used in the written form were evident. The revised draft provided for a limitative summary of the commander's powers; these powers are mandatory and the operator could not put a restriction on them as far as third parties were concerned.[27]

The corrected draft was destined to become the final version of the many drafts which had preceded it and the document became generally known as the Draft Convention on the Legal Status of the Aircraft Commander (as revised in 1947 by the Paris Legal *ad hoc* Committee). However, the corrections applied were actually made unauthorized, since the subject was considered outside the terms of reference of the Legal *ad hoc* Committee. The diplomatic response from the President of the Interim Council to this issue was that some of the Legal *ad hoc* Committee members were particularly well qualified to make such corrections.

In the meantime, the Interim Legal Committee in Montreal had been busy trying to find a reasonable way to convene a conference which could formally finalize and approve both the draft convention on recording of title to aircraft and aircraft mortgages, and the Draft Convention on the Legal Status of the Aircraft Commander. However, at its meeting on 18 March 1947, the Interim Legal Committee considered the Draft Convention on the Legal Status of the Aircraft Commander and thought it most advisable to recommend the Interim Council to immediately circulate the document in order to provide governments

---

26   The PICAO Legal *ad hoc* Committee consisted of Dr. P.A.T. De Smet (Belgium), Major K.M. Beaumont (United Kingdom), who later became *rapporteur* of the ICAO Legal Committee, CITEJA *rapporteur* Mr. A. Garnault (France) and Mr. G.N. Calkins Jr. (United States of America).

27   Van Wijk, A.A. (1982), p. 320.

sufficient time to consider the document before the Assembly. The next step should be a decision on a proposal, with consent of the Assembly, to convene a Conference on International Air Law to consider both the drafts together with the working procedures and methods of the newly appointed (ICAO) Legal Committee.

By receiving the requisite twenty-sixth ratification in March 1947, the Chicago Convention went into effect on 4 April 1947, the date that the provisional aspects of PICAO were no longer relevant and it officially became known as ICAO with a permanent Council. This drastic transition hampered the progress of the proposal in question, resulting in the fact that the outgoing Interim Council did not accept it for reasons of organizational contradictions.

The Interim Legal Committee, at the expense of precedence of the drafts agreed 'that the normal procedure for the consideration of draft conventions on international air law should be through the ICAO Assembly and its Commissions'.

The First Assembly was unable, due to lack of time, to consider the draft on the legal status of the aircraft commander. It was included in the Work Programme of the permanent Legal Committee, albeit with a low priority.

At the first session of the ICAO Assembly, held at Montreal in May 1947, it was resolved that, as mentioned above, in view of the fact that the Chicago Convention had received sufficient ratifications to bring it into force, and with it to bring the permanent ICAO into being, and in view of the forthcoming establishment of a permanent Legal Committee by ICAO, CITEJA should be dissolved in due time and its functions transferred to this Legal Committee, which was formally created by the adoption of Assembly Resolution A1-46. At its establishment, the duty of the Legal Committee was to study any legal matter referred to it by the Council.

The Legal Committee, different from the fully autonomous position of CITEJA, was not to be considered entirely autonomous, since it was established within the framework of ICAO and be subject to certain administrative controls by the ICAO Council, which actually means that it is operating under the supervision of the Council. Its Secretariat has been provided by ICAO. The Legal Committee is not a subsidiary body of the Council but a permanent Committee of ICAO. The Legal Committee is composed of legal experts designated as representatives of and by Contracting States, and shall be open to participation by all Contracting States and certain international organizations, invited by or because of the ICAO Council.

However, it does not have the same independence as its predecessor because the costs of its meetings and the composition and emoluments of the ICAO Legal Bureau, the Legal Committee's Secretariat, are determined by the ICAO Assembly when adopting the ICAO budget. In addition, the ICAO Council exercises a certain control over the work of the Legal Committee by approving the General Work Programme established by the Legal

Committee and determining the agenda, place and time of the meetings of the Legal Committee and its Subcommittees.[28]

As its formal status was just being established during the first session of the ICAO Assembly on 23 May 1947, the Legal Committee, in the early stages of operation, had to work with a limited number of legal experts, while the entrusted legal area was to be quite extensive. It has to deal with public as well as private international air law matters, where CITEJA, in its studies of certain specified subjects, only could deal with questions of private international air law. During the ICAO Assembly, CITEJA held two meetings and adopted resolutions for its liquidation.

Assembly Resolution A1-46, and its Appendix A, also incorporated the Legal Committee's Constitution:

> Constitution of the Legal Committee of ICAO resolved:
> a. That the 'Constitution' of a Legal Committee, in the form of Appendix 'A', be approved;
> b. that the first meeting of the Legal Committee be summoned by the Council at a convenient place and date;
> c. that Commission No. 4 immediately prepare a program of the work to be undertaken by the Legal Committee during the ensuing year.

> Constitution (Assembly Resolution A7-5, authentic text):
> 1. The Legal Committee (hereinafter – in this authentic text – referred to as the Committee) shall be a permanent Committee of the Organization, constituted by the Assembly and responsible to the Council except as otherwise specified herein.
> 2. The duties and functions of the Committee shall be:
>   a. to advice the Council on matters relating to the interpretation and amendment of the Convention on International Civil Aviation, referred to it by the Council;
>   b. to study and make recommendations on such other matters relating to public international air law as may be referred to it by the Council or the Assembly;
>   c. by direction of the Assembly or the Council, or on the initiative of the Committee and subject to the prior approval of the Council, to study problems relating to private air law affecting international civil aviation,

---

28   Mankiewicz, R.H., "The Legal Committee – Its Organization and Working Methods," (1966) 32 *J. Air L. & Com.* 94, pp. 94-95.

to prepare drafts of international air law conventions and to submit reports and recommendations thereon;

d. to make recommendations to the Council as to the representation at sessions of the Committee of non-Contracting States and other international organizations, as to the coordination of the work of the Committee with that of other representative bodies of the Organization and of the Secretariat and also as to such other matters as will be conducive to the effective work of the Organization.

3. The Committee shall be composed of legal experts designated as representatives of and by Contracting States, and shall be open to participation by all Contracting States.

4. Each Contracting State represented in meetings of the Committee shall have one vote.

5. The Committee shall determine, subject to the approval of the Council, the General Work Programme of the Committee and provisional agenda of each session, provided that the Committee may, during a session.

6. Consistently with the provisions of this Constitution, sessions of the Committee shall be convened at such places and times as may be directed or approved by the Council.

7. The Committee shall elect its own officers.

8. The Committee may appoint Subcommittees either to meet concurrently with the Committee or, subject to the approval of the Council, at other times and places as it may deem fit.[29]

The Draft Convention on the Legal Status of the Aircraft Commander was placed on the agenda of Commission No. 4 of the First ICAO Assembly in May 1947.[30] This Commission prepared legal opinions in compliance with requests of the ICAO Assembly and drew up, in collaboration with Commission No. 1, that primarily was concerned with organizational issues, the Constitution of the Legal Committee to function within the framework of ICAO. This was formally required as corollary of the transition by which the Legal Committee had to take over the activities of CITEJA.

---

29 *See* ICAO Assembly Resolution A1-46, A1-P/45, 3 June 1947, pp. 48-49 in ICAO Resolutions Adopted by the First Assembly, 6-27 May 1947 (ICAO Doc. 4411). *See also* ICAO Doc. 7669-LC/139/6 Legal Committee Constitution – Procedure for Approval of Draft Conventions – Rules of Procedure – Sixth Edition 2018, Constitution (Assembly Resolution A7-5), Art. 2. Assembly Resolution A1-46 was revised by Resolution A7-5 (ICAO Doc. 9848), which was superseded by Resolution A31-15. *See also* ICAO Doc. 10022 Assembly Resolutions in Force (as of 4 October 2013). The procedure for the approval of draft conventions is the subject of Resolution A1-48 revised by Resolution A39-11 Appendix B.

30 ICAO Commission No. 4 – Legal Questions – was affiliated with the First Interim Assembly and from 1947 with the First Assembly of ICAO (PICAO Doc. 1649, LE/5, 23 May 1946).

However, apart from the work on the preparation of the legal opinions, the time-consuming considerations on the proposed Convention on the Recognition of Rights in Aircraft, the method of organizing the intended Constitution and the drafting of recommendations pertaining to constitute the Legal Committee, the Commission No. 4 could not find any more available time for a prompt and due consideration to the proposed Draft Convention on the Legal Status of the Aircraft Commander.[31]

In brief, since 1947, the Legal Committee has considered questions of both private and public international air law. This broad legal field, together with the extensive Work Programme, mentioned before, was the reason for the slow progress made by the Legal Committee to discuss the subject regarding the Draft Convention on the Legal Status of the Aircraft Commander, despite its appearance on the agenda at the first full session of the Legal Committee at Brussels (10-25 September 1947).

Earlier, on 24 May 1947, the non-permanent Committee No. 4 on legal questions, instituted in the framework of the First Assembly of ICAO, drew up a synopsis of a constitution, a working procedure and methods for the Legal Committee of ICAO. Part of the Final Report of Commission No. 4 (ICAO Doc. 4382 A1-LE/65) reads:

Appendix E.

Resolution Concerning the Programme of Work of the Legal Committee.

Commission No. 4.

Having been directed by a resolution adopted by the Assembly on May 23rd, to prepare immediately a programme of the work to be undertaken by the Legal Committee during the ensuing year, resolves:

That the following matters be included in the Work Programme of the Legal Committee and that at least the Rules of Procedure of the Legal Committee,[32] and the draft convention concerning the recognition of rights in aircraft should be finalized during the coming year:

Rules of procedure

Draft convention concerning the recognition of rights in aircraft

Revision of the Warsaw Convention

Definitions of terms

Revision of the Rome Convention

Limitation of responsibility

Collision

Draft convention concerning the legal status of the aircraft commander

---

31   Participation of the United States Government in International Conferences, 1 July 1946-30 June 1947, International Conferences: 1946-1947 Aviation. *United States Government Printing Office*, Washington: 1948, p. 128.

32   *See also* ICAO Doc. 7669-LC/139/6, Sixth Edition – 2018.

Settlement of form of consignment note for combined transport

Draft convention concerning assistance to aircraft and by aircraft on land

Convention on assistance and salvage of aircraft by aircraft at sea

Authority of judgements by competent tribunals under conventions in force on air matters and distribution of allowances

Hire and charter

General average (damage)

Remuneration for assistance and postal contribution to such expenses

Abandonment

Jettison

Convention on precautionary arrest of aircraft.

Note: The question of priority of projects would be considered at the first meeting of the Legal Committee.[33]

However, Commission No. 4 came to the following conclusion in this Final Report: Point 8: The Committee reached the following conclusions after consideration of the several items of its agenda: (d) Consideration of the procedure to be followed in dealing with two draft conventions on international air law (Item 4 (a) and 4 (b)): At its first meeting the Commission decided that these two draft conventions should be dealt with by the Commission and that it was not necessary to refer them to a special meeting composed of Contracting as well as non-Contracting States.

Item 4 (a): Draft Convention on the Recognition of Rights in Aircraft.... Item 4 (b): Draft Convention concerning the Legal Status of the Aircraft Commander. The Committee was unable through lack of time to consider this draft convention. This item has been included in the Resolution (Appendix 'E'), concerning the future programme of work of the Legal Committee.[34]

In 1948, further delay was incurred due to the fact that the ICAO Air Transport Committee together with the Air Navigation Commission (ANC) was considering the establishment of the position of the aircraft commander.[35] Progress could only be made if the draft

---

33   *See* ICAO Doc. 4382, A1-LE/65, 24 May 1947. First Assembly, Commission No. 4 – Legal Questions, Final Report of the Commission, Appendix E, pp. 15-16.

34   *See* ICAO Doc. 4382, A1-LE/65 24 May 1947, pp. 2-5.

35   The ICAO Air Navigation Commission (ANC) was established in 1947 pursuant to the provisions of Chapter X of the 1944 Convention on International Civil Aviation. The Interim Agreement on International Civil Aviation was accepted by the ratification of the 26th State on 6 June 1945 creating PICAO. As the main technical body of PICAO, the Committee on Air Navigation (or Air Navigation Commission) was established by the Interim Council on 28 August 1945. At the Fourth Meeting of its Sixth Session, held on 1 February 1949, the ICAO Council adopted Resolution A2-8 on the establishment of what would

convention was forwarded by the Council to these technical bodies for consideration and comments. During the second session of the Legal Committee (May-June 1948), the delegate of the United States understood:

> that the Air Transport Committee and the Air Navigation Commission of ICAO were considering the establishment of the position of the aircraft commander. It would appear to the United States' delegate that a great deal of progress would be made if the draft convention in its present form were submitted to the Council with a request that it be forwarded to the appropriate Committee for consideration and comment so that the technical committees would have the benefit of consideration of the draft and similarly the Legal Committee would have the benefit of the comment of the technical experts.[36]

A UK statement declared that the matter of the aircraft commander might well be regulated by national legislation and that international legislation might not be necessary or desirable, which did not really facilitate the adoption of the draft convention text. With respect to uncertainties about the final inferences on the draft convention, the Chairman of the Legal Committee assured the observers of the International Air Transport Association (IATA) that the possible transmittal of the draft convention text would not mean that it would be considered as having been adopted by the Legal Committee.[37]

To straighten out the matter, the Legal Committee resolved:

> That the text of the Draft Convention on the Legal Status of the Aircraft Commander be sent to the Council with the request that the technical bodies of the Organization be asked for their comments thereon.

A letter from IATA to ICAO, signed by Sir William P. Hildred, Director General, clarified IATA's position on the subject:

The following covering letter has been received by the Secretary General:
   'Sir'

---

      henceforth be recognized as the permanent ICAO ANC. After an overlap, the Interim Committee disposed all necessary business to facilitate the transfer of its functions to the ANC.

36   Review of Second Session of ICAO Legal Committee. The U.S. was represented by Mr. Calkins, Mr. Elwell, and Mr. Tipton of the CAB, the CAA, and the IATA (Source: International), (1949) 16 *J. Air L. & Com.* 327, p. 338.

37   *See* ICAO Doc. 4083, A1-LE/15, 6 May 1947 First Assembly Commission No. 4 – Legal Questions, Agenda Item 4(b). The modern IATA was founded in Havana, Cuba on 19 April 1945. It is the successor to the International Air Traffic Association, founded in The Hague in 1919.

1. I have the honour to inform you that the Draft Convention on the Legal Status of the Aircraft Commander (ICAO Document 4006) has been the subject of careful consideration by the Legal Committee of International Air Transport Association during the past week. The views expressed by the Legal Committee have been endorsed by the Executive Committee of IATA at its recent meeting in Montreal.
2. I enclose herewith a document giving the comments of IATA upon this draft Convention, and I should be grateful if these views could be placed before the appropriate Commission of ICAO at its forthcoming Assembly....

The letter indicates in Item 1:

> The experience of the Members of IATA has not revealed any practical need for the proposed Convention on the Status of the Aircraft Commander. Comments received show that there is no immediate need for a Convention of this character. Many of the subjects dealt with in the Convention are already dealt with in the conditions of carriage, personnel regulations and contracts of employment of the various airlines.
> The present draft would require a great deal of time and effort before it would be in an acceptable form. There is a limit also to the time and attention that governments can devote to a Convention on aeronautical matters and it would seem desirable to allow the proposed Convention to wait until other pressing conventions have been acted upon or until further experience has been accumulated.

The IATA letter ends with a short list of comments on the draft convention articles, mainly based on airline practices. The IATA airlines provided vital input to the work of ICAO, as that Organization drafted its SARPs. By 1949, the drafting process was largely complete and reflected in a number of Annexes to the Chicago Convention.[38]

At the third and fourth sessions of the Legal Committee in 1948 and 1949, the subject of the aircraft commander only appeared on separate occasions related to the commander's practicable obligations as to assistance and SAR. Unfortunately, the subject was not discussed during deliberations on the Work Programme of the Legal Committee during these sessions. Ultimately, the consideration of collisions and the revision of the Warsaw Convention seemed to be of utmost importance.[39]

---

38 *See* ICAO Assembly Resolution A1-31, Definitions of International Standards and Recommended Practices in ICAO Doc. 4411 Resolutions Adopted by the First Assembly, 6-27 May 1947, A1-P/45, 3 June 1947, pp. 27-29. Today, ICAO manages over 12,000 SARPs across the 19 Annexes to the Chicago Convention.
39 Van Wijk, A.A. (1982), p. 322.

In the 1950s, a revival on the legal status of the aircraft commander ensued. Two notable, separate but above all necessary decisions were made regarding the status, in particular, the powers, of the aircraft commander. These involved, in the first place, the issue of appointing a non-piloting aircraft commander to have an overall leadership position on board an aircraft, and in the second place, a resolution submitted by the Canadian airline pilots in order to request explicit clarity about the formal authority of the aircraft commander.

The first issue had its basis in the fact that at that time there was an increasing tendency among European airlines that good use might be made of the accumulated experience of retired aircraft commanders, even after they were declared no longer medically fit to continue their piloting duties. This professional experience could very well be used if these senior ex-pilots were permitted to continue to command an aircraft with the grade of non-piloting aircraft commander. In other words, take advantage of an experienced pilot with a track record in commercial aviation who is, however, no longer legally certified to serve in a piloting capacity. Despite this questionable wording, the non-piloting aircraft commander would be entrusted to command the flight operation while sitting behind the operating pilots.

Within ICAO, attention was shifted to the, rather incoherent, term of non-piloting aircraft commander, the holder of which would not actively pilot an aircraft himself, nor vicariously would attend to navigation or other duties fulfilled by the operating members of the flight crew. Instead, according to the Organization, the non-piloting aircraft commander would solely act in a supervisory capacity, however, with complete control over the other operating members of the flight crew. In the context of enhancing flight safety, the presence in the cockpit of such a more experienced pilot when, for instance, it becomes necessary to select a diversion aerodrome, or to cope with an emergency situation, would be a valuable asset to the younger pilot at the controls.

The ICAO Personnel Licensing (PEL) Division, a technical subcommittee, after careful consideration of the facts, judged that the establishment of the proposed grade of non-piloting aircraft commander was in a practical sense not desirable. In fact, this atypical commanding concept might easily lead to cockpit trouble and potential frustration, since it would be quite difficult for this non-piloting aircraft commander to resist taking over the controls in a challenging situation.

The policy of IATA, established by its own Technical Committee, rejected the idea referring to the fact that older, non-active pilots could be more usefully employed in a (non-flying) ground function such as simulator instructor.[40]

This was emphasized by the opinion of the International Federation of Air Line Pilots' Associations (IFALPA) that the pilot-in-command, the person in command of the flight,

---

40   Ibid., p. 323.

should, with regard to the discussion concerning the non-piloting aircraft commander, be a real pilot, autonomous and resilient, who easily adapts to more comprehensive rules and modern technology. Actually, from 1979, the term 'pilot-in-command' rather than aircraft commander was used by IFALPA, created at a London Conference in April 1948 for the purpose of providing a formal means for the pilots of the world to communicate with ICAO. Logically, one of the first intentions of IFALPA was to clarify the authority of the pilot-in-command or the aircraft commander.[41]

The issue regarding the powers of the aircraft commander and therefore a clear statement of the aircraft commander's authority came from Canadian airline pilots. In the 1950s, Canadian aircraft commanders had been forced by their airlines to admit individuals to the cockpit, often during flight phases with high workload which was rather inconvenient, if not to say unsafe. These inappropriate situations triggered the Canadian Air Line Pilots Association, formed on December 1, 1937, to submit a resolution to the IFALPA Annual Conference, which was held at Chicago from 6 to 10 April 1953.[42] IFALPA shared the views of the Canadian airline pilots and adopted a resolution with a request to ICAO to incorporate an additional Standard in 4.5 of Annex 6 to specify that the pilot-in-command or aircraft commander possesses the authority to exercise the responsibilities referred to in 4.5.1 of the same Annex, namely: the pilot-in-command shall be responsible for the operation and safety of the aircraft and for the safety of all persons on board during flight time.[43]

It should be noted that relevant SARPs for the Operation of Aircraft – International Commercial Air Transport were first adopted by the Council on 10 December 1948 pursuant to the provisions of Article 37 of the Chicago Convention, and designated as Annex 6 to the Chicago Convention (effective on 15 July 1949).

The SARPs were based on recommendations of the PICAO Operations Division at its first session in April 1946, which were further developed at the second session of the PICAO Operations Division in February 1947.[44]

---

41 *See* IFALPA Doc. 80b145, 31 October 1979.

42 In 1996, Air Canada pilots left CALPA and formed their own organization, ACPA. The remaining members of CALPA then arranged a merger with the U.S. Air Line Pilots Association (ALPA) which took effect on 1 February 1997. On 4 March 2023, a statement has been issued by ACPA and ALPA regarding an agreement in principle between the two unions about a potential merger.

43 A provision of this nature as defined in Annex 6 – *Operation of Aircraft – International Commercial Air Transport* has existed in ICAO since the time PICAO was in office.

44 A much later and more comprehensive text in ICAO Annex 6 Part I, Twelfth Edition, July 2022, Chapter 4. Flight Operations, Para. 4.5.1. The pilot-in-command shall be responsible for the safety of all crew members, passengers and cargo on board when the doors are closed. The pilot-in-command shall also be responsible for the operation and safety of the aeroplane from the moment the aeroplane is ready to move for the purpose of taking off until the moment it finally comes to rest at the end of the flight and the engine(s) used as primary propulsion units are shut down.

Since the early days of (P)ICAO's existence, both terms 'pilot-in-command' and 'aircraft commander' were used alternately in official documents, until ICAO standardized the texts of the Annexes in favour of pilot-in-command. Some ICAO documents, like ICAO Doc. 10117, retained or continue to retain the use of the term 'aircraft commander' which is the wording used in the Tokyo Convention of 1963 as amended by the 2014 Montreal Protocol.[45]

For comparison, according to U.S. CFR (Code of Federal Regulations): Title 14 – Aeronautics and Space – Chapter 1, Subchapter A – Definitions and General Requirements, Part 1 – Definitions and Abbreviations, § 1.1 – General definitions:

> Pilot-in-command means the person who:
> 1. Has final authority and responsibility for the operation and safety of the flight;
> 2. has been designated as pilot-in-command before or during the flight;
> 3. holds the appropriate category, class and type rating, if appropriate, for the conduct of the flight.

The incorporation of the additional Standard in Annex 6 regarding the authority of the pilot-in-command still would take some doing. The issue was discussed by the ANC and requested its Secretary to prepare a paper relevant to the IFALPA Conference resolution on the question of the authority vested in the pilot-in-command. This paper (AN-WP/1084), finished on 27 January 1954, stated that

> In conjunction with the provisions covering steps to be taken by the operator for the protection of the flight, one covering the authority of the pilot-in-command would seem to be essential.[46]

It proposed to add a clause to the relevant Annex section, whereby the operator has a responsibility with regard to the composition of the flight crew:

---

45   ICAO Doc. 10117 – Manual on the Legal Aspects of Unruly and Disruptive Passengers, First Edition, 2019, p. 1-1 Introduction, note 5 and ICAO Circular 288 Guidance Material on the Legal Aspects of Unruly/Disruptive Passengers. The full designation of the 2014 Montreal Protocol: Protocol to Amend the Convention on Offences and Certain Other Acts Committed on Board Aircraft.

46   ICAO uses the term "pilot-in-command". *See* ICAO Annex 2, Tenth Edition, July 2005, International Standards Chapter 1. Definitions: The pilot responsible for the operation and safety of the aircraft during flight time. *See also* ICAO Annex 6 Part I, Twelfth Edition, July 2022, International Standards and Recommended Practices Chapter 1. Definitions, Pilot-in-command. The pilot designated by the operator, or in the case of general aviation, the owner, as being in command and charged with the safe conduct of the flight. Flight time – aeroplanes. The total time from the moment the aeroplane first moves for the purpose of taking off until the moment it finally comes to rest at the end of the flight.

4.2.7.1. For each flight, the operator shall designate one pilot to act as pilot-in-command. Same text as in the Twelfth Edition under 4.2.11. Crew: 4.2.11.1. (Additionally, the operator shall ensure that the pilot so designated is given all authority necessary to discharge his responsibilities under the provisions of Annex 6).

On 8 February 1954, the ANC decided to submit the proposal to Contracting States for their consideration. On receipt of the replies on the proposal, the ANC, after a marginal vote gain, recommended to amend Annex 6 by a proposed addition to Annex 6 Paragraph 4.2.7.1.: "...the pilot so designated shall be given all authority necessary to discharge his responsibilities under the provisions of this Annex".

However, the Council, disapproved the text and, after a fascinating debate, returned the proposal to the ANC to improve the text. Then, the Secretariat, after studying the subject, came up with a proposal containing the following addition to Annex 6, incorporating the admission to the cockpit of personnel officially assigned to perform inspections, flight crew proficiency checks, technical duties, etc.:

3.4. The pilot-in-command of an aircraft, during flight time, shall have the final authority for the operation and the safety of the aircraft in flight and the maintenance of discipline with respect to all persons on board.
3.4.1. Subject to the provisions of 3.4, personnel charged with inspection, flight checking or other technical duties during flight time shall not be prohibited from performing the duties to which they have been assigned.

The subject of the status of the aircraft commander has been under consideration for many years. Numerous drafts have been prepared within the framework of CITEJA and ICAO since the time when CITEJA first began to deal with the legal status of the aircraft commander. To mention some dedicated persons (CITEJA *rapporteurs*) who worked on different drafts: Thieffry (1927), Babiński (1930 and 1931) and Garnault (1946), and finally the revised (P)ICAO draft in 1947.

In 1950, a survey demonstrated that more than 30 national aviation legislations contained provisions relating to the legal status of the aircraft commander. These data made clear that the necessity of such regulations was widely recognized. On the other hand, the multiformity of all these regulations accentuated the need for uniformity. Generally, the collection of national aviation laws and regulations has proved very useful in the preparation of careful studies on the technical, economic and legal questions.[47]

---

47 *See* ICAO Doc. 7270, A6-P/1, Report of the Council to the Assembly on the Activities of the Organization in 1951, Montreal, May 1952, Chapter VII Constitutional and Legal Questions, p. 74.

Many respectable authors, lawyers and experts in private international law, who studied the subject within the framework of CITEJA and (P)ICAO, have referred through different approaches to the desirability of a convention on the legal status of the aircraft commander, unlike various suggestions to settle the matter on an international basis by means of SARPs in the Annexes to the Chicago Convention and related ICAO manuals and circulars as well as other documents.

However, the objection to these suggestions is that an Annex offers no guarantee of uniformity, because the Chicago Convention does allow Contracting States to deviate, under circumstances, from international Standards and procedures of an Annex (Art. 38, Departures from international Standards and procedures) through immediate notification obligation to ICAO.

In other words, SARPs do not share the same legal binding forces as the Chicago Convention *per se*, unlike the Annexes A-G (technical regulations) and H (general provisions relative to customs) to the 1919 Paris Convention, having the same legal effect as the treaty itself pursuant to Article 39 of the Paris Convention.[48]

On several occasions, IATA was of the opinion that a Convention on the Status of the Aircraft Commander was considered premature, albeit the objections formulated by IATA were more of a practical than a purely legal character. In this respect, the American CITEJA experts as well as IFALPA were strongly in favour of regularizing the position of the aircraft commander by means of a convention which would also emphasize the importance of the principles involved.

In the 1950s, a substantial growth in international air transportation was observed. An increasing number of passenger aircraft were flying scheduled intercontinental routes, especially but not only over the high seas, and many more intracontinental routes, frequently crossing different territories of contiguous sovereign States.

Inherent in these activities, there were many questions concerning the legal status of aircraft and criminal aspects of problems related to this subject. From a legal point of view, a comprehensive research should be made of the case of criminal acts committed on board aircraft flying through the airspace of a particular State as well as over the high seas. Questions in this regard concerning the jurisdictions of the State of registry, of the State of landing or of the State having sovereignty over the territory being overflown as well as the legal rules concerning the high seas were considered highly relevant.

The importance of the legal status of aircraft would then take precedence over the legal status of the aircraft commander. In the years following this development, the need to prepare an international instrument on criminal acts committed on board aircraft

---

48   Bouvé, C.L., "Regulation of International Air Navigation under the Paris Convention," (1935) 6 *J. Air L. & Com.* 299, pp. 300-305.

therefore became extremely clear. Nevertheless, it would soon appear that the aircraft commander was going to play a major role in this matter.

The first move towards a revival of the Draft Convention on the Legal Status of the Aircraft Commander was made at the sixth session of the Legal Committee in June 1950. As a matter of first priority, Chairman Dr. Enrique M. Loaeza, the Mexican representative to the ICAO Council, who at the same time represented Mexico on the Legal Committee, suggested in his opening speech to add the study of the legal status of aircraft to the Work Programme of the Legal Committee. Mr. John Cobb Cooper, legal adviser of IATA, advocated this move.

Loaeza observed in his speech, among other things, that:

> The definition of the legal status of the aircraft commander also requires immediate attention; and among all those problems, probably one of the most complex, but at the same time the most important and urgent, is the study of the legal status of aircraft, with a view to arriving at a convention. I would suggest that this study be added to our work programme as a matter of first priority.

Loaeza had earlier sought the opinion of other parties, such as the Air Transport Committee and came to the conclusion that such a study is not purely theoretical and presents many problems of considerable importance. The wording of many provisions of the Chicago Convention refers to 'aircraft' and places obligations and rights on 'aircraft'. Hence, clarification of the so-called legal status of the aircraft was very much needed especially in light of an increasingly antagonistic global society and at the same time a more complex international aviation industry in which the authority of the aircraft commander urgently needed a uniform legal basis, if only to prioritize both topics on the agenda.

Notably, the Tokyo Convention had its origin in a 1950 study project of the ICAO Legal Committee and one of its Subcommittees. Upon this basic project, which was originally as conceptually broad as its name 'The Legal Status of the Aircraft', were superimposed parts of a draft convention in being entitled 'The Legal Status of the Aircraft Commander'. The connecting factor between the two topics of the project, to merge into one convention, was their relationship with crimes committed on board aircraft.[49]

An *ad hoc* Subcommittee, considering the Work Programme, recommended that the legal status of the aircraft and the legal status of the aircraft commander be placed as items

---

49   *See* Boyle, R.P., Pulsifer, R., "The Tokyo Convention on Offenses and Certain Other Acts Committed on Board Aircraft," (1964) 30 *J. Air L. & Com.* 305, pp. 306-307 and 316.

three and four on the Work Programme, thus giving more priority than the Legal Committee ultimately indicated. The Legal Committee adopted this opinion taking into account that this combination be placed after topics already on the agenda as Aerial Collisions and a revision of the 1929 Warsaw Convention.[50]

Two *rapporteurs* were appointed: Loaeza for the 'Legal Status of the Aircraft' and Garnault for the 'Legal Status of the Aircraft Commander'. The attention for the legal status of the aircraft commander was based on rather unexpected support from various delegates. IFALPA favoured the enactment of such a convention, while IATA concluded that the experience of its members had not revealed any practical need for the proposed convention. At its seventh session, the Legal Committee considered a report discussing the desirability of a convention on the subject, the questions concerning the legal status of the aircraft commander that can lead to an international solution, and the need for changes in the existing draft text.

The Legal Committee put a request to the Council for advice on the need for a convention as well as the technical and economic aspects of the issues involved. The Council, in preparation to a concluding recommendation, invited interested private international organizations to submit their views on the necessity for such a convention.[51]

The question should provisionally be placed on the agenda of the ninth session of the Legal Committee in 1953 for consideration, if these views would be received in time. At this session, a Subcommittee was appointed only to study the legal status of the aircraft. Its report was adopted as a progress report in September 1954.

It was not before the 10th session of the Assembly at Caracas in 1956 that the direct consistency between the legal status of the aircraft commander and the legal status of the aircraft was first made clear.

Proposals were made to combine both studies as the integral importance of both topics would become significant in international commercial air traffic. The US delegates to the Legal Committee put it this way:

> Every day more than one thousand aircraft registered in the United States were abroad and a large number of foreign aircraft flew over the territory of the United States. There were, therefore, many questions concerning the legal status of these aircraft. An examination should be made of the case of criminal acts committed on board aircraft above the territory of a particular country or

---

50   *See* Boyle, R.P., Pulsifer, R. (1964), p. 308.
51   The International Air Transport Association, the International Federation of Air Line Pilots' Associations, the Fédération Internationale des Transports Aériens Privés (FITAP) and the Fédération Aéronautique Internationale (FAI).

over the high seas. The question of the civil effects of certain acts on board aircraft should also be studied.

Both studies became equivalent active items because the subject of the aircraft commander was now assuming topical importance. Moreover, this topic should therefore be placed in Part A of the Legal Committee's Work Programme.

Regarding the legal status of the aircraft, the US delegation suggested that this subject should be given priority. The reason was that the increase in the number of users of air transportation made it essential to solve the very complex legal problem of determining which law applied to certain acts committed on board aircraft.

Loaeza, wishing to be associated with these comments, recommended that the Legal Committee would deal first with the question of crimes on board aircraft, a matter that would receive a lot of attention in the near future with regard to the drafting process and framework which led to the adoption of the Tokyo Convention in 1963.

A study of the legal status of the aircraft commander would probably require that the Council would also have the question considered from the technical point of view as soon as possible, and that the Council would take the necessary measures in this respect. Loaeza added that the Legal Committee should recommend to the Assembly that it should direct the Council to arrange for a more active technical study of the question of the aircraft commander, as some coordination was required between the rules laid down in the Annexes to the Chicago Convention and the work of the Legal Committee.[52]

Strong support from the US delegation brought about to focus the discussion on the legal status of the aircraft in particular on public law matters, such as criminal offences, rather than private law matters, which incidentally, after a study trajectory parallel to the legal status of aircraft, were largely codified in the 1948 Geneva Convention on rights in aircraft.[53]

The final observation was made by Miss Hazel Alberta Colclaser, aviation lawyer from the United States who suggested that it was necessary to consider the legal status of aircraft and that of the aircraft commander concomitantly, thereby laying the foundation for the draft framework which later became the cornerstone of the Tokyo Convention. Her decisive argument was that considerable work had already been done on the subjects and

---

52 *See* ICAO Doc. 7712, A10-LE/5 10th Session of the Assembly, Caracas, June-July 1956, Report and Minutes of the Legal Commission, p. 4 Part B Subjects on the Work Programme on which no work is at present being done – Legal status of the aircraft commander. *See also* Minutes of Third Meeting, pp. 18-19.

53 Convention on the International Recognition of Rights in Aircraft, signed at Geneva on 19 June 1948. The Convention entered into force on 17 September 1953. *See also*, Honig, J.P., *The Legal Status of Aircraft*, Proefschrift ter Verkrijging van de Graad van Doctor in de Rechtsgeleerdheid aan de Rijksuniversiteit te Leiden, op Gezag van de Rector Magnificus Dr. A. E. van Arkel, Hoogleraar in de Faculteit der Wis- en Natuurkunde, Tegen de Bedenkingen van de Faculteit der Rechtsgeleerdheid te Verdedigen op Woensdag 13 Juni 1956 te 14 Uur (The Hague: Martinus Nijhoff, 1956), Chapter III Rights in Aircraft.

the increase in the number of users of international air transportation made it essential to solve the very complex legal problem of determining which law applied to acts committed on board an aircraft as mentioned earlier.

In line with this, Loaeza pointed out that the authority of the aircraft commander frequently gave rise to discussions and that national laws offered entirely different solutions to the problem. Furthermore, he added that the ICAO Legal Commission (the Legal Commission to the Assembly) should recommend to the Assembly that it should direct the Council to arrange for a more active technical study of the question of the aircraft commander, as some coordination was required between the rules laid down in the Annexes to the Chicago Convention and the work of the Legal Committee.[54]

A report, submitted by Garnault, elected as the legal expert of the Legal Committee and *rapporteur* on the legal status of the aircraft commander, reviewed comments received during the Legal Committee's meetings from a number of delegates and observers of which IFALPA was in favour of a convention on the subject, while IATA concluded, after consultation with its member airlines, that there were no practical benefits to such a proposed convention.

Garnault noted that national legislations, considered all together, had to deal with the following subjects: the necessity for an aircraft commander; his appointment and replacement in case he is unable to act; his general responsibilities; his powers as the agent of the owner or operator, including the limitations or the extensions of these powers; the maintenance of the documents carried on board the aircraft; birth, marriage and death on board the aircraft; customs, sanitary and other regulations; negligence or fault.

Garnault concluded that most of these matters were well capable of international solution, and this would, by facilitating the work of the aircraft commander, have the effect of improving the conditions of civil air transportation. In particular, it is essential to define clearly:

1. the conditions of appointment of an aircraft commander so that his capacity as commander may be recognized by all the Contracting States with the rights and obligations attached to this capacity;
2. the rights and obligations to be recognized uniformly by all Contracting States as belonging to an aircraft commander with their limitations and possible extensions.[55]

However, due to changing circumstances, particularly in the domain of commercial air transportation, and different cultural, societal and legal views of responding Contracting States on the legal status of the aircraft commander, little progress has been made in

---

54   Van Wijk, A.A. (1982), p. 328. *See also* ICAO Doc. 7712, A10-LE/5, pp. 18-19.
55   Boyle, R.P., Pulsifer, R. (1964), pp. 308-309.

working on this subject, as opposed to the establishment of the Tokyo Convention in which a section was devoted to the powers of the aircraft commander.

In November 1964, a number of representatives on the Council had questioned the efficiency of the Legal Committee on the ground that several conventions prepared by that Committee had not been ratified by a great number of Contracting States and that the work of the Legal Committee on its 15th session at Montreal in September 1964 on the Draft Convention on Aerial Collisions had met with strong opposition within the Legal Committee.

Concerns have been raised by representatives of the Legal Committee about the legal work of the Organization from the standpoint not merely of the status of air law conventions prepared by ICAO, but also of the working methods of the Legal Committee and the results it was achieving by those methods. Most of the adopted air law conventions had received an inadequate number of ratifications and there appeared to be little prospect of an improvement in the current situation. It was also stated that this situation had resulted in concern over the working methods of the Legal Committee, expressed by some of its own legal experts.

Altogether, this eventually resulted in a study on the Organization and Working Methods of the Legal Committee by a Working Group of the ICAO Council during the year 1965. The Working Group made various recommendations regarding such items as composition and officers of the Legal Committee, basic principles to be followed in the preparation of draft conventions, creation and maintenance of the Work Programme of the Legal Committee, procedure for the preparation of draft conventions and informal consultations as well as the special role of the ICAO Legal Bureau.

These recommendations, together with the report (ICAO A15-WP/23 LE/4 and C-WP/4160) thereon, were submitted by the Council to the 15th session of the ICAO Assembly which in turn referred the question to its own Legal Commission. Although not unanimously, proposals by the Working Group in the sense of 'the Legal Committee could better increase and coordinate its work' and a different election of representatives did not find favour with the ICAO Legal Commission.

As the starting point of its discussion of Agenda Item 32.1, the Legal Commission took the Report of the Working Group, established by the Council on this particular item. The Report dealt with the Organization and Working Methods of the Legal Committee found in C-WP/4160 attached to A15-WP/23 LE/4. In the opinion of the Working Group, the existing relationship between the Council and the Legal Committee as established in the Constitution of the Legal Committee (Resolution A7-5) existed at the time, required no change. The Legal Commission noted that the Report of the Working Group had been transmitted to the Assembly as a paper for its information when considering Agenda Item 32.1.[56]

The Legal Commission heard a number of general statements on the Report of the Working Group. It considered that the Legal Committee had made a substantial contribution to the development of air law and that progress in that field compared favourably with progress in other fields of international law. Nevertheless, it was recognized that the Organization and Working Methods of the Legal Committee and, for that matter, of any other body could be capable of improvement.

The Legal Commission, having examined the various recommendations made by the Working Group, unanimously determined that the Legal Committee should continue to remain open to representatives of all Contracting States and that there will be no need for the Legal Committee to have a permanent seat in Montreal.

Furthermore, the Legal Commission came to the conclusion that it is not necessary that the Legal Committee should hold permanent sessions, partly contrary to the recommendation of the Working Group, and found that the Constitution and Rules of Procedure of the Legal Committee were sufficiently flexible to permit efficient organization of its work.

Other recommended improvements proposed by the Legal Commission were continuity of participation of the same delegates in work and establishment of national groups or teams of lawyers for consideration of items on the Legal Committee's Agenda. Moreover, the Legal Committee should elect its Chairman and first and second Vice-Chairmen at the beginning of each session to be able to take office immediately, and to hold it for the next two sessions as well as to expedite the work of the Legal Committee.[57] Finally, the Legal Commission decided to refer to the following principles as being of great importance, and recommended that the Legal Committee should continue to observe them:

1. Draft conventions placed before the Legal Committee by Subcommittees should be considered under the procedure found in Rule 28A of the Committee's Rules of Procedure.[58]

---

56   ICAO A15-WP/23 LE/4, 23 April 1965, Agenda Item 32.1 Organization and Working Methods of the Legal Committee. C-WP/4160, 24 February 1965, Report of the Working Group on Organization and Working Methods of the Legal Committee, pp. 9-11. VI Recommendations. *See also* ICAO Doc. 9902 Assembly Resolutions in Force (as of 28 September 2007), p. I-23. A7-5 Revised Constitution of the Legal Committee.
57   ICAO Doc. 8517, A15-LE/10 15th Session of the Assembly, Montreal, 22 June-16 July 1965 – Report and Minutes of the Legal Commission, Agenda item 32.1 Organization and Working Methods of the Legal Committee, pp. 8-10.
58   *See* ICAO Doc. 7669-LC/139/6, Sixth Edition 2018: Rule 28A: Texts by Subcommittees. Where a text for a draft convention has been prepared by a Subcommittee and presented to the Committee, then, unless the Committee shall in any case by a two-thirds majority otherwise decide:
    a.   the text so prepared shall be taken as the basis of discussion;

2. At all stages of the study of a subject, the Legal Committee should make full use of the resources of the Legal Bureau.
3. Questionnaires should be used for the purpose of consulting States and international organizations, although they should be used sparingly.

In order to speed up the work of the Legal Committee and to provide the Council with additional information with respect to draft conventions, the following new rule has been introduced in the Legal Committee's Rules of Procedure:

Each Subcommittee instituted by the Legal Committee to study a draft convention shall include in its report an assessment of the measures of agreement reached and capable of being reached between States upon the problems under consideration, together with an expression of opinion whether the subject is ripe for study by the Legal Committee. That part of the report shall be submitted to the Council as well as to the Legal Committee.[59]

At that time, these reports were submitted only to the Legal Committee although the Council took note when deciding on the agenda and location and date of meetings of the Legal Committee or its Subcommittees, denoting the Council's control over the Legal Committee's work.

The Legal Commission did not suggest any change in the prevailing rules at that time governing preparation and adoption of draft conventions, while it considered that the Chairman of the Legal Committee and the Legal Bureau should be given an increasingly active role in promoting progress of the Legal Committee's work.

1.4 THE AIRCRAFT COMMANDER IN TURBULENT TIMES

In the 1960s and 1970s, known as unprecedented turbulent decades in aviation, the number of aerial hijackings increased alarmingly. The escalation of the severity and multiplicity of unruly behaviour, not to mention unlawful acts, on board aircraft dramatically screwed up good order and discipline on board an aircraft.

Considerably, more than a hundred reported incidents of unlawful seizure of civil aircraft and incidents of violent sabotage and armed attacks, including politically motivated

---

b. any proposals in relation to the text so prepared shall be submitted in the form of amendments to the text.

See also Working Paper Legal Committee – 38th Session LC/38-WP/4-1 Appendix Rules of Procedure, Section VII – Conduct of Business, Rule 28A.

59 See ICAO A15-WP/108 LE/7, 29 June 1965 Assembly – 15th Session – Legal Commission, Agenda item No. 32.1: Organization and Working Methods of the Legal Committee. Proposal of the United Kingdom. See also Mankiewicz, R.H. (1966), pp. 94-96.

acts of sabotage, against civil aircraft and passengers, both in the air and on the ground, occurred.

Because of the dramatic situation, an extraordinary Assembly was held at Montreal from 16 to 30 June 1970. The main topic of conversation was the safety of flight, in particular, measures to combat the spread of aviation terrorism. Clearly, from that time on, the primary objective of each Contracting State was to safeguard its airline passengers, flight crews, ground personnel as well as the general public against any acts of unlawful interference.[60]

In the tenor of crisis and on the legal side, three new multilateral conventions were prepared and concluded in a relatively short period of time. These conventions were widely recognized by the global community in the 1960s and 1970s. In the first place, the Tokyo Convention, thereafter, in 1970, The Hague Convention for the Suppression of Unlawful Seizure of Aircraft (the so-called Anti-Hijacking Convention), which came into force on 14 October 1971, and shortly thereafter, the 1971 Montreal Convention for the Suppression of Unlawful Acts against the Safety of Civil Aviation (the so-called Sabotage Convention), which came into force on 26 January 1973, together designated as the security conventions with the intention to make civil aviation safe again.[61]

The dramatic and desperate incidents of aerial hijackings in those dreadful years was a great and particular concern of IFALPA which was obliged to devote a major part of its efforts and resources to what had become the number one problem in civil aviation. Worldwide concern regarding the hijacking problems required the international community, including governments and organizations such as ICAO, IATA and IFALPA, to take combined prompt and effective international measures to combat this menace to civil aviation. The urgent task was at the time to prepare a convention to ensure that all hijackers, wherever found, would be subject to severe punishment for an act which would endanger the safety and lives of passengers and crew on board as well as people on the ground.

The United States affirmed the support for both the Tokyo Convention and The Hague Convention by the announcement of President Richard M. Nixon on 11 September 1970

---

60   ICAO Doc. 8849-C/990, December 1969. Action by the Council and Other Decisions Taken and Work Done by ICAO on the Subject to Unlawful Interference with International Civil Aviation and its Facilities.

61   The 1971 Montreal Convention (ICAO Doc. 8966) is supplemented by the 1988 Montreal Protocol for the Suppression of Unlawful Acts of Violence at Airports Serving International Civil Aviation (the so-called Airports Protocol), done at Montreal on 24 February 1988 (ICAO Doc. 9518). The 2010 Beijing Convention on the Suppression of Unlawful Acts Relating to International Civil Aviation, adopted on 10 September 2010 that was prompted by the terrorist attacks on 11 September 2001 (ICAO Doc. 9960). The 2010 Beijing Protocol Supplementary to the Convention for the Suppression of Unlawful Seizure of Aircraft, done on 10 September 2010 (ICAO Doc. 9959), supplemented the 1970 The Hague Convention (ICAO Doc. 8920). The 2014 Montreal Protocol to Amend the Convention on Offences and Certain Other Acts Committed on Board Aircraft (the so-called Unruly Passenger Protocol) amended the 1963 Tokyo Convention (ICAO Doc. 8364).

to combat aerial hijacking through a seven-point programme. He directed various government agencies and airlines to develop and implement strict security measures, including new methods for detecting weapons and explosive devices, and called upon other governments to become parties to both conventions. He ordered the State Department and other appropriate agencies to consult with foreign governments and foreign carriers concerning the full range of techniques which they use to foil hijackers. Furthermore, as stated in point 5, he emphasized that it is imperative that all States accept the multilateral convention providing for extradition or punishment of hijackers, the principle of *aut dedere aut judicare*, which would be taken into consideration at the International Conference on Air Law at The Hague in December 1970, under the auspices of ICAO.

Finally, he called upon other governments around the world to take joint action to suspend airline services with those States that persist in refusing to punish or extradite international blackmail hijackers. The UN Security Council has asked all nations to take all possible legal steps to protect against further hijackings or other interference in international civil aviation.[62]

However, governments failed to deal adequately with terrorist actions which took place after the signing of the two new conventions. The international community felt that perpetrators of such acts were not or not appropriately brought to justice, which again gave rise to serious concern and threat to the safety of civil aviation.

The ICAO Council, put under pressure by the United States, had to complete the work on a convention which would provide for sanctions against unwilling States that refused to punish aerial hijackers. This work was hampered because of endless discussions and meetings, without an effective result.

The efforts done by the Legal Committee with respect to the preparation of the conventions preoccupied the Organization in such a way that the progress on the topic of the legal status of the aircraft commander was severely delayed, at least for the time being.

Little progress was made in the early years of the 1970s despite support from various stakeholders to prioritize the topic, which at that time was put in Part B of the Legal Committee's Work Programme. Strong support was expressed by several ICAO Contracting States and IFALPA to make a combination of the legal status of the aircraft and the legal status of the aircraft commander and, to aim for a higher priority.

In 1974, at the twenty-first Assembly of ICAO, the legal status of the aircraft commander continued to receive, albeit, mixed support because of the fact that the situation of aircraft

---

62 *See* Hearings Committee on Foreign Relations of the United States Senate, 92nd Congress, First Session on Executive A, 92nd Congress, First Session. The Convention for the Suppression of Unlawful Seizure of Aircraft, signed at The Hague, 16 December 1970. 7 June and 20 July 1971, pp. 1-3.

commanders was increasingly becoming involved in legal issues so as to require a precise definition of their status in the discharge of their duties.[63] The result was a place in Part A of the Work Programme.

A working paper was submitted by Chile and accordingly its representative within the Legal Commission pointed out that:

> His government, while in the process of developing an aeronautical code in accordance with the requirements of air transport, wished to give particular attention to the question of the legal status of the aircraft commander which was of prime importance, needed urgent study and deserved a higher priority than it had been accorded in the Work Programme of the Legal Committee.[64]

This article resulted in divided reactions. On the one hand, some States expressed doubts, especially about the impending unrealistically extensive Work Programme of the Legal Committee, while on the other hand, some other States, like the United States and Sweden, expressed their full support. The observer from IFALPA also supported the Chilean working paper by pronouncing that although the Tokyo Convention contained a number of important provisions with regard to the legal status of the aircraft commander, so far it had not been universally accepted and did not provide adequate safeguards in many domains. But, the Legal Commission decided not to disturb the pattern of the existing comprehensive Work Programme of the Legal Committee.

Especially aerial hijackings and other terrorist acts on board passenger aircraft had shown how important the critical decisions were that had to be taken by the aircraft commanders dealing with such perilous offences. They unmistakably deserved the corresponding authority and worldwide protection of their status, which, however, would only be possible by global recognition. During the 22nd session of the Legal Committee in 1976, the delegate of the Federal Republic of Germany expressed this alarming reality in an attempt to give the issue a materially higher priority.

Studies conducted by IFALPA and its member associations indicated that the Legal Committee should give its attention to certain problems in this field, such as:

i.   the criminal responsibility of the aircraft commander, which should not be permitted to compromise the technical investigation of an aircraft accident;

---

63   ICAO Doc 9116, A21-LE Report and Minutes of the Legal Commission, Assembly 21st Session, Montreal, 24 September-15 October 1974, 30:1, Part A item 9. Legal Status of the Aircraft Commander, p. 5.
64   Van Wijk, A.A. (1982), p. 331.

ii.   the civil responsibility of the aircraft commander and flight crew members, bearing in mind the interest of ensuring safety by encouraging, during an investigation, full disclosure of all relevant facts;

iii.   the authority of the aircraft commander in respect of ground interventions during acts of unlawful seizure of aircraft;

iv.   the protection of innocent flight crew members from criminal or administrative proceedings in connection with drugs or contraband carried in their aircraft.[65]

Since its creation in 1947 through the adoption of Resolution A1-46 by the ICAO Assembly, the Legal Committee has produced final drafts on various conventions and protocols, while from the early 1960s, its attention was more focused on different high priority items such as the Draft Convention on Aerial Collisions, a study of the revision of the 1952 Rome Convention and of the increase of the limits of liability established by the 1955 The Hague Protocol, as well as a study of the liability of air traffic control (ATC) agencies.[66]

This work was done according to the rather time-consuming Rules of Procedure laid down in the Constitution of the Legal Committee. Among all subjects to be studied, the legal status of the aircraft commander got a high priority one time and a lower rating in the Work Programme in the Legal Field the next time with the result that deliberations about the subject dragged on for years.[67]

It has been stated that the Tokyo Convention had resolved the problem of the legal status of the aircraft commander only partially, namely by defining the powers and authority of the aircraft commander in the case of criminal offences or certain other acts

---

65 ICAO Doc. 9116, A21-Min. LE/3, pp. 20-26.

66 *See* ICAO Doc. 4411, A1-P/45, 3 June 1947, Resolution A1-46 Constitution of the Legal Committee of ICAO. Resolved: (a) That the 'Constitution' of a Legal Committee, in the form of Appendix 'A', be approved; (b) That the first meeting of the Legal Committee be summoned by the Council at a convenient place and date; and (c) That Commission No. 4 immediately prepare a programme of the work to be undertaken by the Legal Committee during the ensuing year, p. 48. The Legal Committee's preparatory work and drafting included, among others, the following private and public international law instruments: Convention on the International Recognition of Rights in Aircraft (Geneva, 1948). Convention on Damage Caused by Foreign Aircraft to Third Parties on the Surface (Rome, 1952). Convention, Supplementary to the Warsaw Convention, for the Unification of Certain Rules Relating to International Carriage by Air Performed by a Person other than the Contracting Carrier (Guadalajara, 1961). Convention on Offences and Certain Other Acts Committed on Board Aircraft (Tokyo, 1963). Protocol to Amend the Convention for the Unification of Certain Rules Relating to International Carriage by Air Signed at Warsaw on 12 October 1929 (The Hague Protocol, 1955).

67 *See* ICAO Doc. 8774, A16-LE, Part B under item 6; ICAO Doc 9116 A21-LE Part A under item 9; ICAO Doc. 9213 A22-LE Part A under item 3, however, as recommended by the Legal Commission to the Assembly to shift the subject to item 6.

committed during flight which might jeopardize the safety of the aircraft, or its occupants or property therein, or the accepted level of good order and discipline on board.[68]

The Legal Commission agreed in Item 27:8 of the Work Programme in the Legal Field, which was established by the Legal Committee at its 22nd session held in October-November 1976, that the problems of unlawful seizure of aircraft and unlawful interference with civil aviation were of continuous concern for the Organization. The Legal Commission endorsed an opinion that it was highly desirable that all Contracting States become parties to the Conventions of Tokyo (1963), The Hague (1970) and Montreal (1971) and resolved to recommend that the Assembly would request the Secretary General to bring again Resolution A21-9 (Expeditious ratification of conventions relating to unlawful interference) to the attention of all Contracting States and that the Council be requested to study ways and means of obtaining widest possible acceptance of those Conventions.[69]

At its 92nd session in November 1977, the Council considered a proposal of the Union of Soviet Socialist Republics (USSR) to include an additional paragraph in ICAO Annex 6, Part I, relating to the authority and responsibility of the aircraft commander (defined as pilot-in-command in applicable ICAO Annexes) subjected to acts of unlawful interference.[70] This proposal was referred to the ANC for study and report on the technical elements of the issue.

Since the authority and responsibility of the aircraft commander were already covered in detail in Annexes 2 and 6, Part I, the ANC first studied these provisions to determine whether further specifications were needed to cover the case of unlawful interference during flight time. As a result of this study, the ANC concluded that the existing provisions were adequate.

In order to reach this conclusion, the ANC expressed the view that existing ICAO specifications covered undeniable duties of the pilot-in-command before and after flight time, but they did not provide for the exercise of command authority and responsibility in respect of the aircraft, persons or property on board the aircraft during these periods.

The ANC considered that before flight time, the pilot-in-command practically could do little in respect of protection against acts of unlawful interference, making an extension

---

68   See ICAO Doc. 9213, A22-Min. LE/2, p. 23 under item 10.
69   ICAO Doc. 9213, A22-LE, Work Programme in the Legal Field, p. 7, Agenda Item 27:8. See also ICAO Doc. 9118, A21-RES, p. 40.
70   See ICAO Doc. Council Working Paper C-WP/6636 (8 November 1977) and ICAO Doc. Council Working Paper C-WP/6946, 26 October 1979, Study on the Legal Status of the Aircraft Commander, Para. 3.5 Responsibility of the Pilot-in-Command during Flight of ICAO Annex 6, Part I, Twelfth Edition, July 2022, should be amended by: The pilot-in-command shall apply the operator's programme to ensure protection against acts of unlawful interference with civil aviation until such time as the appropriate authorities of the State where the aircraft is located assume responsibility for the aircraft and for the persons and property on board. During this period, any decision taken by the pilot-in-command to safeguard the aircraft and the persons and property on board against acts of unlawful interference shall be final.

of the relevant authority and responsibility in order to prevent an act of unlawful interference to be unwarranted and ineffectual. In addition, while the ANC was aware of many of the problems involving command authority and responsibility after flight time in the case of unlawful interference where, for example, an aircraft has been immobilized at an airport with all occupants kept on board, the Commission did not believe that consideration to extend the authority and responsibility of the pilot-in-command in such cases would involve significant technical matters to be dealt with in Annex 6.

The ANC concluded in detail that:

a. the proposal appeared to extend the scope of the authority and responsibility of the pilot-in-command before, during and after flight time to cover matters of a non-technical nature;

b. existing specifications contained in Annexes 2 and 6 adequately covered the authority and responsibility of the pilot-in-command for all technical matters concerning the operation and safety of the aeroplane and for the safety of all persons on board during flight time;

c. on technical grounds, it is not practical to develop detailed regulations concerning the authority and responsibility of the pilot-in-command during acts of unlawful interference because of the great variability and critical nature of such acts. In such cases the pilot-in-command must be permitted to apply his own initiative and best judgement on the basis of existing regulations and the operator's programme.

In March 1978, after taking note of the conclusion, the Council decided to refer the matter to the ICAO Committee on Unlawful Interference (CUI) for further study. This body sought advice of the ANC on the following proposed text to be suitable, according to the CUI, to insert in Annex 6, Part I:

> In the event of an act of unlawful interference, the pilot-in-command shall use his best judgement so as to protect the safety of the passengers, crew members and the aircraft until such a time as the appropriate authorities of the State on whose territory the aircraft has landed take over the responsibility for the aircraft and for the persons on board.

The ANC studied the text and concluded that it was not appropriate for inclusion in Annex 6. The ANC, through President Mr. E. K. Kasara from Uganda, responded on the request of the CUI as follows:

> In consideration of the limited applicability of Annex 6, Part I, to only those aeroplanes (as opposed to aircraft) engaged in scheduled international air services and non-scheduled international air transport operations for

remuneration or hire, it is not believed that the proposed specifications would accomplish the intended purpose. Furthermore, the proposal raises a number of issues concerning the responsibilities of the pilot-in-command beyond those currently addressed in Annex 6, Part I and Part II, or in Annex 2. Any change in the currently defined pilot-in-command responsibilities could have far-reaching consequences in other areas and would be difficult to assess without considerable study of all the factors involved. Accordingly, it appears that even if the proposed specification is located in Annex 17 similar problems would result and it is, therefore, the opinion of the Commission that the overall subject of pilot-in-command responsibility and authority need to be studied carefully before changes are made.

The proposal also raises other significant issues, such as the requirement of the State to take over responsibility from the pilot-in-command, which were discussed in considerable detail by the Commission. However, a number of these issues involve matters outside the normal technical competence of the Commission and it was therefore extremely difficult in the short time available to develop constructive suggestions to the Unlawful Interference Committee for alternative courses of action.

Finally, both bodies felt that altogether there were too many legal aspects to the proposal.[71]

At its 94th session on 29 June 1978, the Council decided to refer to the Legal Committee the question of the authority and responsibility of the pilot-in-command of an aircraft during acts of unlawful interference with a paper outlining the history of the subject and the views of the CUI, the ANC and the Council. It was further agreed to request the Legal Committee to study this item within the framework of Item 6, Part A of the Legal Committee's Work Programme and to decide on its priority. At its 24th session in May 1979, the Legal Committee decided that this item be given highest priority as Item 1 of Part A of the General Work Programme.

On 13 June 1979, the Council decided by Council Decision 79/6 to request the Secretary General to have a Secretariat study on the subject of the legal status of the aircraft commander prepared for presentation to the 98th session of the Council together with suggestions for further course of action. A few month later, on 26 October, the Secretary General presented a practical factual and descriptive study on the subject to the Council. One month later, the Council examined the study in its working paper C-WP/6946, and

---

71   ICAO A23-WP/31 P/12, 10 July 1980 Assembly – 23rd Session, Plenary, Agenda Item 7: Annual Reports of the Council to the Assembly for 1977, 1978 and 1979 and Work Programme for 1981-1983 and their reference to the Executive Committee as a whole and to Commissions as necessary – Legal status of the aircraft commander, pp. 1-3 and Attachment A (26 May 1978).

made two modifications in the text, including the proposal from the working paper of Chile.

Having considered the study prepared by the Secretariat, the Council decided, on 28 November 1979 during its 98th session, to establish in due time a Panel of Experts in the operational and legal fields. The working method of this Panel of Experts (formally known as: the 1980 ICAO Panel of Experts on the Legal Status of the Aircraft Commander, hereinafter referred to as the Panel of Experts) was based on the following terms of reference at that time:

a. to study the subject 'Legal Status of the Aircraft Commander' on the basis of the Secretariat study and in the light of comments from States and international organizations;

b. to prepare a list of operational and legal problems related to this subject which, in the opinion of the Panel, require a solution;

c. to suggest any specific solutions for further consideration by the appropriate bodies of ICAO;

d. to make every effort to complete the work during its meeting in April 1980 so that its report could be considered during the 100th Session of the Council.

The Secretariat study outlined the more than 50 years of history of consideration on the subject within the framework of CITEJA, PICAO and ICAO, as far as legal work was concerned. While the main focus has been on specific recent proposals, done at meetings of the Legal Committee, the history of the subject indicated that this legal matter could not be handled in an isolationist way, but needed a review by various domains at the international level. A key point was that this review should not disturb the international order, namely the existing instruments. Initially, the Panel of Experts had to consider those issues that would pose practical problems and where international regulation turned out to be needed.

Some members of the Panel of Experts expressed the view that the study should be carried out very cautiously. It was recalled that the subject to a large degree had been covered in some legal instruments such as the Annexes to the Chicago Convention and Chapter III of the Tokyo Convention, all which contain detailed elements concerning the duties and powers of the aircraft commander. Another important view was expressed that the existing regulations contained in national legislation should not be overlooked since many aspects of this particular subject were governed by national laws at the time.

A Questionnaire was provided in the final part of the Secretariat study. After the Council considered the study and believed that an interdisciplinary approach was needed, the Secretary General was requested to dispatch the study, including the attached Questionnaire, to ICAO Member States and to international organizations, including IFALPA, IATA and the UN advisory body Ibero-American Institute of Aeronautic and

Space Law (*Instituto Iberoamericano de Derecho Aeronáutico y del Espacio*) for their comments.[72]

Moreover, the Council, after consulting the ANC and the CUI, agreed to leave the deliberations to the Panel of Experts, which eventually met at Montreal from 9 to 22 April 1980, and approved the terms of reference set out in paragraphs 4.2 (a), (b) and (c) of ICAO Doc. C-WP/6946 with an additional provision suggested by the representative of the USSR, stating:

> [...] (d) to make every effort to complete the work during the meeting of the Panel of Experts in April 1980, so that its report could be considered during the 100th Session of the Council.

The meeting of the Panel of Experts dealing with the legal status of the aircraft commander turned out to be the highlight of the legal work within ICAO in terms of unification of international air law. Member States of all continents participated in the Panel of Experts.[73]

The Panel of Experts considered the questions formulated in the Secretariat study and then considered a number of additional identified questions. Furthermore, it examined a report submitted by an informal Working Group, created to facilitate and expedite the task of the Panel of Experts on operational matters related to the legal status of the aircraft commander within the framework as determined by the specific terms of reference (to consider operational problems associated with the legal status of the aircraft commander).[74]

A crucial Questionnaire question that needed to be answered by ICAO Contracting States and aviation organizations was:

---

72   Milde, M., "News from international organizations – ICAO forthcoming Panel of Experts on the legal status of the aircraft commander, 9-22 April 1980," (1980) 5 *Air Space L*. 1, pp. 53-54.

73   Acting under the delegated authority, the President of the Council appointed to the Panel as members the Chairman and Vice-Chairman of the Legal Committee (United Kingdom, Canada, Czechoslovakia and Venezuela) and further invited the following States to nominate an operational or legal expert: Cameroon, Chile, Federal Republic of Germany, Finland, France, India, Japan, Kenya, Lebanon, Netherlands, Philippines, Trinidad and Tobago, Union of Soviet Socialist Republics, United States of America and observers from IFALPA and IATA. Kenya and Philippines were not represented on the Panel while Trinidad and Tobago was represented only by an observer. An expert from Tanzania was later appointed. Observers came from Australia, Brazil, Egypt, Senegal and Yugoslavia. Members of the informal Working Group on operational matters related to the legal status of the aircraft commander came from Australia, Canada, Finland, France, Japan, United Kingdom, United States of America, Venezuela and observers from IATA and IFALPA.

74   The Working Group was composed of members from Australia, Canada, Finland, France, Japan, United Kingdom, United States of America, Venezuela and observers from IATA and IFALPA.

> Is there a practical need for an international regulation of the legal status of the aircraft commander in addition to the existing international regulations (Chicago Convention – SARPs – Tokyo Convention) referred to in paragraphs 5.1-5.4 of the Secretariat study on the subject.[75]

The question was clearly related to this domain that had been discussed earlier in a Council Decision of 15 June 1956. In this decision, cited in attachment F of the Secretariat study, Contracting States were invited

> to study the question whether their national laws and regulations were adequate, or required any improvements, to enable operators and pilots-in-command of aircraft, including, in particular, aircraft of foreign registry, to discharge effectively their duties and responsibilities, particularly as specified in Annexes to the Chicago Convention, with relation to the safety of their aircraft and any person or property on board and the prevention of any unauthorized act with respect thereto.[76]

On the same day, the Council adopted a resolution stating the following, in part:

> The Council invites Contracting States to study the question whether their national regulations are adequate, or require any improvement, to enable operators and pilots-in-command of aircraft, including, in particular, aircraft of foreign registry, to discharge effectively their duties and responsibilities in ensuring the safety of their aircraft and any person or thing on board and preventing any unauthorized act with respect thereto, and recommends that States undertake such measures to amend their national regulations as may be necessary to ensure the above-mentioned objectives.[77]

---

75 Questionnaire of the study on the legal status of the aircraft commander provided for by the ICAO Secretariat, transmitted to States by State Letter LE 4/38.1-79/233 of 28 December 1979.

76 Other attachments to the Secretariat study were: Attachment A. Draft Convention on the Legal Status of the Aircraft Commander (as revised by the Paris Legal *ad hoc* Committee of PICAO, February 1947. Attachment B. Comments submitted by IFALPA to the 22nd Session of the ICAO Legal Committee (19 October-5 November 1976) LC/Working Draft No. 855-1. Attachment C. Draft International Statute of the Aircraft Commander (Spanish text), developed by the Ibero-American Institute of Aeronautics and Space Law (1973). Attachment D. Proposal presented by Chile to the 24th Session of the ICAO Legal Committee (May 1979), LC/Working Draft No. 868-3. Attachment E. Comments submitted by IFALPA to the 24th Session of the ICAO Legal Committee (May 1979) LC/Working Draft 868-2.

77 *See also* ICAO Doc. 8565-LC/1522-2, International Conference on Air Law, Tokyo, August-September 1963, Volume II, Documents, Montreal 1966, pp. 65-66.

Regarding the last item, unauthorized acts, the question at that time focused mainly on the adequacy to respond to the situation of international civil aviation, given the increasing number and gravity of acts of unlawful interference, which had adverse implications for the safety of the aircraft and of crew and passengers on board.

The draft convention (the PICAO version, Doc. 2417 of 12 December 1946) was provided as background material of the Secretariat study. Following the meeting of the Panel of Experts in April 1980, the Report of the Legal Commission to the Assembly at its 23rd session from 16 September to 7 October 1980, presented its 1979 examination of the Part A current study items of the Legal Committee's General Work Programme, including the first posted subject on the legal status of the aircraft commander:

Part A.
a.   Legal Status of the Aircraft Commander
b.   Liability of Air Traffic Control Agencies
c.   Aerial Collisions
d.   Study of the Status of the Instruments of the Warsaw System

Part B.
Problem of Liability for Damaged Caused by Noise and Sonic Boom.

The Legal Commission discussed in great detail the subject which has been on the Work Programme of the Legal Committee since 1947 and was given, as mentioned before, in May 1979, the highest priority as Item 1 of Part A of the General Work Programme. The Legal Commission noted the Report of the Panel of Experts, which met in April 1980, and also noted that the Council deferred a decision on the further course of action on the subject pending the review of the Work Programme in the Legal Field by the 23rd session of the Assembly.

Several delegations stated that, although the majority of the Panel of Experts held the view that there was no practical need for the legal regulation, in the form of a new international instrument regarding the legal status of the aircraft commander, a minority had emphasized that there was a need to clarify in the appropriate ICAO Annexes and other relevant ICAO documents the role of the pilot-in-command, particularly regarding acts of unlawful interference, SAR operations and measures of assistance to aircraft in distress.

Other delegations emphasized that there were many legal and operational problems associated with the legal status of the aircraft commander requiring a solution, in particular the rights and duties of the pilot-in-command during the pre-flight and post-flight phases, search on board an aircraft, security and safety measures on board, etc.[78]

Several delegations emphasized the importance of the Tokyo Convention to strengthen the authority of the aircraft commander in cases of seizure and other acts of unlawful interference. It was in particular necessary to invite all Contracting States which had not yet become Party to the Tokyo Convention to do so.

Some other delegations agreed with the conclusions of the Panel of Experts. They also believed that unless problems of sufficient magnitude and practical importance were revealed, no further study would be justified on this item. Moreover, they were of the opinion that certain proposals, such as exercise of specific functions by the aircraft commander in a foreign State, would infringe the sovereignty of States. Another delegation expressed the opinion that the issue of State sovereignty was not involved in this case; it was a question of mere cooperation between the aircraft commander and the local authorities to safeguard flight safety.[79]

As a result of a lengthy discussion on this item, the Legal Commission decided by consensus to recommend to the Plenary:

a. to retain the subject of the 'Legal Status of the Aircraft Commander' as an important item in the General Work Programme of the Legal Committee;

b. that the Report of the Panel of Experts should be forwarded to Contracting States and international organizations;

c. that Contracting States and international organizations should be requested by the Council to reply to a detailed and precise Questionnaire which would elicit a statement of legal problems of sufficient magnitude to require urgent action, together with an indication of possible solutions.

The Legal Commission also noted paragraph 36 of the Report of the Panel of Experts which reads as follows:

> The Panel also agreed that the Council, taking into consideration the competence of the States, the role of the operators, the airport authorities and others, may wish to consider whether there is a need to clarify in the appropriate ICAO Annexes and any other relevant ICAO documents the role of the pilot-in-command in determining that the flight cannot be made safely because of the lack of security and safety measures.

---

78 The terms 'aircraft commander' and 'pilot-in-command' were still used interchangeably in connection with documentation, the Tokyo Convention Regime and ICAO Annexes.

79 ICAO Doc. 9314, A23-Min. LE/2 Legal Commission Report and Minutes, p. 24.

The Legal Commission also agreed that the Secretariat should prepare a comprehensive compilation of all the provisions in the Annexes and international conventions relating to the legal status, functions and duties of the aircraft commander; it was believed that such a compilation will facilitate the task of States in replying to the Questionnaire mentioned above.[80]

Other issues, formulated in the Secretariat study, to be studied with a view to possible adoption of a new international regulation, were:
– Terminology to be used and definition of the aircraft commander.
– Conditions of appointment of an aircraft commander, duration, international recognition and termination of his responsibility and authority.
– Operational (technical) authority and responsibility of the aircraft commander for the safe operation of the aircraft before, during and after the flight.
– Authority and responsibility of the aircraft commander as an agent of the State of registry (administrative and other functions on behalf of the State of registry with respect to authorities of other States and other entities, status as custodian of the diplomatic bag, functions and duties with respect to occurrences on board, etc.).[81]
– Authority and responsibility of the aircraft commander as an agent of the operator in the private law field with respect to passengers, baggage, cargo, commercial transactions with respect to the aircraft and its servicing, etc.
– Authority and responsibility of the aircraft commander with respect to persons on board (enforcement of law and order, powers foreseen by the Tokyo Convention, etc.) and other persons, before, during and after the flight.
– Authority and responsibility of the aircraft commander with respect to authorities outside the aircraft – in particular in connection with the concurrent or overlapping authority of the ATC agencies and aviation security agencies of different States.

The Panel of Experts then identified a certain number of questions which should be examined, and it was agreed that they would consider them point by point:
– Responsibility of the aircraft commander for any offence against customs, emigration and immigration, sanitary or medical legislation of any State without proof of guilt on his part.
– Transfer of responsibility of the aircraft commander in case of his incapacitation.

---

80   ICAO Doc. 9314, A23-LE Assembly 23rd Session, Montreal 16 September to 7 October 1980, Legal Commission Report and Minutes, pp. 7-8. Note: in this document, the two descriptions for the commanding officer, *viz*: aircraft commander and pilot-in-command, are mentioned in particular.
81   The State of registry or the State of registration is the State on whose register the aircraft is entered (ICAO Annex 7 – *Aircraft Nationality and Registration Marks*, Sixth Edition 2012, International Standards 1. Definitions).

- Suspension of the aircraft commander by the operator or by other authority.
- Assistance to be given to the aircraft commander by public authorities when the aircraft is subject to an act of unlawful interference and is 'in distress' (Art. 25 of the Chicago Convention and Art. 11 of the Tokyo Convention).[82]
- Civil liability of the aircraft commander and limits of such liability.
- Rights and duties of the aircraft commander in case of carriage of dangerous goods.
- Rights and duties of the aircraft commander in case of carriage and use of weapons on board an aircraft.
- Carriage of persons in custody.
- Problems of lease, charter and interchange of aircraft.
- 'Consolidation of penal procedural provisions' relating to penal proceedings against the aircraft commander following an aircraft incident or accident abroad.

Regarding the Questionnaire drawn up in the Secretariat study, only 20 respondents out of a total of 146 notified States and organizations had answered. The written comments received from those States at the beginning of the meeting indicated a mild cooperative but also a 'watching and waiting' attitude towards the subject matter on the Panel of Experts' Agenda. The moment the Panel of Experts started its deliberations on the legal status of the aircraft commander, it became quite clear that a majority of the replies from the Contracting States were in the affirmative.[83]

The bottom line was that, to their rational opinion, the predominant objection to the current situation was, according to the Contracting States, that existing regulations were scattered in multiple instruments as opposed to a potentially elaborate draft convention that would dissolve most of the issues, in particular the dominant question about the authority and responsibility of the aircraft commander prior to, during and after the flight.

Some members of the Panel of Experts stated that poor response was indicative of lack or total absence of interest in the subject and that Contracting States generally did not experience any practical legal problems in this field. Some other Panel members did not agree with the interpretation of the reactions of Contracting States to the Questionnaire.

Furthermore, the opinion was expressed that, in considering all the problems involved, a pragmatic approach was recommended, and that, consequently, it would be appropriate

---

82 Art. 25, Chicago Convention. Aircraft in distress. Each Contracting State undertakes to provide such measures of assistance to aircraft in distress in its territory as it may find practicable, and to permit, subject to control by its own authorities, the owners of the aircraft or authorities of the State in which the aircraft is registered to provide such measures of assistance as may be necessitated by the circumstances. Each Contracting State, when undertaking the search for a missing aircraft, will collaborate in coordinated measures which may be recommended from time to time pursuant to this Convention.

83 States in favour of an international instrument of the legal status of the aircraft commander were: Cuba, Czechoslovakia, Finland, Greece, Hungary, India, Iraq, Ireland, Lebanon, Mauritania, Mexico, Seychelles, Sweden and Yugoslavia.

to decide whether there was a need to add anything to the existing regulations. It was also stated that specific aspects of an operational nature were already dealt with in the Annexes to the Chicago Convention and that it would not be proper to list them from the Annexes in order to produce a single instrument.[84] An interesting divergence from its earlier views on the subject of the legal status of the aircraft commander was the argumentation done by IATA, rather mildly, in its working paper for submission to the Panel of Experts, that *inter alia*:

> Depending on the nature of any problems identified as a result of the review of the various replies to subsequent questions (of the Questionnaire prepared by the ICAO Secretariat), there may well be a practical need for an international regulation of this subject in addition to or possibly in lieu of existing regulations. It is, therefore, premature to take a final position as to the necessity for an international convention.[85]

In summary, after considering all aspects of the issues, the majority of the Panel of Experts was of the opinion that no practical need existed for a legal regulation along the lines of a new international instrument. The Panel of Experts did not identify any specific operational or legal problems which, in its view, required a solution.

Furthermore, the Panel of Experts noted that most questions regarding the authority of the aircraft commander with respect to offences and other acts committed on board aircraft are satisfactorily covered in the Tokyo Convention. Apart from possible improvements of certain rules in ICAO Annexes, no further study of the legal status of the aircraft commander was necessary at that time.[86]

After considering all aspects, the Panel of Experts agreed that the ICAO Council might consider whether it would be necessary to clarify the role of the aircraft commander in determining that a flight could not be made in a safe manner because of lack of security and safety measures, bearing in mind that resolving certain issues, where applicable, would be closely related to matters of national sovereignty. Given the slowness of decision making at the international level and the possible apparent disinterest on the part of Contracting States, a large number of States unhesitatingly defined the role of the aircraft commander, inherent to contemporary reality, in their national regulations, albeit hampering applicable legislation, apart from reaching consensus, at the international

---

84 ICAO A23-WP/23 LE 1 Assembly – 23rd Session 30 June 1980 Legal Commission, Annex I to Attachment PE/AIRCO Report, 22 April 1980, p. 16.
85 *See* Doc. PE/AIRCO-WD/7, 28 February 1980.
86 Van Wijk, A.A. (1982), p. 334.

level. States found the international discussions on the subject too long winded and often not suitable for compromise due to previously developed rigid national regulations.

However, a minority (three members) of the Panel of Experts was of the opinion that future study on this issue probably might reveal, in discussions in the forum of the Legal Committee, that there would, however, be a need for such an international instrument.[87]

In June 1980, the ICAO Council noted the Report of the Panel of Experts on the subject and decided to submit the Report to the Assembly for review by its Legal Commission and the Technical Commission. The latter was informed by IFALPA that some of its associations were experiencing difficulties with respect to existing national regulations.

The Assembly agreed that ICAO should publish a comprehensive list of ICAO references relating to the legal status of the aircraft commander as a starting point for further study of the case. The Assembly preserved this topic as an item on the Legal Committee's Work Programme, which, however, was due to be completely reviewed.[88]

The fact that more than one hundred Contracting States did not even reply on the Questionnaire showed a rather thin line to adhere to drawing up a sound and widely supported convention. Considering this state of affairs, the Panel of Experts eventually concluded that no follow-up study was needed at that particular time. Remarkably, in 1947, an observation of the UK delegation stated with reference to the aircraft commander's issue:

> It requires consideration whether this subject matter is more appropriately dealt with by a convention or by an Annex under Chapter VI – International Standards and Recommended Practices – to the Chicago Convention.[89]

In the context of the significant growth of international aviation expected in the 1980s and the following decades, the need for regulations in the field of safety and security increased proportionally. Especially, the aircraft commander engaged in international air transportation had to face constantly increasing challenges which justified the high priority of the subject regarding the legal status of the aircraft commander in the Work Programme of the Legal Committee. As a matter of fact, relevant provisions or applicable regulations were still scattered in various existing instruments (Chicago Convention and SARPs in Annexes 2, 6, 9 and 12, as well as the Tokyo, The Hague and Montreal

---

87   Milde, M., "News from international organizations – ICAO Report on the meeting of the Panel of Experts – legal status of the aircraft commander, Montreal, 9-22 April, 1980," (1980) 5 *Air Space L.* 3, pp. 187-188.

88   U.S. Participation in the U.N. Report by the President to the Congress for the Year 1980. Panel of Experts on the Legal Status of the Aircraft Commander. Department of State Publication 9222 International Organization and Conference Series 153, November 1981, pp. 268-269.

89   ICAO Doc. 4123, A1-LE/23, 9 May 1947 Agenda Item 4 (b), point 1. *See also* point 2 Title: It is suggested that a more appropriate title might be 'Draft Convention on the Rights and Duties of the Aircraft Commander'.

Conventions), without the prospect of consolidating the subject of the legal status of the aircraft commander in one single instrument, for example, an additional Annex to the Chicago Convention.[90]

However, the Canadian delegate pointed out that the Legal Commission was not really in a position to ask the Council to initiate studies with a view to preparing an Annex to the Chicago Convention in which the various provisions relating to the legal status of the aircraft commander would be brought together. His argument was that this kind of method was beyond the purview of the Legal Commission, but supported the suggestion that Contracting States and international organizations should be requested to provide detailed and precise information, documented by practical examples, on any legal problems of sufficient magnitude to require urgent international action. States should further be consulted as to whether they wished to suggest specific solutions regarding the questions raised in the Questionnaire, but he emphasized that the question of the authority and responsibility of the aircraft commander with respect to State authorities outside the aircraft was a sensitive point. After addressing the principle of State sovereignty, the Canadian delegate added that the drafters of the Tokyo Convention had achieved a delicate balance between the powers of the aircraft commander and the powers of the sovereign State which should not be impaired.[91]

Delegates from various States to the Legal Commission had different opinions with respect to an international solution. The UK delegate also stated that Chapter III of the Tokyo Convention had achieved a delicate balance of the authority of the aircraft commander and the ground authorities. This balance should not be disturbed by an international instrument, and that some matters that States wanted to be resolved in an international instrument were of political nature which, if dealt with an international regulation, would infringe the sovereignty of States. He agreed that the Secretariat could prepare for information of States a text of convenience which would assemble all the relevant provisions or regulations scattered in the various existing instruments.[92]

At the outset of the discussion within the Legal Commission on the Work Programme in the Legal Field, the delegations of Denmark, Finland, Iceland, Norway and Sweden (the Nordic delegations) presented a proposal which stated that the General Work Programme of the Legal Committee should reflect the needs of international civil aviation in the 1980s, that a number of subjects in the Work Programme have been studied for many years and that there was little prospect of concluding the work on these subjects and that it was

---

90   A large number of the delegates of the Legal Commission agreed that universal acceptance of the Tokyo, The Hague and Montreal Conventions was important. It was also essential that these Conventions be fully implemented.

91   ICAO Doc. 9314, A23-Min. LE/3, Minutes of the Third Meeting – Summary of Discussion, p. 30.

92   ICAO Doc. 9314, A23-Min. LE/3, p. 28.

necessary to carry out a more detailed examination of the General Work Programme, which would take more time than the present 23rd session of the Assembly.[93]

The Nordic delegations proposed a postponement of the work on the subjects and that the Council should be directed to develop, at an early date, a fundamentally revised General Work Programme reflecting the above-mentioned needs, a cleanup of the Work Programme of such subjects which did not reflect the practical needs of States or on which there was no possibility of an agreed solution.

For this purpose:

> it was decided to invite the views of the States and to consult with the Chairman and two Vice-Chairmen of the Legal Committee, the Secretariat and other experts in the legal and other fields as the Council may deem appropriate. Such consultations should be carried out, if the Council so decides, by means of a panel that should communicate, as soon as possible, the revised General Work Programme to the Legal Committee.

The delegation of India formally proposed that the Legal Commission should in principle accept the ideas expressed in the proposal of the Nordic delegations without prejudice to any conclusion that could have arisen from the discussion of the previously established Work Programme.

A newly appointed Panel of Experts, that specifically focused on the General Working Programme of the Legal Committee, met at Montreal from 8 to 16 June 1981. The task of this Panel was as follows: to study and analyse the replies from States and international organizations to the questionnaires prepared under the instructions of the 23rd session of the Assembly on the legal status of the aircraft commander and some other priority items in Part A of the General Working Programme, to study and analyse States' comments on the Report of the Panel of Experts on the Legal Status of the Aircraft Commander and the views of States concerning any subject that might be added or removed from the General Working Programme, and to make recommendations to the Council on this programme in the context of the Assembly decisions and related comments from States, including recommendations on the relative priority of the subjects in this programme.

On 26 October 1981, the Council noted the Report of the Panel of Experts and, in light of the conclusions and recommendations thereof, requested the Secretariat to prepare detailed studies and research material and to collect information on the following subjects: liability of ATC agencies, the status of the legal instruments of the Warsaw System, the legal implications of aircraft accident and incident investigation and the development of

---

93   ICAO A23-WP/54, LE/3, 18 September 1980.

standard contracts on the lease, charter and interchange of aircraft. The Council decided to await the progress of the work undertaken by the Secretariat on the above-mentioned subjects before deciding whether to convene a meeting of the Legal Committee.

The Council agreed with the Panel's recommendation that the first two subjects should remain in Part A of the Legal Committee's General Working Programme, and, consequently, to downgrade the priority of the subject on the legal status of the aircraft commander.[94]

In the 1980s, the legal topics shifted more and more to the misuse of civil aviation. For example, in A26-WP/56 Agenda Item 21: Work Programme in the Legal Field – it was noted by a large number of delegations that, in the interests of ensuring the safety of civil aviation and developing international cooperation in this field in accordance with the Chicago Convention, this important problem must continue to be studied so that it is covered fully and in all aspects, like the outcome of a Secretariat's report on the problem. The work thus accomplished, according to the delegations, would then help in undertaking a detailed examination of the question of formulating appropriate measures to prevent the misuse of civil aviation.

In this respect, the USSR delegation believed that a thorough study on the problem of misuse of civil aviation within the framework of the Legal Committee would make an important contribution to enhancing safety in civil aviation as a whole while meeting the requirements of respecting the sovereignty and law and order of States.[95]

The threat of attacks on aircraft and airports, aerial hijackings, incidents involving unruly and disruptive passenger behaviour, which might jeopardize the safety of the aircraft, or persons or property therein, or jeopardize good order and discipline on board, have unfortunately made international civil aviation a vulnerable mode of transportation. A shift to priority issues, such as worldwide protective security measures, other than an elaborate pragmatic codification of the legal status of the aircraft commander, has taken place over time.

The objective, after so many years of studies and discussions, to reach consensus on a Convention Supplementary to the Tokyo Convention or amendments of appropriate Annexes to the Chicago Convention with regard to the legal status of the aircraft commander, which deserved wider acceptance, unfortunately turned out to be a step too far.

---

94   ICAO Doc. 9356, Annual Report of the Council – 1981, Chapter VI Constitutional and Legal Questions, pp. 146-148.
95   ICAO A26-WP/56 LE/3 12 September 1986 Working Paper on the question of misuse of civil aviation.

1.5   CONCLUDING REMARKS

In the early days of aviation, the original intention of studies and discussions on the legal status of the aircraft commander in international air transportation was to regulate his position in private law – in other words, his legal and business powers to perform as a representative of the air carrier.

At that time, flying internationally was an adventurous endeavour that required a lead aviator, traditionally a male person, with, obviously, extraordinary abilities to cope with challenging events along the routes and at airports in remote areas.

The designation 'he' in ancient documents and even in texts of prevailing aviation conventions showed that in the early days of aviation, there must have been a typical 'man's bastion' that restricted most women to work in support roles in the aviation industry. Only a few managed to become pilots, making impressive historic flights. Brave women like Bessie Coleman, Amelia Earhart, Amy Johnson and Jacqueline Cochran contributed to the first steps towards emancipation in aviation.

> Someday, I dare say, women can be flyers and yet not be regarded as curiosities!
> (Amelia Earhart)[96]

Nevertheless, it took until the 1970s, a decade of societal changes, before there was a substantial influx of female pilots to commercial airlines, practically all over the world, which was one of the signs of emerging equal rights, legal standards and values regardless of gender, which is a fundamental human right.

In the 1980s, Captain Lynn Rippelmeyer from the United States became the first woman to fly a trans-Atlantic Boeing 747, and, some years later, became the first woman to serve as aircraft commander on the 'queen of the skies'. She and her iconic predecessors inspired countless young women to earn a pilot's licence in order to finally get that coveted left seat in the cockpit. Today, the number of female aircraft commanders and first officers has increased considerably, although the aviation sector in general and flight crews in particular still continue to have one of the poorest gender balances, according to the Royal Aeronautical Society and IFALPA.[97] This phenomena certainly was, and possibly still is, the case for the permanent bodies of ICAO, such as the Legal Committee, according to a survey on the gender of the representatives (legal experts) in the decades following its

---

96   Earhart, A.M., *The Fun of It* (New York: Harcourt Brace and Company, 1932), p. 95. *See also* Lieutenant Colonel Samuelson, N.B., "Equality in the Cockpit, a Brief History of Women in Aviation," (May-June 1984) 35 *Air Univ. Rev.* 4.

97   *See* IFALPA Position Paper 21POS09, 30 September 2021, Women in Aviation: Why Diversity, Equity, and Inclusion Matter. *See also* Royal Aeronautical Society, "Redressing the Balance. Why Do so Few Women Decide to Become Pilots?" *Industry News* 8 November 2016.

creation. The vast majority of the representatives of the Contracting States consisted then of men.

CITEJA, the ICAO Legal Committee and international organizations have done a lot of work through studies, discussions and deliberations at various meetings to make repeated attempts at the feasibility of a Draft Convention on the Legal Status of the Aircraft Commander.

However, as international air carriers in the course of time started to use their own station managers, local representatives and technical service repair facilities at their outstations, supported by contemporary telecommunication networks, the essential private air law element of the aircraft commander's statutory powers in that domain faded into the background. The administrative and representative functions gave way to the principal powers, namely the authority and responsibility in respect of the safety of the aircraft, crew, passengers or property therein.

Moreover, the changing global social landscape, the general increase in violence, especially emerging criminal acts such as aerial hijacking, unruly and disruptive behaviour of persons on board civil aircraft made the legal status of the aircraft commander to adapt to this 'new order'. The public law element in the cockpit could no longer be ignored because it does not come as a surprise that the aircraft commander as the competent authority on board the aircraft should curb these offences in a careful manner with the intention of trying, often with the assistance from the crew and passengers, to de-escalate the situation on board so as not to endanger the safety of the aircraft and its occupants. However, countless efforts in the field of public international air law have not been able to achieve consensus on a fully codified Legal Status of the Aircraft Commander.

The question arises whether there is still a manner to achieve universal coherence regarding a comprehensive Legal Status of the Aircraft Commander, being the pivotal figure in flight operations around the world. Trying to reach consensus through one of the sources of international law, for example, an international air law convention or protocol, means that consent of potential State Parties is required which usually needs a compromise or, in case of widely divergent interests, a *modus vivendi*. This, in turn, may easily lead to differences in States' interpretations of the provisions, especially words, phrases and definitions. A side effect taken into consideration is that the establishment trajectory of such an international legal instrument can be considerably lengthy, let alone the question whether there will be a practical need for such an instrument containing all legal specifications related to the aircraft commander.

Nonetheless, the lengthy and in-depth process of discussing, studying, drafting and negotiating in the past on a draft of the legal status of the aircraft commander has implicitly enriched the international air law system.

On the other hand, the conclusion must be drawn that the issue of the complicated international Legal Status of the Aircraft Commander is only partially regulated. At the international level, there are legal instruments as the Tokyo Convention (and the 2014 Montreal Protocol as an amending instrument) and ICAO Annexes that deal with this particular subject. However, the Standards in these Annexes are regarded as quasi-law, qualified as semi-binding, subject to derogation by Contracting States (which means a notification obligation or opt-out treaty clause), however explicitly binding through exclusive rulemaking for flying above the high seas (Annex 2, laying down the *Rules of the Air*).

There are, however, disadvantages associated with an international instrument. For example, the important powers and immunity of the aircraft commander conferred by the Tokyo Convention (to be discussed in Chapter 2), will only apply whenever this convention is applicable.

Notwithstanding this reality, there must be a need, at the international level, for a newly created comprehensive convention or protocol on the legal status of the aircraft commander to the present and future time frame. This possible realization of such an instrument can build on the remaining available studies and documents from the work history of the Legal Committee. On the other hand, bearing all considerations in mind, it is highly doubtful that there will be sufficient support for such a strenuous and long-term exercise on the subject. A Questionnaire submitted by the ICAO Secretariat to all Contracting States, as has been done in the past, could make a difference.

Another more practical thought is to create an ICAO Annex including technical SARPs, currently scattered in the Annexes, standing operating procedures in various documents and other legal regulations devoted to the powers, duties and responsibilities of the pilot-in-command, as defined in most of the ICAO documents. SARPs, which together form a large part of international air law, and relevant for the exploitation of international air transportation, are characterized by ambiguous legal effect. This statement has been made because of the Council's law-making powers considered in a 'quasi-legislative sense'.

In view of the mild (putative) enforcement or sanction mechanisms such as Article 54(j) of the Chicago Convention with respect to infractions or ICAO's Universal Safety Oversight Audit Programme regarding noncompliance with regulations and SARPs, these SARPs can be considered soft law. Implementation of international law in national law can only be explained in view of different international, constitutional and other national legal principles with divergent approaches such as a monistic, dualistic or modest form about the applicability of international norms as SARPs. According to the monistic approach, international legal rules do not require transformation into national law since international law, which, however, is of a higher order (*lex superior derogat legi inferiori*), and national law form a single legal system. International rules are directly applicable. The dualistic approach assumes that both legal spheres are separate, resulting in the transformation of international rules into national law having the same ranking.

In both approaches, SARPs, especially Standards that are highly authoritative in practice, are considered (indirectly) enforceable, sometimes conditionally self-executing depending on the purpose and wording of the relevant provisions. This description means that they must be sufficiently clear and not exclusively regulate the responsibility of Contracting States. However, the legal status of SARPs under international law is not as clear as it should be, taking into account the essentiality for uniformity in order to protect and enhance the safe operation of international air transportation.

Regarding these compact outlines concerning the potential full-fledged or semi-legislative instruments, a modern international convention or an exclusive ICAO all-Standards Annex, preference should be given to decisive characteristics such as safety, desirability, proportionality, feasibility, clarity, efficiency, uniformity, legal basis and global implementation without any reservation.

Incidentally, a rather inconvenient, if not highly problematic, albeit futuristic issue is looming, namely the absence of an authoritative person on board an unmanned (pilotless) passenger carrying civil aircraft (discussed further in Chapter 3).

2 International Instruments and Documents on the Legal Status of the Aircraft Commander

2.1 The Increase in Violence on Board Aircraft

In the early days of civil aviation, no major incidents occurred as a result of criminal offences committed on board civilian aircraft by individual or conspiracy terrorists. In those seemingly unworried days, civil air travel was reserved for the wealthy whereby security was by no means a top priority. Even non-passengers were allowed to proceed to the airport concourses to meet their relatives, partners or friends at the arrival gates without any inexorable security restrictions.

> Civil aviation fulfills a noble mission in our time because of its contribution to the understanding among nations which fosters peace and universal harmony. It is to the efforts and perseverance of the pioneers of aviation that we owe the message of brotherhood that links continents and disseminates in the most remote corners of the globe the reciprocal cultures which strengthen man's intellect and breed friendship among peoples....
> Every State treasures its own sovereignty, and, even though civil aviation requires greater freedom, nations must regulate air navigation and air traffic so as to prevent violations of accepted principles and enable their own airlines to develop without the unregulated competition that may unduly hamper their activities....[1]

Following the relaxed first decades of civil aviation, friendliness and respectfulness had to make way for the threat of possible aggressive behaviour and certain other acts on board aircraft, that could jeopardize flight safety. Notably, it was CITEJA that had already discussed the growing concern about aviation-related terrorism and security breaches since 1926. In the following years after these formal discussions, there was not only an increase in violations on board civil aircraft, but also in one specific form of terrorism

---

1   Agenda Item 2: Addresses of Welcome by the Governmental Authorities of the Host State and Reply thereto by the President of the Council – Speech (abbreviated) by the Minister of Communications of Venezuela, Colonel Luis Felipe Llovera Paez. ICAO Doc. 7708-1 A10-P/17-1, 10th Session of the ICAO Assembly, Caracas, June-July 1956.

against civil aviation, namely aerial hijacking. These criminal acts have not only tarnished the glorious image of international air transportation, but it still is a worldwide issue to the safe growth of this mode of transport. Undeniably, in such a terrifying predicament as the hijacking of an aircraft, the aircraft commander takes up a vital, intricate, but above all, decisive position.

The first reported aerial hijacking, which was actually a hostage-taking, took place on 21 February 1931, just after landing at the airport of Arequipa, the second largest city in Peru, when armed Peruvian revolutionaries surrounded and seized a Pan-American Airways mail aircraft. In subsequent years, more aircraft hijacking incidents occurred, albeit mainly amateurish.

However, the vulnerability of civil air transportation in this respect became especially evident from 1948 when aircraft hijacking increased considerably at the regional level, especially for reasons of political asylum. Yet, from an international point of view, the seizure of a commercial aircraft represented a rare event in civil air transportation.

Because of rather inadequate security measures, it was apparently easy to hijack a civil aircraft. During the Cold War (1945-1989), in particular in the late 1960s, hijacking of aircraft was soon to become common practice.[2] This was clearly demonstrated by a large number of Cuban refugee-hijackings, first of all from Cuba to other destinations, mainly located in the United States, followed by vice versa flights, the so-called Fly-me-to-Cuba hijackings. These incidents were at their peak between 1968 and 1972.

Towards the mid-1970s, the number of hijackings in the Caribbean region gradually decreased due to more stringent measures and a joint agreement between the United States and Cuba to extradite or prosecute aircraft hijackers. Despite curbing these law violations, an astonishing large number of subsequent aircraft hijacking incidents have taken place between both countries until the late 1990s.[3]

Obviously, this rather metaphorical contagious phenomenon was present in practically all regions of the world. In the 1960s and 1970s, the number of aircraft hijackings, acts of sabotage and armed attacks on aircraft around the world had risen to extraordinary proportions. In 1961, the former Federal Aviation Agency (FAA) issued a directive prohibiting unauthorized persons from carrying concealed firearms and interfering with crew members' duties on board commercial aircraft.[4]

---

2   The Cold War began shortly after the end of World War II and ended in December 1989 with the Malta Summit Declaration, a few weeks after the fall of the Berlin Wall. The Cold War was a decades-long struggle for supremacy between the United States and its Allies on one side, and the Soviet Union and its satellite States on the other.

3   *See also* Hijacking Accord between the United States and Cuba. Hearing before the Subcommittee on Inter-American Affairs of the Committee on Foreign Affairs, House of Representatives, 93rd Congress, First Session, Tuesday, 20 February 1973, U.S. Government Printing Office, Washington: 1973.

4   Created on 23 August 1958, the new Federal Aviation Agency was responsible for civil aviation safety. On 1 April 1967, the FAA became one of several modal organizations within the new Department of Transport

In September 1961, President John F. Kennedy signed an amendment to the Federal Aviation Act of 1958, which made it a crime to hijack an aircraft, interfere with an active flight crew or carry a dangerous weapon aboard an air carrier aircraft. For those seizing control of such an aircraft, severe penalties would be imposed. In 1964, the FAA adopted a rule requiring that cockpit doors on commercial aircraft be kept locked at all times.[5]

> The recent hijackings of air carrier aircraft have highlighted a necessity to provide additional controls over the conduct of passengers in order to avoid a serious threat to the safety of flights and persons aboard them. The FAA has the responsibility to see that air carriers take such steps as are possible to prevent such occurrences. The FAA has requested the air carriers to take every practicable precaution to prevent passengers from having access to the pilot compartment. In addition, the FAA was then about to adopt a regulation which will prohibit any person, except one who is specifically authorized to carry arms, from carrying on or about his person while aboard an air carrier aircraft a concealed deadly or dangerous weapon. The regulation being adopted will also make it a violation of the CARs (Civil Air Regulations) for any person to assault, threaten, intimidate, or interfere with a crew member in the performance of his or her duties aboard an air carrier aircraft or to attempt to or cause a flight crew member to divert the flight from its intended course or destination.[6]

In September 1970, a total of five commercial aircraft were hijacked by members of the Popular Front for the Liberation of Palestine (PFLP) in European airspace. The hijackings were actually prompted by the Palestinian Liberation Organization (PLO). By means of these actions, this organization wanted to call for worldwide attention to the deplorable, hopeless situation of the Palestinian people. The hijackings were used as blackmail to achieve self-determination for the Palestinians.

(DOT), and received a new name, the Federal Aviation Administration.

5   On 6 August 1964, a FAA Rule, effective this date, required the closing and locking of crew compartment doors of scheduled air carriers and other large commercial aircraft in flight to deter passengers from entering the flight deck. Reference is made to an incident on board a Pacific Air Lines Fairchild F-27A, N2770R, on 6 May 1964 en route from Reno Airport, NV, via Stockton Airport, CA, to San Francisco International Airport, CA, when on the second stretch, close to Oakland, a passenger gained access to the flight deck and shot the Captain and First Officer. The aircraft crashed near San Ramon, CA, killing all 44 occupants. *See also* 14 CFR § 121.587 – Closing and locking of flight crew compartment door.

6   Preamble to Special Civil Air Regulation No. SR-448A, issued by the FAA on 28 July 1961 (Source: Volpe, J.A. & Stewart, J.T.Jr., "Aircraft Hijacking: Some Domestic and International Responses," (2017) 59 *Kentucky L. J.* 2, Art. 3, pp. 275-276.

During this mass hijacking, one aircraft was foiled by killing one hijacker, and his partner, Leila Khaled, was subdued by using force and handed over to the British authorities in London. Another aircraft ended up via Beirut in Cairo, while three aircraft relentlessly ended up, although without any casualties, on a remote desert airstrip named Dawson's Field in Jordan.

While the majority of the 310 hostages were transferred to Amman and freed on 11 September, the PFLP segregated the flight crews and Jewish passengers, keeping the 56 Jewish and American hostages in custody, while releasing the non-Jews. Prior to their announced deadline, the PFLP used explosives to destroy the empty aircraft, as they anticipated a counterattack. Due to a deal negotiated by the government of Jordan, the remaining hostages were released on 1 October 1970 in exchange for Leila Khaled and three other PFLP members held captive in a Swiss prison.[7]

The rising wave of terrorist attacks culminated in a series of four coordinated terrorist hijackings and suicide attacks by 19 militants associated with the Islamic extremist group al-Qaeda on 11 September 2001, terrifying the American people, if not the whole world community, totally disrupting the international civil airline industry, creating a global economic recession and urging governments around the world to strengthen their anti-terrorism legislation.

On that tragic day, almost 3000 innocent people were killed by four airline hijackings of which two commercial aircraft impacted the Twin Towers of the World Trade Center complex in Lower Manhattan, New York City. Another commercial aircraft hit the Pentagon (the headquarters of the US military), in Arlington, VA, just outside Washington, D.C.

The fourth commercial aircraft crashed into a field near Shanksville, PA, after the passengers attempted to retake the aircraft from the resisting hijackers. This courageous action prevented the hijackers from reaching Washington, D.C. with the intention to hit a federal government building, either the US Capitol or the White House. *Nota bene*, each of the four hijacking groups had one hijacker who had received flight training to be able to take control of each aircraft. All 19 terrorists died.

The rise of extremely violent terrorism such as unlawful seizure of commercial aircraft and the use of those aircraft as lethal weapons caused an irrevocable and abrupt end to the ever so primary comfort and reliability of the international airline industry, previously experienced by politicians, air travellers, airline operators and aircraft crew members.

To curb this altered reality, legal instruments were deemed urgently needed. Without any doubt, aircraft hijacking was not a new phenomenon. In the past, aircraft hijacking was more or less an action by an individual or a small group of persons to demand, for

---

7   Source: https://dbpedia.org/page/Dawson%27s_Field_hijackings.

example, political asylum, a ransom or release of conspiracy prisoners, sometimes considered contagious behaviour and thus most probably repetitive. As a matter of fact, at the time of this emerging phenomenon, most governments had little control over these crimes, especially with regard to occurrences on international flights.

Logically, ICAO, which has as its objective the development of international civil aviation along safe and orderly lines, is in the position to contribute to the adoption of international norms, in the form of conventions, in various fields of international air law. Regarding jurisdictional concerns over offences committed on board the aircraft and the powers of the aircraft commander over acts which could jeopardize the safety of the aircraft or of persons or property therein, widespread government acceptance on relevant international instruments had to be achieved.

2.2   STUDY ON THE LEGAL STATUS OF BOTH AIRCRAFT AND AIRCRAFT COMMANDER

The Tokyo Convention (ICAO Doc. 8364) had its origin in a study project of the ICAO Legal Committee. This study was initiated in 1950, based on provisions and study results of both the subjects of the Draft Convention of the Legal Status of the Aircraft and the Draft Convention on the Legal Status of the Aircraft Commander, which actually was a revised CITEJA draft version done by the PICAO Legal *ad hoc* Committee at Paris in 1947.[8]

The study project was to try to define the legal status of the aircraft and to establish both judicial jurisdiction and the applicable substantive law to govern alleged offences committed on board an aircraft in flight. Both Draft Convention studies were part of the Work Programme of the Legal Committee in a time where civil air transportation was undergoing a practically inevitable negative transition from a post-war free and leisurely atmosphere to a more violence-sensitive transport mode.

The revised CITEJA version was lagging since 1947, obviously with Article 2 in particular being worded too broadly and at the same time restrictively, if not unclear in some of the paragraphs, and thus failing to reach the distinction made clear years later by the provisions of the Tokyo Convention, especially with regard to the conferred authority

---

8   Aspects of United States Participation in International Civil Aviation, Department of State, Publication 3209, International Organization and Conference Series IV, International Civil Aviation Organization 2 – CITEJA and the Legal Committee of ICAO, pp. 96-100. ICAO Doc. 4494, LC/3, 2 July 1947, includes the revised text, identical with Annex I to Appendix "F" of the Final Report of Commission IV, Doc. 4382, A1-LE/65, 24 May 1947.

and powers of the aircraft commander with respect to certain incidents on board the aircraft in flight.[9]

Draft Convention on the Legal Status of the Aircraft Commander (as revised by the Paris Legal *ad hoc* Committee (PICAO), February 1947), Article 2:

1. Within the periods specified in Article 5 below, the aircraft commander:
   a. shall be in charge of the aircraft, the crew, the passengers, and the cargo;
   b. has the right and the duty to control and direct the crew and the passengers to the full extent necessary to ensure order and safety;
   c. has the right, for good reason, to disembark any number of the crew, or passengers at an intermediate stop;
   d. has disciplinary power over members of the crew within the scope of their duties; in case of necessity, of which he shall be sole judge, he may assign temporarily any member of the crew to duties other than those for which he is engaged.[10]

Within ICAO, up to 1950, no valid reasons were presented to establish the need for an upcoming 'Convention on Offences and Other Acts Occurring on Board Aircraft'. However, because of advancing insight, attention was given to the question whether international legislation was required with regard to offences committed on board an aircraft. Obviously, in the 1950s, the phenomenon of aircraft hijacking was a known fact, albeit on a small scale. Yet, the increase of violent terrorism against civil aircraft, in this case the offence of hijacking, in other words the unlawful seizure of civil aircraft by the use of force or by threats of any kind, or the exercise of control of civil aircraft, became an essential policy element of international aviation organizations like ICAO, IATA, IFALPA, Airports Council International (ACI) and national institutions as the FAA and supranational bodies as the European Civil Aviation Conference (ECAC).

---

9   Kamminga, M.S. (1953), pp. 135-140. On page 137, Kamminga noticed the following: An apparent defect of the present wording is that a stowaway is neither a member of the crew nor a passenger, and consequently the commander would really have no jurisdiction over him. It might therefore be better to amend the wording in such a way that paragraphs *a, b* and *c* refer to "all persons on board".

10 Revised Draft by the PICAO *ad hoc* Legal Committee, February 1947: Art. 5: (1) The beginning and at the end of the period during which the Commander maintains disciplinary control over the crew may be fixed by the operator. In any case, he is entitled to exercise such control as soon as the crew embarks. At all stopping places, including the end of the trip, he continues to be entitled at least until the formalities of arrival are completed or until his command is taken over by another person. (2) The powers of the Commander over the aircraft, the passengers and the cargo on board come into force as soon as the aircraft, with passengers and cargo, are handed over to him at the beginning of the trip. They expire at the end of the trip when the aircraft, the passengers and the cargo have been respectively handed over to the operator's representative or other qualified authority.

After deliberations between ICAO legal experts and representatives of Contracting States, an international legal instrument like the 'Convention on Offences and Certain Other Acts Committed on Board Aircraft' was desirable for the following reasons:

1. One characteristic of aviation is that aircraft fly over the high seas or over areas having no territorial sovereign. While national laws of some States confer jurisdiction on their courts to try offences committed on aircraft during such flights, this was not the case in others, and there was no internationally agreed system which would coordinate the exercise of national jurisdiction in such cases. Further, with (the) high speed of modern aircraft and having regard to the great altitudes at which they fly as well as other factors, such as meteorological conditions and, in certain parts of the world, the fact that several States may be flown over by aircraft within a small space of time, there could be occasions when it would be impossible to establish the territory (*lex loci delicti*) in which the aircraft was at the (exact) time a crime was committed on board. There was, therefore, the factual possibility that in such a case, and in the absence of an internationally recognized system regarding the exercise of national jurisdiction, the offender may go unpunished.

2. National jurisdictions in respect of criminal acts are based on criteria which are not uniform; for example, on nationality of the offender, or nationality of the victim, on the locality where the offence was committed, or on nationality of the aircraft on which the crime occurred. Thus, several States may claim jurisdiction over the same offence committed on board aircraft, in certain cases. Such conflict of jurisdictions could be avoided only by international agreement.

3. The possibility that the same offence may be triable in different States might result in the offender being punished more than once for the same offence (*ne bis in idem*). This undesirable possibility could be avoided by a suitable provision in the Convention.[11]

During its Ninth Session, from 25 August to 12 September 1953 at Rio de Janeiro, the ICAO Legal Committee officially appointed a Subcommittee on the subject of the legal status of aircraft to study the problems associated with crimes committed on board aircraft.[12] The initial objective of this appointment was, however, the study and revision by this Subcommittee of the text of the Draft Convention of 1952, intended to replace the outdated 1929 Warsaw Convention.

During the 10th session (September 1954) of the Legal Committee, the Legal Status of the Aircraft Subcommittee (the Subcommittee) held several exploratory meetings to

---

11   Boyle, R.P., Pulsifer, R. (1964), pp. 316-317.
12   *See* ICAO Doc. 7450-LC/136, Vol. I-Minutes, p. XVIII, Para. (4) (b), Ninth Session of the Legal Committee, Rio de Janeiro, 25 August to 12 September 1953.

determine the best procedure to be followed in the further consideration of the legal issues involved in studying the legal status of the aircraft.[13]

In the fullness of time, it was determined that the most useful approach would be to consider first those circumstances of most frequent occurrence on aircraft which would raise issues with regard to the legal status of the aircraft and give preliminary consideration to the problem of what law does, or should, regulate for those acts under different circumstances.

This was preferred to an approach which first studied the status of aircraft in law and then applied that conclusion to the several acts and circumstances occurring on aircraft to determine the applicable law governing the particular act under the circumstances in which it occurred. The several types of acts, criminal related and various civil matters, and related regulatory laws which the Subcommittee considered appropriate for its study were:

1. Acts which are crimes under the law of the State of registry of the aircraft and the law of the State in which the act occurred.
2. Acts which are crimes according to the law of the two States mentioned in (1) above.
3. Acts for which a licence is required by the law of either or both States described in (1), such as sale and service of alcoholic beverages, sale and service of food, carriage of firearms, carriage and use of various types of drugs and medicines, etc.
4. Acts which are tortious according to the law of either or both States described in (1) above.
5. Acts which constitute the formation of contracts according to the law of either or both of the two States described in (1) above.
6. Acts which constitute the execution, revocation, or modification of wills according to the law of either or both States described in (1) above.
7. Acts which affect the status of persons such as birth, death, marriage, etc.[14]

Only two acts involved crimes under the law of the State of registry and the State in which the act occurred, or one but not both States. The other acts relate to civil matters such as contracts, licensing requirements, torts and official actions under both the law of the State of registry and the territorial or subjacent State.

Since aircraft will cross national boundaries and airspaces of subjacent States or make stopovers in a particular State, which implies different movements and regulations, the

---

13 The ICAO Legal Committee's Subcommittees were occasionally (during its Sessions) established as appropriate for legal studies and preparatory work for draft conventions on primary agenda items on the current Working Programme of the Legal Committee. The Legal Status of the Aircraft Subcommittee also decided to consider that portion of the Legal Committee agenda item entitled the "Legal Status of the Aircraft Commander" insofar as it related to crimes committed on board aircraft.

14 Boyle, R.P., Pulsifer, R. (1964), p. 311. See also ICAO Doc. 8565-LC/152-2, International Conference on Air Law, Tokyo, August-September 1963, Montreal 1966, Vol. II Documents, Doc. No. 5, pp. 24-25.

Subcommittee determined that all these acts should be studied in relation to realistic, factual circumstances in which the aircraft may be at the time of the particular act to be able to define the applicable laws that affect that act.

The six factual or physical circumstances, in which the aircraft may be at the time of the relevant act, include:

- The aircraft is in transit non-stop in the airspace above the geographical boundaries of a State other than the State of registry of the aircraft.
- The aircraft is in the airspace above the geographical boundaries of a State other than the State of registry of the aircraft and a subsequent landing is to be effected in that State.
- The aircraft is in the airspace above the geographical boundaries of a State other than the State of registry of the aircraft but has made a prior landing in such State.
- The aircraft is in the airspace above the geographical boundaries of a State other than the State of registry of the aircraft but the aircraft has made a prior landing in such State and a subsequent landing in such State is intended.
- The aircraft is over the high seas.
- The aircraft is on the ground at an airport in the State of registry of the aircraft.[15]

The United States prepared a paper on criminal acts on board aircraft which included, in fact, the two types of acts on the list to be studied by the Subcommittee. Since the remaining acts on the list, related to a civil law nature, were excluded from the scope of the study and subsequently of the Draft Convention on issues associated with crimes on aircraft, the US paper, submitted to the Subcommittee on 13 April 1956, became the principal basis of continued study by the Subcommittee on the subject.[16]

This paper, called 'A Study of the Jurisdiction and Law to be Applied to Crimes on Board Aircraft' examined, more or less in detail, five bases or principles for the exercise of penal jurisdiction and law as to aircraft. These principles are:

- The principle that the laws and jurisdiction of the State in the territorial airspace of which the criminal act takes place should apply, based on the rule of international law that each State has complete and absolute sovereignty over its airspace as defined in Article 1 of the Chicago Convention.
- The principle that the law's jurisdiction of the State in which the aircraft is registered should be applicable at all times, or in any event when the aircraft is not in sovereign airspace, for instance over the high seas or lands having no sovereignty.

---

15   Van Wijk, A.A. (1982), pp. 346-347.
16   ICAO Doc. 8565-LC/152, International Conference on Air Law, Tokyo, August-September 1963, Montreal 1966, Vol. I, Minutes, Preparatory work, p. (xi). *See also* ICAO Doc. 8565-LC/152-2, pp. 23-27.

- The principle that the jurisdiction and law of the State of which the accused or the victim is a national should be applicable.
- The principle that the State of first landing should apply its jurisdiction and law.
- The principle that the State from whence the aircraft last took off should have jurisdiction and should apply its laws.[17]

The first two principles, the territorial or subjacent State and the State of registry, are generally recognized as correct as well as desirable and have found almost unanimous acceptance in the practice of States. The US paper study concluded that some form of concurrent jurisdiction would be the most effective security feature for the punishment of crime. Derived from this conclusion, the concept of dual competence consisting of a combination involving the State of registry and the subjacent State was favoured. A concept of multiple competencies, on the other hand, would serve only to perpetuate undesirable jurisdictional conflicts.[18]

Each principle is analysed in accordance with the six factual circumstances, and the advantages as well as disadvantages of each is weighed in terms of practicality, State and air transportation interests, and the probability of conflict between States adhering to different principles.

2.3 THE IMPETUS TO THE TOKYO CONVENTION AND THE POWERS OF THE AIRCRAFT COMMANDER

One of several States that volunteered to submit papers analysing one or more of the seven types of acts in relation to the six sets of circumstances was the United States which undertook to prepare a report on criminal acts committed on board aircraft. This paper, that examined in some detail the bases for the exercise of penal jurisdiction and law as to aircraft, became the principal basis of further work on the legal status of aircraft.

In September 1956, it was decided at an independent meeting of the Subcommittee at Geneva that the study on the subject should be aimed at the convergence of the legal status of the aircraft and that of the aircraft commander, insofar as it related to crimes committed on board aircraft, eventually resulting in a merger of both topics.[19]

The criminal aspect was regarded as one independent element, thereby limiting the scope of the subject of the legal status of the aircraft which originally would cover several substantial aspects like the nationality of an aircraft, rights in aircraft, contracts, damage

---

17 *See also* ICAO Doc. 8565-LC/152-1, Tokyo 1963, Vol. I Minutes, Agenda Item 11, pp. 100-101.
18 Denaro, J.M., "In-Flight Crimes, The Tokyo Convention, and Federal Judicial Jurisdiction," (1969) 35 J. Air L. & Com. 171, p. 184.
19 Boyle, R.P., Pulsifer, R. (1964), pp. 311-316.

on the surface caused by foreign aircraft, etc. This 'by-pass' method might have helped to concentrate the efforts on the criminal aspect of the study.[20] Regarding the scope of the Draft Convention, the Subcommittee decided that it should:

> Apply to any act or omission by a person on board an aircraft which is punishable under penal law, and that no distinction should be made between serious or minor offences; be limited to aircraft in flight, the term to be later defined; be applicable only to persons, who, having committed the offence, were on board at the time the act or omission claimed of occurred; and not apply to State aircraft.

Moreover, the Subcommittee generally agreed that:

> The aim of such a Convention should not be to establish or create jurisdiction; on the contrary, the main objective of the Convention would be the recognition, by international agreement, of the competence of States to establish jurisdiction of their courts under national laws.[21]

As a matter of fact, the Tokyo Convention adheres to the definitions with regard to the question of priorities of jurisdiction as stated in the proposed Convention, as described above.

Because of different opinions and prioritizing other more advanced topics, such as the Draft Convention on Aerial Collisions, little progress was made in 1957 on the study on criminal acts committed on board aircraft until the US delegation of the Legal Committee returned to Washington to deliberate the issue of conflicts of jurisdiction with the US Air Coordinating Committee. This Committee decided to prepare a Draft Convention on the subject for use at the 1958 meeting of the Subcommittee, to be held at Montreal, for the purpose of expediting ICAO action towards the development of a convention. The 1958 US Draft Convention was made applicable to civil aircraft in flight, formulated as: from the moment power is applied for the purpose of actual take-off until the moment when the landing run ends. It became the precursor of the final ICAO Draft of 1963.[22]

---

20   Shubber, S., *Jurisdiction over Crimes on Board Aircraft* (The Hague: Martinus Nijhoff, 1973), pp. 7-8. *See also* ICAO Doc. 8279 A14-LE/11, 14th Session of the Assembly, Rome 21 August-15 September 1962, Report and Minutes of the Legal Commission, p. 20 Legal Status of the Aircraft Commander, items 27-31.

21   Boyle, R.P., Pulsifer, R. (1964), p. 317.

22   *See* Annual Report to the President by the Air Coordinating Committee 1958, Air Coordinating Committee, Department of Commerce Building, 1711 New York Avenue NW, Washington D.C., 31 January 1959, pp. 49-51.

The priority consideration of the United States on this subject was prompted by the increasing volume of international traffic handled by civil aircraft, and especially the need to address the growing frequency of unruly, disruptive and criminal passenger behaviour. In order to achieve a quick but well-considered settlement, the United States proposed extensive jurisdiction conferred to the State of registry, within the status of forces agreements (SOFAs) in effect between States. Under international law, a status of forces agreement differs from military occupation.[23]

In this special case, according to this legal construction, if concurrent jurisdiction does exist between one or more States, one such State is given the primary right to exercise jurisdiction over criminal acts whenever in view of the circumstances of the offence that State has the paramount interest.[24]

The Draft Convention, approved at the 1958 Montreal Subcommittee meeting, gives international recognition to two bases of criminal jurisdiction: (1) the State of registry of the aircraft and (2) the State in whose territorial airspace the offence was committed (the subjacent State). Although in the Draft Convention a condition of concurrent jurisdiction is created, this legal construction will avert conflicts. Moreover, the State having the primary right to exercise its jurisdiction may waive its jurisdiction in favour of other converging States.

The Draft Convention, prepared by the United States, included four bases or principles of concurrent jurisdiction:
1. The territorial or airspace State.
2. The State of registry of the aircraft.
3. The State whose national security has been violated, or against the person of whose sovereign the offence is committed (passive personality principle).[25]
4. The State of the suspected offender's nationality.

Eventually, disagreement about the system of priorities persisted for some time among the members of the Subcommittee. Yet, the Draft Convention was made applicable to offences punishable under the penal laws of the four States having jurisdiction. A proposed provision against the *ne bis in idem* principle did not survive the final text of the 1963 Draft Convention due to an exclusion decision at the Tokyo International Conference on Air Law (hereinafter referred to as Tokyo Conference).[26]

---

23 A Status of Forces Agreement (SOFA) is an agreement between a host State and a foreign State stationing military forces as part of a comprehensive security arrangement in that State. Politically, SOFAs often will cause mixed feelings among host States (South Korea, Japan, etc.), in particular regarding the presence of foreign bases on their territory.

24 Boyle, R.P., Pulsifer, R. (1964), p. 319.

25 In international law, this principle allows a State, in limited cases, to assert jurisdiction to try a foreign national for an offence committed against its national anywhere in the world.

26 Boyle, R.P., Pulsifer, R. (1964), p. 319-320.

In view of the very first mandatory provisions regarding the legal status of the aircraft commander in a detailed international legal instrument, the first Draft Convention on offences, criminal jurisdiction and the rights and duties of the aircraft commander, under the auspices of ICAO, was produced by the Subcommittee at Montreal between 9 and 20 September 1958.

The content of this Draft Convention went beyond the subject of the legal status of the aircraft in that it also covered part of another subject on the Work Programme of the Legal Committee, *viz.*, the legal status of the aircraft commander.[27]

In the draft, entitled 'Legal Status of the Aircraft', careful attention was paid to the important item of the powers and duties of the aircraft commander. It was recognized that consideration should be given to include some provisions in the Draft Convention pertaining to the exercise of certain powers by the aircraft commander of an aircraft in flight, for example restraint or arrest in respect of any act prejudicial to security or constituting an offence or attempted offence against persons or property on board or the aircraft itself.

The following text of the Draft Convention, approved at Montreal in 1958, included Articles 5 to 10 covering the powers and related immunity of the aircraft commander:

Article 5.
The individual responsible for the operation and safety of the aircraft (hereinafter called the aircraft commander) shall have the right to impose upon any person whom he has reasonable grounds to believe has committed an offence on board the aircraft, or whom he has reasonable grounds to believe will jeopardize by his actions the safety of the passengers, crew, cargo or aircraft, measures of restraint when these seem necessary to protect the safety of the passengers, crew, cargo or aircraft, or to enable the aircraft commander to deliver the person so restrained to competent authorities.

Article 6.
The aircraft commander shall have the right to request or authorize the assistance of other crew members and of passengers to restrain any person whom under Article 5 he has the right to restrain. Any crew member may also impose such restraint without authorization when immediate restraint reasonably appears to be necessary to protect the safety of the passengers, crew, cargo or aircraft.
Article 7.

---

27   ICAO Doc. 8565-LC/152-2, Tokyo 1963, Vol. II Documents, p. 55, Doc. No. 5 Appendix IV, item 2 Scope of the draft Convention.

1. The aircraft commander shall have the right to deliver to the competent authorities of any Contracting State in the territory of which the aircraft lands any person whom he has reasonable grounds to believe has committed an offence on board the aircraft.

2. The aircraft commander shall have the right to detain the suspected offender until the aircraft lands in a place in a Contracting State where the authorities agree to detain him.

3. The aircraft commander shall also have the right to deliver any person to the competent authorities of any State in the territory of which the aircraft lands if the safety of the passengers, crew, cargo or aircraft requires that such person be removed from the aircraft.

Article 8.

1. The aircraft commander shall retain for delivery to appropriate authorities anything which he considers to be evidence in connection with any apparent offence. The aircraft commander may collect information from any person on board the aircraft in regard to the offence.

2. The aircraft commander shall transmit to the authorities to whom any suspected offender is delivered anything which he has retained as evidence and any information which he has obtained in accordance with Paragraph 1.

Article 9.

1. The aircraft commander shall report to the appropriate authorities of the State of registry of the aircraft the fact that an apparent offence has occurred on board, any restraint of any person, and any other action taken by him pursuant to this Convention, in such manner as the State of registry may require.

2. The aircraft commander shall, as soon as practicable, notify the appropriate authorities of any Contracting State in which the aircraft lands of the fact that an apparent offence involving violence or an act endangering the safety of the passengers, crew, cargo or aircraft has occurred and that the suspected offender is on board.

Article 10.

Neither the aircraft commander, other member of the crew, a passenger, the owner nor the operator of the aircraft, shall be liable in any proceedings, civil or criminal, brought in respect either of any reasonable restraint imposed under the circumstances stated in Articles 5 and 6 of this Convention or of other actions authorized by Articles 7, 8 and 9.[28]

Normally, an aircraft pilot, whether it is an aircraft commander or a first officer, lacks a pure legal background or advanced knowledge in that field. His ready knowledge is primarily technical and operational in nature. The Subcommittee formulated his powers in relation to illegal acts which are prejudicial to the safety of an aircraft or persons or property therein or to good order and discipline on board. In respect to such acts, the aircraft commander may impose necessary measures as arrest or restraint on the actor, under the applicable code of criminal procedure *casu quo* international customary law, and may require or authorize the assistance of other crew members and may even request or authorize the assistance of passengers to also carry out these custodial actions.

Without such authorization, assisting crew and passengers may also take reasonable preventive measures when the aircraft commander has reasonable grounds to believe that such actions must be immediately necessary to protect the safety of the aircraft, or persons or property therein.

IATA, in the meantime, indicated that the conclusion of an international Convention on the subject was not warranted. This statement, expressed because of doubts within ICAO about the need for such an instrument, was based on studies done by the IATA Legal Committee referring to actual experience of scheduled international air carriers. However, this was contrary to the opinions of both IFALPA and the International Law Association (ILA) that implied to support the development of such a Convention. The Subcommittee noted, after due deliberations of all relevant aspects, including safety, that such a Convention was needed for two obvious reasons:

1. The lack of an international rule concerning extra-territorial jurisdiction of a State in regard to offences committed on aircraft of its nationality engaged in international air navigation.
2. Problems of conflict of criminal jurisdictions, and the need to define the powers of the aircraft commander to take necessary measures in respect of acts on board endangering the safety of flight and for the preservation of order over the community on board.[29]

With regard to the term 'community', the Subcommittee noted at that time: 'that in this connection such community is expected to increase significantly when aircraft of larger types will be operating in the near future'.

---

28   ICAO Doc. 8565-LC/152-2, Tokyo 1963, Vol. II Documents, Doc. No. 5 Appendix II, pp. 47-49.
29   ICAO Doc. 8565-LC/152-2, Tokyo 1963, Vol. II Documents, Doc. No. 5 Appendix VI, Need for a Convention, p. 77, Note (1): Para. 3.1 of LC/WD No. 583. *See also* Boyle, R.P., Pulsifer, R. (1964), p. 320.

With respect to the powers and duties of the aircraft commander, the ever-present mantra is the safety of the aircraft. It was considered meaningful that there should be internationally adopted rules which would enable aircraft commanders to maintain order on board, whether in respect of offences or of any acts jeopardizing the safety of an aircraft or persons or property on board an aircraft engaged in international air navigation.

In addition, it was decided to ensure the protection of the aircraft commander or other persons concerned from liability in any proceedings when acting pursuant to such international rules. The intention was that no liability proceedings, civil or criminal nor any proceedings of an administrative character, such as revocation of a licence, should be taken in respect of any reasonable restraint or the reasonable performance of other action in Article 9 of the Draft Convention.[30]

For the first time, a theme was articulated that would later become dominant: that the Convention should have, as a principal purpose, the enhancement of aviation safety which was translated as the scope of the Convention stating that the Convention shall apply to 'offences against penal law' as well as 'acts which, whether or not they are offences, may or do jeopardize safety [...]'.

Other principles in the Draft Convention, subsequently retained in succeeding drafts and ultimately adopted at the Tokyo Conference, relate to the delivery procedure by the aircraft commander of a suspected offender or dangerous person, the obligation of a Contracting State to take such a person into custody under certain circumstances, and those relating to the collection of evidence by the aircraft commander.[31]

For information, the following text is the authentic text of Article 9 adopted at the Tokyo Conference:

1. The aircraft commander may deliver to the competent authorities of any Contracting State in the territory of which the aircraft lands any person whom he has reasonable grounds to believe has committed on board the aircraft an act which, in his opinion, is a serious offence according to the penal law of the State of registration of the aircraft.

2. The aircraft commander shall as soon as practicable and if possible before landing in the territory of a Contracting State with a person on board whom the aircraft commander intends to deliver in accordance with the preceding paragraph, notify the authorities of such State of his intention to deliver such person and the reasons thereof.

3. The aircraft commander shall furnish the authorities to whom any suspected offender is delivered in accordance with the provisions of this Article with evidence and

---

30 See Art. 10, Tokyo Convention (authentic text): for actions taken in accordance with this Convention, neither the aircraft commander, any other member of the crew, any passenger, the owner or operator of the aircraft, nor the person on whose behalf the flight was performed shall be held responsible in any proceeding on account of the treatment undergone by the person against whom the actions were taken.

31 Boyle, R.P., Pulsifer, R. (1964), p. 321. See also Tokyo Convention Chapter V Powers and Duties of States.

information which, under the law of the State of registration of the aircraft, are lawfully in his possession.

The very first draft was understood to be based on the US Draft Convention, the purpose of which was to expedite the ICAO work on the development of a convention, although no indication or reference of that effect has been confirmed.

In August 1959, at its 12th Session at Munich, the Legal Committee undertook a substantive consideration on the subject of the legal status of the aircraft and the Draft Convention developed by the Subcommittee, dealing with the legal status of the aircraft. This work resulted in the adoption by the Legal Committee's own, rather comprehensive, so-called Munich draft entitled: 'The Draft Convention on Offences and Certain Other Acts Occurring on Board Aircraft'.

After examining this draft, the Legal Committee determined that the State of registry is competent to exercise jurisdiction over offences committed on board an aircraft and that such a legal rule would not prejudice other legal grounds such as the jurisdiction of the State in whose territorial airspace the aircraft was at the time of the offence.

Whether the State of registry could refrain from actually exercising its jurisdiction in any given case or would be required to take legal action, based on its jurisdiction, remained, however, an unanswered question. The Tokyo Convention provides that each Contracting State shall take such measures as may be necessary to establish its jurisdiction as the State of registry over offences committed on board an aircraft registered in such State.[32]

Another debate item was conflicts of criminal jurisdiction to the extent that a majority of the Legal Committee asserted, regarding the troublesome issue of priority, that the Tokyo Convention should not go beyond recognizing the jurisdiction of the State of registry and to limiting, under certain conditions, the jurisdiction of the State flown over, in whose airspace the act occurred. Or to put it differently, although the Tokyo Convention does not provide a specific rule governing the priority of States to exercise jurisdiction, it implies a priority of the State of registry.[33]

---

32   Art. 3.2, Tokyo Convention.
33   The formulation of the Legal Committee with respect to limiting the jurisdiction of the State overflown is according to the following rules (*See also* Art. 4, Tokyo Convention and for comparison: Art. 19, Para. 1, of the Convention on the Territorial Sea and the Contiguous Zone of 1958, concerning the restrictions on the criminal jurisdiction of the coastal State in relation to offences on board a foreign ship passing through the territorial waters of that State): The criminal jurisdiction of a State in whose airspace the offence was committed, if such State is not the State of registry of the aircraft or the State where the aircraft lands, shall not be exercised in connection with the offence committed on an aircraft in flight, except in the following cases:
  a.   if the offence has effect on the territory of such State;
  b.   if the offence has been committed by or against a national of such State;
  c.   if the offence is against the national security of such State;

The Legal Committee carefully examined the particular part of the Draft Convention dealing with the powers and duties of the aircraft commander as well as the conditions of the applicability, especially the formulation of 'aircraft in flight' which means that 'in flight' has been defined in accordance with the original proposal of the United States. This wording does not affect the jurisdiction of the State territorially involved in respect of any offence committed on board while the aircraft is at rest or moving on the ground for taxiing or for any other purpose than for actual take-off.

Regarding the position of the aircraft commander, the Legal Committee formulated his powers in relation to acts which are prejudicial to the safety of the aircraft. In respect to such acts, the aircraft commander may impose necessary measures of restraint on the actor, and may require or authorize other crew members to do the same. Moreover, in a similar way, he could authorize passengers.

After landing, the commander is entitled to disembark and or deliver, under certain conditions, any person whom he has reasonable grounds to believe has committed on board during flight a serious offence or an act detrimental to the safety. Regarding the difference between the mere concept of disembarkation of a passenger, who may be subjected to this action, and the concept of delivery of a passenger to the competent authority, addressed in the debates of the Tokyo Conference, convened in 1963, the machinery of disembarkation was considered a simpler one than the machinery of delivery. The Rome draft of 1962 assumed that the procedure of disembarkation was to be used to protect safety, while that of delivery has as its objective repression of serious crimes, in particular, such crimes as might be found to be extraditable. These concepts should be very clearly separated throughout the Tokyo Convention.[34]

At least in the legal system of the United States, the expression 'reasonable grounds' has a substantial legal significance. Within the general concept of US law, this expression would give the impression that the aircraft commander would be required to have a substantial basis for his belief, that he could not act on the basis of facts which were inadequate to support his belief to the effect that a person had committed or was about to commit the kind of act under consideration. In other words, the aircraft commander cannot act arbitrarily or capriciously.[35]

If the expression 'serious grounds' might be considered heavier than 'reasonable grounds', then, in US law, the aircraft commander would be held to quite a severe test

---

d.　if the offence consists of a breach of any rules and regulations relating to the flight and manoeuvre of aircraft in force in such State;

e.　if the exercise of jurisdiction is necessary to ensure the observance of any obligation of such State under an international agreement.

34　See ICAO Doc. 8565-LC/152-1, Tokyo Convention (1963), Vol. I, Minutes, Item 42, p. 176. See also ICAO Doc. 8302-LC/150-1, Vol. I, Minutes of the 14th Session of the ICAO Legal Committee, p. XIX.

35　, See ICAO Doc. 8565-LC/152-1, Tokyo 1963, Vol. I, Minutes, Comment of Mr. Boyle (United States of America) in Item 67, p. 155.

which would go beyond a reasonable doubt. The word 'serious' would have fairly severe consequences in the legal system in the United States as in more States. A suggestion from IATA to use the word 'appropriate' instead of 'reasonable' was not accepted by the delegations.

Subsequently, after being convinced, on reasonable grounds, of a serious offence according to the penal law of the State of registry of the aircraft, the aircraft commander may deliver the actor to the competent authorities of the State in which the first port of call is located. As soon as practicable and if possible before landing, the aircraft commander shall notify the authorities of such State of his intention to deliver the offender and the reasons, thereof. After the alleged offender's delivery, which is lawfully in the possession of the aircraft commander in accordance with the law of the State of registry, the receiving State must then treat this person in custody according to its laws and is obliged to notify certain other States. In addition, in case of a delivery act, the Draft Convention requires the aircraft commander to hand over all evidence to the receiving State.

The Legal Committee understood that legal problems could actually arise in the event of aircraft registered in one State and to be operated under a dry-lease contract, charter or interchange by an operator of another State. Complicated lease structures required additional studies and legal comments by air navigation-related international institutes and organizations. During the Tokyo Conference, the subject of chartering or (dry) leasing of aircraft and the consequences regarding applicable exercises of jurisdiction was raised, causing the delegations to have different positions with respect to solutions and inclusion of related provisions.[36]

The solutions in regard to the question of chartered aircraft, as contained in one of the Reports (Part II) of the Legal Committee's Subcommittee on Resolution B of the Guadalajara Conference,[37] were:

Solution 1.
An aircraft chartered on a barehull basis to an operator who is a national of a State other than the State of registry shall be treated for the purpose of this Convention as if throughout the period of the charter it was registered in that other State.

---

36   *See* ICAO Doc. 8565-LC/152-1, Tokyo 1963, Vol. I Minutes, Problems concerning the case of aircraft chartered on a barehull basis, pp. 128-131.

37   The Subcommittee on Resolution B of the Guadalajara Conference, established by the Legal Committee at its Fourteenth Session, had to study two legal questions and present the findings in reports entitled Part I: Legal problems affecting the regulation and enforcement of air safety which have been experienced by certain States when an aircraft registered in one State is operated by an operator belonging to another. Part II: Problems concerning charter on a barehull basis in relation to the draft Convention on Offences and Certain Other Acts Occurring on Board Aircraft.

Solution 2.

No action should be taken to include in the Draft Convention provision for jurisdiction of the State of the lessee.

Solution 3.

To include in Article 2 of the Draft Convention a specific provision embodying the principle of the concurrent jurisdiction of the State of the lessee. (Note: '*When an aircraft without crew is leased to a person who is a national of a State other than the State of registry of that aircraft, the State in which such person is a national may also be competent to exercise jurisdiction over offences committed on board the aircraft*'.)

During the Tokyo Conference deliberations, it was pointed out that the Guadalajara Conference had dealt with charters, but not with leases. However, in Part II, an attempt was being made to solve problems in the case of leases and, in particular, in the case of a barehull lease, which was confirmed by the Chairman of the Subcommittee saying that the inclusion of the case of lease of an aircraft with crew was outside the terms of reference of the Subcommittee.

While the IATA observer's position implied that the Draft Convention should cover not only lease without crew (dry lease), but also lease with crew (wet lease), the following considerations on aircraft lease and applicable jurisdiction were discussed during the Tokyo Conference. First of all, a reason for including a provision on the lease of aircraft was related to the duties and obligations of the aircraft commander as laid down by the provisions of the Draft Convention. These duties are, to some extent, linked to the laws of the State of registry. If leases were the common practice in air transportation, the aircraft commander would have to face the situation that he might fly aircraft registered in a State whose laws were remote and unacquainted. This issue would place a heavier burden on the aircraft commander.[38]

The Tokyo Conference deliberations continued more explicitly. Where the control was handed over by the lessor to the lessee, one was referring to a lease. It was just conceivable that the lease could be done with crew. Furthermore, it was conceivable that some type of aircraft was operated by a specialized crew trained to operate that type of aircraft. In the circumstances where the lessee did not have a proficient crew for that type of aircraft, the lessor might make the lease with crew even though he did not wish to retain control of the aircraft.

However, the Subcommittee on Resolution B of the Guadalajara Conference, during its meeting at Montreal, had wisely decided to recommend only the inclusion of the case of lease without crew since, only in such circumstances, there was really a need to cover the situation. Where, for example, there was a crew of the State of registry, that crew might

---

38   *See* ICAO Doc. 8565-LC/152-1, Tokyo 1963, Vol. I Minutes, Item 75, p. 132.

know or especially should know how to take action in accordance with the law of that State.

In particular, the task of the aircraft commander would be simplified if he did not have to refer to the law of a particular State, not merely because he was not a lawyer, but because he might not be a national of that State. Anyway, it appears that the aircraft commander would have to evaluate the offence on a legal basis as if he were a judge. The justification lies in the fact that when the aircraft commander would take an action in accordance with the provisions of the Tokyo Convention, he would be within his legitimate rights in the fulfilment of his functions.

No specific provision is made by the lessor to an airline company (the lessee) in the case that an aircraft is leased in a State other than the State of registry. Apparently, priority-wise, the only State required to establish its jurisdiction over activities on board an aircraft while it is operated by the lessee is the State of registry, even if the aircraft is operated by a crew provided by the lessee, which is not uncommon.

This way of operation might be undesirable because the State with which an aircraft, and its aircraft commander, is most closely connected is the State in which the lessee has its principal place of business, or if he has no such place, his permanent residence. The State of registry would continue to have jurisdiction since the jurisdiction of the State whose national decided to operate a leased aircraft was facultative rather than mandatory.[39]

Another statement proclaimed that the Tokyo Convention should not provide that the nationality of the lessee should determine the nationality of the aircraft. A different approach to the question yielded cause for concern that since a lease was an agreement in civil law, which means a private law matter, such a matter should not determine the question of jurisdiction of a State.[40]

The US comments on the so-called Munich Draft Convention of 1959 included a proposal that only offences which would jeopardize aviation safety should be made cognizable under the Convention, a solution to conflicts of jurisdiction and to add two further descriptions in the Draft Convention to be adopted by the Legal Committee.[41]

---

39   *See also* Protocol Relating to an Amendment to the Convention on International Civil Aviation, Art. 83 *bis*, signed at Montreal on 6 October 1980. This Protocol provides for the transfer of certain functions and duties from the State of registry to the State of the operator. The transfer of certain functions and duties from the State of registry to the State of the operator of leased, chartered or interchanged aircraft as provided for by Art. 83 *bis* clarifies safety responsibilities, simplifies procedures and enhances aviation safety. Art. 83 *bis* came into force on 20 June 1997.

40   A provision on the issue of (dry) lease of aircraft is included in Art. 5 of the 1970 Montreal Convention for the Suppression of Unlawful Acts Against the Safety of Civil Aviation.

41   The draft Convention should contain an article to the effect that: (1) nothing in the Convention shall be deemed to create a right to request extradition of any person, and (2) the term jurisdiction in any arrangements respecting extradition between Contracting States over crimes committed in their airspace shall, with respect to an offence to which the Convention applies, be taken to include the jurisdiction of the

Another proposal of the United States, motivated by the increase of aircraft hijacking incidents, was submitted to ICAO and the Subcommittee for consideration during its next meeting in 1962. This resulted in additional provisions, dealing with forcible seizure of aircraft, somewhat similar to piracy on ships, being incorporated in the Draft Convention, and is contained in Article 16 of the Tokyo Convention.

In 1959, at its 12th Session held in Munich, the Legal Committee considered the report of the Subcommittee together with its proposed Draft Convention. During the course of the session, a proposal was made to the effect that the scope of the Convention should be reduced so as to exclude the treatment of problems relating to the essential offences committed on board, and to deal only with such acts, whether or not they constituted an offence, as were prejudicial to the safety of the aircraft or persons or property therein or to good order and discipline on board.

The argumentation in support of the proposal was that a convention, limited to such prejudicial acts committed on board and to the powers of the aircraft commander with respect to such acts, would better match the objectives of ICAO, specifically, safety of international air navigation. However, the proposal was opposed on the ground, *inter alia*, that, in the view of the Subcommittee, there was a need for rules on offences committed on board an aircraft to be laid down on an international basis and, moreover, a need for the unification of national rules on the subject. The report of the Legal Committee contained the following statement on this point:

> The Committee noted the view of the Subcommittee that there is a need for an international agreement on the subject of offences committed on aircraft, and the reasons adduced therefore in its report. The Legal Committee agreed with this view, taking into account, in particular, the disparity in the provisions of various national laws related to such matters, the lack in several instances of a law equivalent in the case of aircraft to the rule of international law relating to the application of the law of the flag in the case of ships, and the desirability of unification of certain rules on the subject.[42]

After expanding the scope of the Draft Convention by introducing new elements, the Legal Committee was prepared to adopt a comprehensive Draft Convention entitled 'Convention on Offences and Other Acts Occurring on Board Aircraft'. This newly adopted

---

State of registry of the aircraft. *See also* Art. 16 of the Tokyo Convention: (1) Offences committed on aircraft registered in a Contracting State shall be treated, for the purpose of extradition, as if they had been committed not only in the place in which they have occurred but also in the territory of the State of registration of the aircraft, (2) Without prejudice to the provisions of the preceding paragraph, nothing in this Convention shall be deemed to create an obligation to grant extradition.

42   ICAO Doc. 8565-LC/152-2, Tokyo 1963, Vol. II, pp. 7-8.

draft contained provisions with respect to jurisdiction over offences and other acts committed on board an aircraft, exceptions concerning the exercise of criminal jurisdiction (*ne bis in idem* principle), the rights and duties of the aircraft commander, members of the crew and passengers, rights and obligations of Contracting States and immunity issues.

Some principles and elements were of historical origin. As early as 1902, Paul A.J. Fauchille, a French lawyer and one of the pioneers of air law, discussed the question of which State should exercise jurisdiction over Criminal and Other Acts Occurring on Board Aircraft while in flight. He adopted nationality (*viz.* the law of the flag) as the norm governing the law and jurisdiction in respect of occurrences on board an aircraft.[43]

During the 1910 Paris International Air Navigation Conference on the regulation of air navigation, the First Committee resolved that nationality should be used to establish State responsibility for, as well as diplomatic protection to, civil aircraft. However, nationality was considered not to form any basis for resolving conflicts of law and competence. Unfortunately, the Paris Conference came to a final disagreement between participating governments.

In 1919, in the wake of World War I, governments, represented at the (Paris Peace Conference) Aeronautical Commission, addressed political obstacles and complexities involved in international air navigation. The governments made proposals as to the method of determining which State should have jurisdiction over offences committed on board an aircraft while in flight. The overall result was the 1919 Paris Convention, however, without a solid solution for the subject of crimes in the air.

As it appeared, the Munich Draft Convention was based on a system of concurrent jurisdiction, while the question of priority was excluded, due to a lack of agreement on the order of priority among the States concerned and the fact that the priority matter would generally be governed by the extent to which extradition treaties existed at the time. From the aircraft commander's position, the Munich draft introduced for the first time in the history of international air law a new series of norms regarding the powers, rights and duties of the aircraft commander to take necessary action in the event that the safety of the aircraft, and its occupants, was jeopardized by the act of someone on board. It also dealt with the immunity under the Convention.[44]

In view of the complexity of the problems related to the subject, the Legal Committee regarded the Munich draft, tentatively under the same title as previously mentioned, as only a provisional document and requested the Council to circulate the draft to Contracting

---

43 De Saussure, H. & Fenston, J., "Conflicts in the Competence and Jurisdiction of Courts of Different States to Deal with Crimes Committed on Board Aircraft," (1952) I *McGill L. J.* 66, p. 69.
44 Shubber, S. (1973), pp. 9-11.

States and international organizations for the purpose of obtaining their comments. Shortly after, the action requested was taken by the Council and comments were received on the Munich draft from various States and international organizations.

At Montreal, a newly formed Subcommittee convened from 26 March to 5 April 1962. It considered and reviewed the received comments and came to the conclusion to keep the Munich draft text basically intact. However, the Subcommittee proposed certain substitutional and additional provisions, resulting in a redraft.[45]

The Legal Committee made the final revisions during its 14th Session at Rome in 1962, and made a number of amendments, changes and deletions such as the *ne bis in idem* principle, and introduced a new article (Art. 11, Unlawful Seizure of Aircraft) about the issue of aerial hijacking. The objectives of such a provision would be to secure the collaboration of States to take all appropriate measures to restore control of the aircraft to its lawful aircraft commander or to preserve his control of the aircraft, that the passengers and crew shall be permitted to continue their journey as soon as possible and that the aircraft and the property therein shall be returned to the persons lawfully entitled to their possession.

It was agreed that a provision should be included concerning hijacking of aircraft to the effect that, whenever, through the use or threat of violence against the aircraft, the aircraft commander lost control, or was in danger of losing control, over the aircraft, all Contracting States should agree to take appropriate measures to restore control of the aircraft to its lawful commander.[46]

The Legal Committee stated that the final draft, which was formally entitled 'Draft Convention on Offences and Certain Other Acts Committed on Board Aircraft' and the accompanying report, provided with a few subtle yet emphatic modifications, was ready for presentation to States and transmission to the ICAO Council for further action in accordance with Assembly Resolution A7-6 (superseded by A31-15).

The Draft Convention was eventually adopted by the Tokyo Conference (Diplomatic Conference) convened by the Council from 20 August to 14 September 1963. Both the subject of the legal status of the aircraft and the legal status of the aircraft commander formed the foundation of the Tokyo Convention which was applicable only to civil, and not State, aircraft.

The Tokyo Convention (ICAO Doc. 8364), entered into force in 1969 on 4 December. With regard to increased security in aviation, the Tokyo Convention, established under the auspices and successful work of the ICAO Council, was a first step in what would

---

45   ICAO Doc. 8565-LC/152-2, Tokyo 1963, Vol. II Documents, Doc. No. 2, pp. 13-14, Doc. No. 5 Appendix VII, pp. 104-107.

46   *See* ICAO Doc. 8565-LC/152-2, Tokyo 1963, Vol. II Documents, p. 14.

become an outstanding international effort to eventually curb global aviation terrorism as far as possible.

2.4   THE TOKYO CONVENTION REGIME

The purpose of the Tokyo Convention was to protect the safety of the aircraft and of the persons or property therein and to maintain good order and discipline on board, while the aircraft is engaged in international air navigation. The activities regulated under the Convention fall into two categories: (a) offences against penal law and (b) acts which, whether or not they are offences, may or do jeopardize the safety of an aircraft or persons or property therein or which jeopardize good order and discipline on board.[47]

The Convention provides for cases of seizure of aircraft by violence (hijacking) and gives the aircraft commander extensive powers to act when safety or order on board the aircraft are at stake. Offences against penal law committed in flight are treated as though they had occurred in the State of registry. The Convention does not define the term 'offences' due to the fact that such a definition was thought to serve no useful purpose, and it does not impose an obligation on a State to grant extradition because such an act is governed by existing national laws and treaties of State Parties to the Convention. A multitude and diversity of national laws involved were insurmountable obstacles in achieving a universally acceptable formulation of offences.[48]

The Tokyo Convention does not have application in strictly domestic cases, and acts and offences committed in the airspace of the State of registry are excluded except when the point of departure or intended landing lies outside that State, or the aircraft enters into the airspace of a State other than the State of registry as, for instance, on a domestic flight traversing the boundary of another State.[49]

The aircraft commander, other crew members and, under specific conditions, even passengers on board, are empowered to prevent the commission of acts, which in the opinion of the aircraft commander are considered serious offences according to the penal law of the State of registry of the aircraft, and to restrain the alleged person (or persons) concerned. The aircraft commander may also disembark that person or, if to his judgement, the offence in question is serious, deliver that person to the competent authorities of any Contracting State in the territory of which the aircraft has landed. For actions taken in accordance with this Convention, neither the aircraft commander, any other member of the crew, any (assisting) passenger, nor the person on whose behalf the flight was

---

47   *See* Art. 1, Tokyo Convention.
48   *See* Mendes de Leon, P.M.J., *Introduction to Air Law*, Eleventh Edition (Alphen aan den Rijn: Kluwer Law International, 2022), 2.4 The Powers of the Aircraft Commander.
49   *See* Art. 5, Tokyo Convention.

performed shall be held responsible in any proceeding on account of the treatment undergone by the person against whom the actions were taken.[50]

The Tokyo Convention had its early origin in discussions and studies on both the legal status of the aircraft and the legal status of the aircraft commander as well as air law rather than concerns regarding unlawful interference.

Whereas the Tokyo Convention in the first place applies to offences and other acts prejudicial to good order and discipline on board an aircraft, the swift increase of unlawful seizure of aircraft by violence, sabotage and armed attacks on civil aviation targets in the sixties and seventies of the twentieth century called for a much wider range of security measures. In other words, safety to aircraft crew, passengers, ground personnel and the general public shall be the primary objective of each Contracting State in all matters related to safeguarding against acts of unlawful interference with international air transportation.

Supplementary legal instruments have been adopted and ratified to urgently undertake further efforts with a view to ensuring security and safety of the aviation industry and preventing acts of unlawful seizure, sabotage and attacks on civil aircraft and airport facilities.

In December 1969, the UN General Assembly adopted Resolution 2551, in which it emphasized its deep concern over acts of unlawful interference with international civil aviation. On 9 September 1970, the UN Security Council adopted Resolution 286, calling upon States to take all possible legal steps to prevent further hijacking or any other interference with international air transportation. On 25 November 1970, the UN General Assembly adopted Resolution 2645 (XXV) which condemned, without exception whatsoever, all aerial hijackings or other interferences caused by criminal threat, usually accompanied by severe aggression, use of force and or intimidation.[51]

To drastically address these horrifying crimes, two new conventions, following the Tokyo Convention, were prepared. From 1 to 16 December 1970, 77 States and 12 international organizations met in The Hague for a Diplomatic Conference on Air Law, under the auspices of ICAO, which was concluded with the signing of The Hague Convention for the Suppression of Unlawful Seizure of Aircraft (the so-called Anti-Hijacking Convention) which came into force on 14 October 1971 (ICAO Doc. 8920).

The Hague Convention, ratified on a large scale, attempted to rectify shortcomings of the Tokyo Convention like the failure to define aerial hijacking as an act of terrorism, and therefore designated hijacking of aircraft as a distinct criminal offence, calling for severe

---

50   *See* Arts. 6-10, Tokyo Convention.
51   United Nations Assembly Resolution 2645 (XXV) Aerial Hijacking or Interference with Civil Air Travel, adopted at the 1914th Plenary Meeting on 25 November 1970.

punishment of aircraft hijackers. Other shortcomings of the Tokyo Convention, especially with regard to unruly passenger incidents on board aircraft, are: the absence of definitions of the offences or acts that may jeopardize good order and discipline on board an aircraft; a dual regime definition of 'in-flight'; no definition of 'good order' and 'discipline', terms which may be regarded as imprecise and may be subject to conflicting judicial interpretation; lack of mandatory jurisdictions of States other than the State of registry; uncertainties about leased aircraft; the jurisdictional gap which means that numerous unruly persons are left unpunished due to lack of jurisdiction; uncertainties as to the legal standard to be applied in respect of the immunity of the aircraft commander; the issues of disembarkation and delivery; lack of guidance on persons removed from the aircraft, extradition and unlawful seizure of aircraft; and insufficient coverage in the area of international cooperation.[52] Nevertheless, the Tokyo Convention has certainly laid down the foundations for a legal framework for the international civil aviation community.

The Hague Convention specifies the action to be taken by States whenever an aircraft has been unlawfully seized. The Hague Convention defines an offence as:

Article 1
Any person who on board an aircraft in flight:
(a) unlawfully, by force or threat thereof, or by any other form of intimidation, seizes, or exercises control of, that aircraft, or attempts to perform any such act, or (b) is an accomplice of a person who performs or attempts to perform any such act commits an offence.

Article 2
Each Contracting State undertakes to make the offence punishable by severe penalties.

This Anti-Hijacking Convention represents a singularly significant development in international law. The Hague Convention ensures that Contracting States will subject aerial hijackers to severe punishment, regardless of where the act of aerial hijacking takes place.

The next convention, the 1971 Montreal Convention for the Suppression of Unlawful Acts against the Safety of Civil Aviation (ICAO Doc. 8966), was opened for signature at the International Conference on Air Law, convened at Montreal, and adopted on 23 September 1971. It came into force on 26 January 1973. The Montreal Convention is a multilateral treaty by which States agree to prohibit and punish behaviour which may

---

52   Source: ICAO Working Paper LC/SC-MOT-WP/1, 7 May 2012.

threaten the safety of civil air transportation. In particular, it is dealing with a different, emerging terrorist threat, to wit aircraft sabotage. The provisions apply also to aircraft on the surface, even if the offender is not physically present in the aircraft.

Both conventions cover much wider and different areas than the scope of the Tokyo Convention. None of the three conventions, however, has formulated the offence of aircraft hijacking in specific terms. It must be said that further in time, new elements of hijacking were to be added, such as malicious cyberattacks on aircraft communication and navigation systems, ground-based air traffic control (ATC) centres, other ground facilities, although these vital systems are necessarily very well protected against such criminal attacks.

However, the aviation landscape is subject to continuous change in time, resulting in new security challenges in that domain. States Parties to the Tokyo Convention regime have committed themselves to the provisions in order to enhance aviation safety by preserving security throughout the aviation industry. An undeniable fact is that this form of security extends to new developments in air transportation such as commercial unmanned aircraft (UA).

Fairly new targets are remote pilot stations (RPS) which nowadays have full control over, initially, cargo carrying remotely piloted aircraft (RPA), the flying component of the remotely piloted aircraft systems (RPAS), a subcategory of unmanned aircraft systems (UAS) which include futuristic passenger carrying aerial vehicles, similar to RPA, as well as fully autonomous passenger and parcel carrying aircraft systems, better known as pilotless (highly automated) professional air taxis carrying passengers and freight at lower altitudes (below 120 m/400 ft AGL) in urban and suburban areas, part of the urban air mobility (UAM) market, including, *inter alia*, last-mile parcel delivery, air metro and eVTOL air taxi.[53]

Eventually, UAS will operate in non-segregated airspace alongside traditional manned aircraft, a merging facilitated by the so-called U-space framework, consisting of a set of advanced services relying on an ultra-high level of digitalization and automation of functions and specific procedures designed to support safe, efficient and secure access to non-segregated airspace and at aerodromes for a large number of UAS.

---

53 Urban Air Mobility (UAM), on demand automated passenger or cargo-carrying air transportation services around cities and urban areas, is a subset of a broader Advanced Air Mobility (AAM) concept that includes (inter)national inter-city commercial and private air transport by UAS in U-space. However, public acceptance for this mode of transport is a key aspect which relies on a number of factors, including passenger safety risks and security concerns in the absence of flight crew members, cyber security, insurances, liability, the absence of a person vested with powers similar to the aircraft commander or pilot-in-command and social equity, which in this case means the high costs of UAM services which could prove to be prejudicial to public opinion, especially as the affordability of services and technologies is not guaranteed.

UAS, such as pilotless air taxis, are a breakthrough in air transportation, but not if the international aviation industry can guarantee maximum reliability. A special point of interest is the question of sufficient confidence, not only among the general public, but above all, among the rather reliant air taxi passengers.

With the introduction of passengers carrying RPA and autonomous UAS flights, in the sense of pilotless or 'uncrewed' flights, the question may arise to what extent international legal instruments as the Tokyo Convention, governing the authority over passengers, good order and discipline and the safety on board the aircraft, including Chapter III dealing with the powers of the aircraft commander, the 2014 Montreal Protocol to expand the scope of the Tokyo Convention, as well as The Hague Convention, dealing with aerial hijacking, can be applied to these UAS flights for the same reason as to traditional civil aircraft, namely to punish at an international level onboard crimes. The question is obvious, since these international legal instruments are supposed to apply exclusively to unlawful acts committed on board traditional manned aircraft carrying passengers.

UAS are generally considered as aircraft since these vehicles meet the characteristics of an aircraft, defined as: any machine that can derive support in the atmosphere from the reactions of the air other than the reactions of the air against Earth's surface.[54] However, while UAS can be considered as aircraft, there is a difference in control and the safety aspect during flight. The safety aspect of traditional manned aircraft during flight is being supported, among others, by the provisions dealing with the powers of the aircraft commander.

UAS operations, autonomous and pilotless, the very new mode of air transportation, once certified, legalized and publicly accepted, lack an onboard aircraft commander or any other person who could fulfil all the powers conferred under the Tokyo Convention regime. Consequently, this innovative mode of air transportation requires, at an international level, coordinated modifications of applicable legal instruments to cope with crimes committed in flight onboard UAS. With regard to domestic UAS, mainly UAM flights, national laws (modified) will most likely prevail.

To extend the provisions of the 1971 Montreal Convention to include attacks on airports, the Montreal Protocol, the so-called Airport Protocol (ICAO Doc. 9518) was adopted in 1988. In 2010, the Beijing Convention (ICAO Doc. 9960) and the Beijing Protocol (ICAO Doc. 9959), partly prompted by the terrorist attacks on 11 September 2001 on targets in the United States, were both adopted, in order to complement the shortcomings of the existing legal instruments. These international legal instruments were succeeded by the

---

54   *See* ICAO Annex 6 Part I, Twelfth Edition, July 2022, International Standards and Recommended Practices Chapter 1.1 Definitions.

2014 Montreal Protocol (ICAO Doc. 10034), the so-called Unruly Passenger Protocol to amend the outdated Tokyo Convention.[55]

The Tokyo Convention was considered ineffective, no longer up-to-date and too easily avoided to empower air carriers to take remedial actions against unruly passengers. The Tokyo Convention failed to provide a suitable deterrent to unruly passengers because, under its terms, the State of registry of the aircraft concerned was at first instance the State to exercise, although not exclusively, its jurisdiction to try unruly passengers.[56] However, in many cases, this rule has become rather obsolete through the complex leasing contracts which modern aircraft are subject to.

In case of aircraft leasing, the State of the operator could be different from the State of registry, especially in the case of a short-term dry lease when an aircraft retains its original registration as recorded in the national civil aircraft register.

This type of leasing normally means that an aircraft is operated by the operator's own flight crew of which the aircraft commander generally is a national of a State other than the State of registry of the aircraft. Assuming the aircraft commander is not a lawyer, he may have difficulty in understanding the penal laws of his home State, let alone to have any knowledge of the penal laws of a foreign State, in this case, the State of registry.

The question concerning the judgement of the aircraft commander was apparent in considerations of the delegations to the Tokyo Conference in 1963. One of the starting points was devoted to the deliberations about the subjective words 'in his opinion' and 'reasonable grounds', for instance, with respect to the decision to deliver a person to the competent authorities of a State where the landing takes place (State of landing). The opinion of the aircraft commander refers to the committed act as being a serious offence according to the penal laws of the State of registry of the aircraft (Art. 9, Tokyo Convention). The words 'in his opinion' seem less fortunate. In matters like delivering a suspect (offender) to the competent authorities of any Contracting State, the subjective opinion should not be accentuated.

However, if the words were deleted, the aircraft commander would have to evaluate the offence on a legal basis as if he were a judge. On the other hand, some delegates were of the opinion that the words were a dangerous qualification because the aircraft commander would then be enabled to deliver a person because the latter had done something which the aircraft commander considered to be a serious offence, but which was not a serious

---

55 According to ICAO Doc. 10117 Manual on the Legal Aspects of Unruly and Disruptive Passengers, First Edition, 2019, Chapter I, Introduction 1.2, the terms unruly and disruptive passengers are commonly understood as referring to passengers who fail to respect the rules of conduct on board aircraft or to follow the instructions of crew members and thereby create a threat to flight safety and/or disturb the good order and discipline on board aircraft.

56 *See also* Tokyo Convention, Art. 3.3. This Convention does not exclude any criminal jurisdiction exercised in accordance with national law.

offence under the penal laws of the majority of States. It would be much simpler for the aircraft commander if he were not required to refer to the law of a particular State, but were required merely to use his general judgement. In a question of personal freedom, the legality should be the only basis of judgement.

Before the immense growth of civil aircraft leasing on a global scale, the distinction between the State of the operator and the State of registry was largely irrelevant because they were generally the same State. Unlike this rather conservative condition, today, it is more common for the State of registry and the State of the operator to be different jurisdictions as a result of widespread use of international aircraft leasing and financing. Entering into aircraft leasing contracts between airline operators from different States requires jurisdictional, societal and political stability in those States, especially in view of issues like repossession, responsibilities, registration and safety oversight.

Arrangements made according to Article 83*bis* – *Transfer of Certain Functions and Duties*, a 1980 amendment to the Chicago Convention, function as successful tools in the dynamic domain of aircraft leasing. It provides a framework to allow the State of registry to transfer supervisory responsibilities for one or a fleet of aircraft to the State of the operator.[57]

Because of this amendment to the Chicago Convention, the *rapporteur*, the Panel of Experts, the Special Subcommittee of the Legal Committee on the subject and the 23rd Session of the Legal Committee considered possible problems arising out of aircraft lease, charter and interchange with respect to the Tokyo Convention. However, the Legal Commission was not convinced that further work on the subject was necessary. It was considered undesirable to implement an amendment to the Tokyo Convention, ratified by so many State Parties, with respect to hypothetical problems which have never given any proven practical difficulty.

It was also recalled that in the Legal Committee, doubts were raised whether a private law agreement such as aircraft lease or charter could properly confer criminal jurisdiction on the State of the operator of the aircraft. In view of the foregoing, the Legal Commission decided unanimously to recommend to the Plenary that this item be deleted from the General Work Programme of the Legal Committee, leaving the provisions of the Tokyo Convention, including the powers of the aircraft commander, especially concerning his judgement, in effect.[58]

---

57   Protocol Relating to an Amendment to the Convention on International Civil Aviation, signed at Montreal on 6 October 1980 (Art. 83*bis*). *See also* ICAO Doc. 9316 A23-RES, Assembly 23rd Session, Montreal, 16 September to 7 October 1980. Resolutions Adopted by the Assembly and Index to Documentation, A23-2, pp. 35-37.

58   ICAO Doc. 9314 A23-LE Assembly 23rd Session, Montreal, 16 September to 7 October 1980 Legal Commission, Report and Minutes. Lease, Charter and Interchange of Aircraft in International Operations (Resolution B of the Guadalajara Conference) – Problems with respect to the Tokyo Convention, p. 12.

ICAO identified the widespread phenomenon of unruly passengers as a major issue for civil aviation since these kind of people could very well endanger the safety of both passengers and crew members, which would soon justify a stronger international legal framework to curb this culpable behaviour.

In September 2009, the ICAO Legal Committee recommended the reactivation of the Secretariat Study Group on Unruly Passengers. The Study Group recommended the Council to convene a Special Subcommittee of the Legal Committee at Montreal in May 2012 to review the Tokyo Convention, with particular reference to the issue of unruly passengers. While the Tokyo Convention is considered a thoroughly successful instrument with 185 States Parties, as of 2012, it is almost 50 years old, and there is a practical need to consider whether it is still adequate to respond to the current situation of international air transportation given the increasing number and gravity of incidents of unruly and disruptive passengers on board an aircraft, which have adverse implications for aircraft safety and for all occupants therein, as well as in light of the modernization of other conventions and protocols of Beijing and Montreal.

In spite of ICAO guidance material on unruly passengers and the encouragement of States to enact authorization legislation to deal with unruly or disruptive passengers, there are constant appeals from the civil aviation industry to consider going beyond voluntary measures and moving to develop a global framework that is codified in an international instrument.[59]

Appropriate issues to be considered are, among other things, the powers and duties of the aircraft commander and crew members and their immunity from liability. The Subcommittee, while examining these issues, should strive to achieve the necessary balance between the need for safe, secure and orderly flights and the protection of the rights of passengers.

International civil aviation safety and security have always been the goals of ICAO. Due to societal and political tranquillity, any protection whatsoever against criminal acts committed on board an aircraft in the early days of international air transportation was considered as low profile. However, this seemingly peaceful status quo changed quickly in the second half of the twentieth century. Aircraft hijacking was the order of the day. In most aircraft hijackings, the aircraft commander was forced to adhere to the orders given by the hijackers. Occasionally, the hijackers took over control to fly the aircraft themselves as during the 11 September 2001 attacks.

Especially after these highly terrifying terrorist hijacking in the United States, security measures in international civil aviation were drastically scaled up worldwide. These extremely stringent security measures were not only intended to prevent potential

---

59   ICAO Circular 288, 1 January 2002. *See also* ICAO Doc. 10117, 2019, Chapter 4.

hijackings, but also, generally speaking, offences against penal laws and acts which, considered as whether or not offences, could endanger the safety of the aircraft or of persons or property therein or jeopardize good order and discipline on board.

2.5   IN-FLIGHT CRIMES, THE TOKYO CONVENTION AND THE MONTREAL PROTOCOL

At the 1944 Chicago Conference, the delegates could hardly have imagined that, one day sometime in the future, aircraft hijackers and terrorists could abuse the operational vulnerability and the fundamental openness as well as easy access, so self-evident in the history of civil aviation until that particular horrible day in September 2001.

With the rise of extremely violent terrorism and unlawful seizure of aircraft, aviation security became a key element of ICAO's role in the world. Together with a number of organizations including IATA, IFALPA, ACI, FAA and ECAC, ICAO made important progress in combating unlawful interference in international air navigation.

Although less violent but highly annoying, not to say sometimes highly threatening, is the unruly behaviour of persons on board an aircraft during flight. Incidents involving unruly or disruptive behaviour of passengers or even crew members, albeit rarely, is a growing concern within the international aviation community. This kind of behaviour is due to the unprecedented growth in the number of people flying. However, other factors may underlie this emerging phenomenon.

Bad experiences on the ground such as poor customer service, delayed flights, denied boarding and being rerouted, being downgraded and intrusive security measures are only part of the factors. Limited room to move during flight, claustrophobia, stress, insufficient leg room, fear of flying and smoking bans are typical onboard factors. On top of that, consumption of alcohol and use of illegal drugs on the ground but certainly in the air at high altitude may all contribute to disruptive behaviour.

Unquestionably, a minor infraction which may be inconsequential on the ground may produce disastrous effects in flight. In light of these potentially detrimental effects on aviation safety, the Tokyo Convention allows the aircraft commander, as the internal executive authority, certain prerogatives to handle passengers in those situations where they have already committed or are about to commit a criminal offence or an act that may jeopardize the safety of the aircraft.

The objectives of the Tokyo Convention cover a variety of subjects with the intention of providing safety on board an aircraft, protection of life and property on board, and generally protecting the security concerning civil aviation. Given the various national laws providing different scenarios for the extra-territorial application of rules of jurisdiction over crimes committed on board an aircraft, the intention of the drafters of the Tokyo Convention was to achieve some degree of international uniformity in the rules applicable to the prosecution of offences committed on board an aircraft.

In this respect, the Tokyo Convention provides for maintaining law and order on board an aircraft engaged in international air navigation, protection of persons acting in accordance with the provisions of the Convention, protection of the interests of disembarked persons and the quest for justice. The Tokyo Convention entered into force on 4 December 1969, bringing (temporary) closure to ICAO's tremendous efforts on the subject since the 1950s.

In the years since 1968, the number of aircraft hijackings increased significantly. This number was further enlarged by politically motivated acts of sabotage against aircraft, crew and passengers both in flight and on the surface. Deep concern prevailed in the world over these acts of unlawful interference with international air transportation.

This concern was the reason to convene an extraordinary ICAO Assembly (17th), which was held at Montreal from 16 to 30 June 1970, specifically on the subject of aviation security. The Assembly produced a series of resolutions dealing with a wide range of security measures, eventually leading to the adoption of a completely new Annex. On 22 March 1974, the ICAO Council adopted the First Edition of Annex 17 – *Standards and Recommended Practices – Security – Safeguarding International Civil Aviation against Acts of Unlawful Interference*, pursuant to the provisions of Article 37 of the Chicago Convention.[60]

Annex 17 lays down the following objectives:
– Each Contracting State shall have as its primary objective the safety of passengers, crew, ground personnel and the general public in all matters related to safeguarding against acts of unlawful interference with civil aviation.
– Each Contracting State shall establish an organization and develop and implement regulations, practices and procedures to safeguard civil aviation against acts of unlawful interference taking into account the safety, regularity and efficiency of flights.
– Each Contracting State shall ensure that such an organization and such regulations, practices and procedures: (a) protect the safety of passengers, crew, ground personnel and the general public in all matters related to safeguarding against acts of unlawful interference with civil aviation; and (b) are capable of responding rapidly to meet any increased security threat.
– Each Contracting State shall ensure appropriate protection of sensitive aviation security information.[61]

---

60   ICAO Annex 17, Twelfth Edition, July 2022, Foreword – Historical background.
61   ICAO Annex 17, Twelfth Edition, July 2022, Chapter 2, General Principles, 2.1 Objectives.

The Tokyo Convention covers, except as provided in Chapter III – Powers of the Aircraft Commander, offences committed or acts done by a person on board any aircraft registered in a Contracting State, while that aircraft is in flight or on the surface of the high seas or of any other area outside the territory of any State.

Article 5, Paragraph 1 of Chapter III states:

> The provisions of this Chapter shall not apply to offences and acts committed or about to be committed by a person on board an aircraft in flight in the airspace of the State of registry or over the high seas or any other area outside the territory of any State unless the last point of take-off or the next point of intended landing is situated in a State other than that of registration, or the aircraft subsequently flies in the airspace of a State other than that of registry with such person still on board.[62]

Article 1, Paragraph 2 provided a practical solution to what was a practical problem. It was, in practice, necessary to deal with the cases of crimes committed over the high seas and over land areas when it was uncertain over exactly what State the offence had been committed.[63]

There is no geographical limit to the application of the Tokyo Convention. However, the Convention does not create or define particular offences. It is left to national law to determine the description of certain offences.

The Tokyo Convention has four principal purposes:

- The Convention makes it clear that the State of registry of an aircraft has the authority to apply its laws to events occurring on board its aircraft while in flight, no matter where it might be.
- The Convention provides the aircraft commander with the necessary authority to deal with persons who have committed, or are about to commit, a crime or an act jeopardizing safety on board an aircraft through the use of reasonable force when required and without fear of subsequent retaliation through civil suit or otherwise.
- The Convention delineates the duties and responsibilities of the Contracting State in which an aircraft lands after the commission of a crime on board, including its authority over, and responsibility to, any offenders that may be either disembarked within the territory of that State or delivered to its authorities.

---

62 For the purpose of the Tokyo Convention, an aircraft is considered to be in flight from the moment when power is applied for the purpose of take-off until the moment when the landing run ends (Art. 1, Para. 3).
63 Art. 1, Para. 2: Except as provided in Chapter III, this Convention shall apply in respect of offences committed or acts done by a person on board any aircraft registered in a Contracting State, while that aircraft is in flight or on the surface of the high seas or of any other area outside the territory of any State.

- The Convention is dealing with an emerging issue which is the crime of hijacking, however, not being prioritized.

Concerning the question of which penal law actually will be applicable, five theories, based on a US study submitted in 1956,[64] can be distinguished:

1. The territorial theory. This theory follows the territorial basis in international law on which each State is assumed to have complete and exclusive sovereignty over the airspace above its territory and the territorial waters adjacent thereto.[65] The law of the State in whose airspace the offence has taken place will be applied by its national courts. In fact, the offence is subject to the concurrent jurisdiction between the State of registry (normally the flag State) and the subjacent State. Overlapping or concurrent jurisdictions may exist. In principle, each Contracting State as the State of registry has the competence to exercise jurisdiction (Chapter II, Jurisdiction, Art. 3, Paras. 2 and 3). The enforcement power of the subjacent State will be restricted by Article 4, except in the case of defined conditions.

> Article 4 of the Tokyo Convention:
> A Contracting State which is not the State of registry may not interfere with an aircraft in flight in order to exercise its criminal jurisdiction over an offence committed on board except in the following cases:
> a. the offence has effect on the territory of such State;
> b. the offence has been committed by or against a national or permanent resident of such State;
> c. the offence is against the security of such State;
> d. the offence consists of a breach of any rules or regulations relating to the flight or manoeuvre of aircraft in force in such State;
> e. the exercise of jurisdiction is necessary to ensure the observance of any obligation of such State under a multilateral international agreement.

However, the determination of the exact geographical position (GPS instant longitude-latitude data) of the aircraft, travelling with high subsonic airspeed (approximately 8 NM per minute) at high altitudes through different sovereign airspaces, at the time the offence actually has been committed, is not always clear, possibly depending on the cause and course of the incident, the attempt to initially subdue it by the cabin crew and the time it

---

64 Study of the Jurisdiction and Law to be Applied to Crimes on Board Aircraft, submitted by the US Delegation to the ICAO Legal Status of the Aircraft Subcommittee on 13 April 1956.

65 *See also* Convention Relating to the Regulation of Aerial Navigation, signed at Paris, 13 October, 1919 (Paris Convention), Art. 1. The High Contracting Parties recognize that every Power has complete and exclusive sovereignty over the air space above its territory.

takes to notify the aircraft commander, whether through the intercom or physically. For that very reason, it is generally impracticable for a State to base its jurisdiction solely on the territorial principle. Especially for flights over the high seas or above *terra nullius*, the territorial principle turns out to be ineffective.

Mr. Lodewijk Hulsman (ICAO Legal Committee representative of the Netherlands) said

> that the question under consideration (to give the Convention a more restricted scope or a much broader scope) should be discussed by drawing a distinction between questions of jurisdiction and cooperation between States (for instance, in the field of extradition which was related to the question of jurisdiction) and the question of the powers of the aircraft commander. In regard to the question of penal jurisdiction, it was not practicable to restrict the Convention to offences which jeopardized the safety of the aircraft. Such a restriction would add a new element to the various aspects of offences which would make the application of jurisdiction very difficult. Moreover, such restriction would prevent the successful accomplishment of the task before the Tokyo Conference. That task was not only to take into account the safety of aviation, but to settle other difficulties that arose out of the specific nature of aviation.[66]

In this regard, Hulsman observed that penal law which was, in general, based on the concept of territoriality, could no longer be applied in the case of a fast-moving aircraft since it was no longer possible, in a great number of cases, to determine exactly where a crime had been committed.

2. The national theory. The law of the State where the aircraft is registered must be applied under all circumstances, according to this theory. The nationality rule is of special importance when flying over the high seas or over other areas having no territorial sovereign, for instance, areas such as Antarctica, Earth's south polar land mass, based on the Common Heritage of Mankind (CHM) principle.[67]

3. The mixed basis theory. The law of the nationality of the aircraft in flight, and or the law of the State over which territory the aircraft is flying, next to each other (concurrent),

---

66   ICAO Doc. 8565-LC/152-1, Tokyo 1963, Vol. I Minutes, Second meeting, p. 19, Item 31. *See* Hufnagel, S., *Cross-border Cooperation in Criminal Matters* (New York: Oxford University Press, Oxford Bibliographies International Law, Transnational Criminal Law, 2014).

67   This principle of international law, applicable to areas beyond the limits of national jurisdiction, constitutes an alternative to the traditional *res nullius* approach for determining property rights among States (Source: Herber, B.P., "The Common Heritage Principle: Antarctica and the Developing Nations," (1991) 50 *Am. J. Econ. Sociol.* 4).

are enforceable whenever the security or public order of such State is jeopardized by offences committed on board an aircraft.

This theory has already been described in a proposal concerning the resolution of conflicts of competence and jurisdiction contained in excerpts from the Draft Convention on Jurisdiction with Respect to Crime of the Harvard Research in International Law.[68]

4. The departure theory. The theory of the applicable law of the State of departure.
5. The arrival or landing theory. This is the theory of the applicable law of the State of landing.

The departure and arrival theories confer jurisdiction on the State from which the aircraft has departed, respectively on the State in which the aircraft has landed. The departure theory does not leave the aircraft commander any choice of jurisdiction, while the arrival or landing theory confers the aircraft commander the power to inform the appropriate authorities by any means of communication the delivery of any person whom he has reasonable grounds to believe has committed on board an aircraft an act which, in his or her opinion, is a serious offence according to the penal law of the State of registry of the aircraft, and alert the airport officials for assistance and to scale up security measures (Art. 9, Tokyo Convention).

In all cases, the aircraft commander will retain full authority in selecting which airport in which State is adequately equipped, and thus whose law will eventually be applied to the committed offence (Art. 8, Tokyo Convention).[69]

Criminal jurisdiction may be exercised by Contracting States other than the State of registry under limited conditions, *viz.* when the exercise of jurisdiction is required under multilateral international obligations, in the interest of national security, etc.

The Tokyo Convention recognizes, for the first time in the history of international air law, certain powers and immunities of the aircraft commander who, on international flights, may impose rational measures including restraint when he has reasonable grounds to believe that a person has committed or is about to commit, on board an aircraft in flight, an offence against penal law or an act which is, whether or not is an offence, liable to

---

68 Boyle, R.P., Pulsifer, R. (1964), pp. 311-314, Concurrent Jurisdiction. The 1935 Harvard Draft Convention on Criminal Jurisdiction would vest jurisdiction in States over crimes committed within their airspace and aircraft which have their national character. The drafters specifically rejected any provision assigning priority to either State. Art. 3. A State has jurisdiction with respect to any crime committed in whole or in part within its territory. Art. 4. A State has jurisdiction with respect to any crime committed in whole or in part upon a public or private ship or aircraft which has its national character. Thus, with respect to all crimes on aircraft regardless where they might be, there would be two competent jurisdictions.

69 Diederiks-Verschoor, I.H.Ph., Butler, M.A. (Legal advisor), *An Introduction to Air Law*, Eighth Revised Edition (Alphen aan den Rijn: Kluwer Law International, 2006), pp. 290-291.

interfere with the safety of persons or property on board an aircraft or is jeopardizing good order and discipline.

Under general legal principles, an intentional or unlawful act of interference on board an aircraft can be regarded as a crime. The question of whether a particular act is lawful or unlawful is to be judged by the law of the State of registry of the aircraft or the law of the subjacent State at the time the aircraft is flying in its airspace. By the use of this sub construction, it is unnecessary for the Tokyo Convention to try by international law to dictate a particular act as criminal.

To avoid any legal confusion, the Tokyo Convention will rely upon the existing applicable criminal codes of the Contracting States.[70] A crime has been identified as: "the intentional commission of an act usually deemed socially harmful or dangerous and specifically defined, prohibited, and punishable under criminal law".[71]

In retrospect of the Draft Convention on the Legal Status of the Aircraft Commander (as revised by the PICAO Legal *ad hoc* Committee, February 1947), some rules apply to the powers of the aircraft commander, albeit there is no clear explanation of any measures against offences or other acts endangering the safety of the aircraft and its occupants. Article 2 of this draft stated that:

1. Within the periods, specified in Article 5 below, the aircraft commander:
    a. shall be in charge of the aircraft, the crew, the passengers, and the cargo;
    b. has the right and the duty to control and direct the crew and the passengers to the full extent necessary to ensure order and safety;
    c. has the right, for good reason, to disembark any number of the crew, or passengers at an intermediate stop;
    d. has disciplinary power over the members of the crew within the scope of their duties; in case of necessity, of which he shall be sole judge, he may assign temporarily any member of the crew to duties other than those for which he is engaged.

Article 5 stated in Paragraph 2:

> The powers of the aircraft commander over the aircraft, the passengers and the cargo on board come into force as soon as the aircraft, with passengers and cargo, are handed over to him at the beginning of the trip. They expire at the end of the trip when the aircraft, the passengers and the cargo have been respectively handed over to the operator's representative or other qualified authority.

---

70   Boyle, R.P., Pulsifer, R. (1964), p. 345.
71   www.britannica.com/topic/crime-law.

The Tokyo Convention does not define the term 'trip'. However, for the purpose of this Convention, an aircraft is considered to be in flight from the moment when power is applied for the purpose of take-off until the moment when the landing run ends (Art. 1, Para. 3, Tokyo Convention), albeit for the purpose of Chapter III – Powers of the Aircraft Commander – only, a modification for the delineation of responsibilities has been implemented that reads: an aircraft shall be considered to be in flight at any time from the moment when all its external doors are closed following embarkation until the moment when any such door is opened for disembarkation. In the case of a forced landing, the provisions of this chapter shall continue to apply with respect to offences and acts committed on board until competent authorities of a State take over the responsibility for the aircraft and for the persons and property on board (Art. 5, Para. 2, Tokyo Convention).[72]

Thus, if the aircraft commander makes a forced landing outside the airport and he is unable to deliver the offender to the competent authorities, the authority of the aircraft commander will not be disrupted as, under the Convention, in that particular situation, he is considered the international executive authority. The rationale of this provision is that a criminal or a group of criminals (offenders) who are on board the aircraft might, after a forced landing, force the doors to open, including any aircraft over-wing exit or service-door (which is a broad interpretation of 'any such door' stated in Art. 5, Para. 2, Tokyo Convention), and that action would instantly cease the exercise of the powers of the aircraft commander, which under those circumstances, however, would be highly undesirable, especially since it is quite possible that there might be no competent authorities at the scene to whom the aircraft commander could directly deliver the offender(s).[73]

The powers of the aircraft commander in Articles 6 to 9 of the Tokyo Convention are mainly focused on the imposition of reasonable measures including restraint upon a person believed to have committed or is about to commit an offence or act, described in Article 1, Paragraph 1, Tokyo Convention, on requiring respectively requesting assistance

---

72   *See* the 1952 Rome Convention on Damage Caused by Foreign Aircraft to Third Parties on the Surface (ICAO Doc. 7364), Art. 1(2): For the purpose of this Convention an aircraft is considered to be in flight from the moment when power is applied for the purpose of actual take-off until the moment when the landing run ends. *See also* the 1971 Montreal Convention, Art. 2: For the purpose of this Convention: (a) an aircraft is considered to be in flight at any time from the moment when all its external doors are closed following embarkation until the moment when any such door is opened for disembarkation; in the case of a forced landing, the flight shall be deemed to continue until the competent authorities take over the responsibility for the aircraft and for persons and property on board. (b) an aircraft is considered to be in service from the beginning of the preflight preparation of the aircraft by ground personnel or by the crew for a specific flight until twenty-four hours after any landing; the period of service shall, in any event, extend for the entire period during which the aircraft is in flight as defined in paragraph (a) of this article.

73   ICAO Doc. 8565-LC/152-1, Tokyo 1963, Vol. I Minutes, pp. 169-170 and ICAO Doc. 8565-LC/152-2, Tokyo 1963, Vol. II Documents, p. 74.

of other crew members and passengers to restrain such a person, and after landing followed by disembarkation and delivery to the competent authorities at the first port of call, which stands for any Contracting State.

In case of aircraft hijacking, which means when a person on board has unlawfully committed by force or threat thereof an act of interference, seizure, or other wrongful exercise of control of an aircraft in flight or when such act is about to be committed, Contracting States shall take all appropriate measures to restore control of the aircraft to its lawful commander or to preserve his control of the aircraft. The Contracting State in which the aircraft lands shall permit its passengers and crew to continue their journey as soon as practicable, and shall return the aircraft and its cargo to the persons lawfully entitled to possession (Art. 11, Tokyo Convention).

These provisions, however, do not oblige all States Parties to the Tokyo Convention to prohibit or punish aircraft hijacking. They merely require them to take all appropriate measures to restore control of the aircraft. Remarkably, aircraft hijacking has not been defined in the provisions of the Tokyo Convention.

The Tokyo Convention actually deals with four major issues: penal jurisdiction, the police powers and immunities of the aircraft commander, duties of the custodial State as well as unlawful seizure of an aircraft (aerial hijacking). In this context, the Tokyo Convention obliges States to take appropriate measures, subject to State restrictions on feasibility and legality, in order to restore or maintain control of the aircraft to the aircraft commander.

With respect to unlawful seizure of aircraft, the Tokyo Convention spells out minimal obligations to ensure safety and security of passengers and crew and the return of the hijacked aircraft to its lawful commander. According to the provisions of the Tokyo Convention, no security measures will be imposed on Contracting States. At the time, it was believed that hijacking could be stopped by legal deterrence.

At the 16th Session of the ICAO Assembly, Resolution A16-37 concerning unlawful seizure of civil aircraft was adopted. It states:

> Whereas unlawful seizure of civil aircraft has a serious adverse effect on the safety, efficiency and regularity of air navigation;
> The Assembly,
> Noting that Article 11 of the Tokyo Convention on Offences and Certain Other Acts Committed on Board Aircraft provides certain remedies for the situation envisaged; being of the opinion, however, that this article does not provide a complete remedy,
> 1. urges all States to become parties as soon as possible to the Tokyo Convention;

2. invites States, even before ratification of, or adherence to, the Tokyo Convention, to give effect to the principles of Article 11 of that Convention; and

3. requests the Council, at the earliest possible date, to institute a study of other measures to cope with the problem of unlawful seizure.[74]

The Tokyo Convention did no more than to reformulate customary international law obligations already existing for quite some time. In fact, the anti-hijacking provisions, particularly laid down in Article 11 were considered to be weak to provide effective sanctions for their enforcement. The Tokyo Convention only addressed the hijacking issue incidentally. Consequently, it was not a pronounced anti-hijacking treaty.

With the adoption of two additional international conventions addressing acts of unlawful interference, in this case terrorist acts against international civil aviation, the modern era of international counter-terrorism agreements, providing for assistance in law enforcement questions, started as of 1970 with The Hague Convention followed by the Montreal Convention in 1971, by a supplement in 1988, the Montreal Protocol, by the Beijing Convention and Beijing Protocol in 2010 and an instrument called the Montreal Protocol of 2014, to amend and modernize the Tokyo Convention, making the system a coherent international jurisdictional regime. The last instrument in a row of the Tokyo Convention regime, the Montreal Protocol of 2014, resulted from the desire of many States to assist each other in curbing the escalation and frequency of unruly behaviour and restoring good order and discipline on board an aircraft.[75]

The Hague Convention, which reflected a changing international scene marked by an alarming increase in the number of aircraft hijackings, designated this violation of the law as a distinct criminal act. The Montreal Convention is a multilateral treaty by which State Parties agree to prohibit and punish behaviour which may threaten the safety of civil aviation. It was aimed at attacks on aircraft, whether in flight or on the surface. To cover attacks on airports, the scope of the Montreal Convention was widened by the adoption of the Montreal Protocol in 1988.[76]

The Beijing Convention and Beijing Protocol complement the shortcomings in the existing international legal instruments, respectively, on the subjects of Suppression of

---

74 ICAO Doc. 8770, Assembly Resolutions in Force (as of 26 September 1968), p. 109. *See also* ICAO Doc. 8775 A16-Min. P/1-9 Minutes of the Plenary Meetings, 16th Session of the Assembly, Buenos Aires, 3-26 September 1968, pp. 80-81.

75 The 1971 Montreal Convention (ICAO Doc. 8966) is supplemented by the 1988 Montreal Protocol (ICAO Doc. 9518). The 2010 Beijing Convention (ICAO Doc. 9960). The 2010 Beijing Protocol (ICAO Doc. 9959) supplementary to the 1970 The Hague Convention (ICAO Doc. 8920). The 2014 Montreal Protocol (ICAO Doc. 10034) to amend the 1963 Tokyo Convention (ICAO Doc. 8364).

76 Wallis, R., *How Safe Are Our Skies? Assessing the Airlines' Response to Terrorism* (Westport, CT: Praeger Publishers, 2003), p. 59.

Unlawful Acts relating to international civil aviation and on supplementing The Hague Convention.

Article 1, Paragraph 1, subparagraph (a) of the Montreal Convention and Article 1, subparagraph (a) of the Beijing Convention provide that:

> Any person commits an offence if he/that person unlawfully and intentionally performs an act of violence against a person on board an aircraft in flight if that act is likely to endanger the safety of that aircraft.

These provisions may also be applied in cases involving safety threatening acts of violence committed on board by unruly and disruptive passengers. The Montreal Protocol of 2014, which came into force on 1 January 2020 following the ratification of 22 States, modernized the outdated Tokyo Convention by expanding the grounds of jurisdiction by recognizing, under certain conditions, the competence of the State of landing and the State of the operator to exercise jurisdiction over offences and acts on board an aircraft. In addition, it updated the definition of 'in flight', equivalent to other applicable instruments.[77]

Undeniably, the powers and duties of the aircraft commander, outlined in the Tokyo Convention, are to be continued in these international legal instruments, if applicable, in particular in the Montreal Protocol. However, the weaknesses of the provisions of the Tokyo Convention had left major questions unanswered with regard to extradition enforcement, custody and prosecution of aircraft hijackers. It applied only to aircraft in flight without considering possible attacks or acts of sabotage on aviation-related facilities and parked aircraft at airports. Needless to say that the Tokyo Convention, and subsequent treaties on the subject, would only apply to those States that ratified it, which made it rather limited in its international application.[78]

Whereas the Tokyo Convention only grants jurisdiction over offences and certain other acts committed on board an aircraft to the State of registry of the aircraft concerned, the Montreal Protocol confers mandatory jurisdiction to the intended State of landing, however, with two included guarantees to reflect the concerns of some States with respect to legal certainty and proportionality. First of all, the character of the offence must be sufficiently serious, in the sense that the safety of the aircraft or persons or property therein, or good order and discipline on board are unmistakably jeopardized. Secondly, the State of landing must consider if the offence is an offence in the State of the operator.

---

77   *See* Montreal Protocol Chapter II – Jurisdiction, Art. 3, and for the definition of "in flight" Art. 1, Para. 3 (a).
78   Mackenzie, D., *A History of the International Civil Aviation Organization* (Toronto: University of Toronto Press, 2010), pp. 253-255.

The Montreal Protocol further implies that where the severity of the incident is such that the aircraft commander decides to divert the aircraft to an airport in a State not being the destination airport according to schedule, that State has competence to assert and exercise jurisdiction. Since in many cases, the State of registry is necessarily not the State of the operator, due to an increasing number of aircraft for short- and long-term lease, mandatory jurisdiction for the State of the operator is established by the Montreal Protocol.

Once it is widely ratified, the Montreal Protocol will close the jurisdictional gaps of the Tokyo Convention and will ensure that States have the tools to deal with unruly and disruptive passengers that land in their territory irrespective of where the aircraft is registered. However, even in cases where jurisdiction is not an issue, there is often a reluctance to pursue criminal prosecutions against unruly and disruptive passengers, especially for offences and certain acts that, for various reasons, are considered to be less serious, allowing these passengers to escape prosecution. Lack of response from the authorities after an incident will impair deterrence. A strict civil penalty system should be the remedy.[79]

The Montreal Protocol clearly identifies certain behaviours which should at least be considered as an offence which in turn will lead to appropriate criminal or other legal proceedings by States to be taken. These include physical assault or a threat to commit such assault against a crew member, and refusal to obey a lawful instruction given by or on behalf of the aircraft commander in view of aviation safety (Art. 15 *bis*).

This definition and simplification make the powers of the aircraft commander much clearer, and certainly will increase the likelihood that the aircraft commander shall feel duly authorized to take appropriate and legitimate action against unruly and disruptive passengers. Furthermore, the aircraft commander may request, but not require, the assistance of an in-flight security officer (IFSO) to restrain any person whom he or she is entitled to restrain, according to Article 6, Paragraph 2 of the Montreal Protocol.[80]

IATA data, collected on a regular basis from its airline members on reported incidents, involved various types of onboard offences as well as unruly and disruptive acts, including assault on flight and cabin crew members and/or passengers, fights among intoxicated passengers, child molestation, sexual harassment and assault, disorderly conduct as a result of alcohol and/or drugs intoxication, ransacking and sometimes vandalizing of aircraft seats and cabin interior, unauthorized use of portable electronic devices, destruction of safety equipment on board and other disorderly or riotous conduct. In a

---

79   ICAO A40-WP/335 LE/9, 2 August 1919 Assembly – 40th Session Legal Commission, p. 3 – Item 2. Resolving Jurisdictional Gaps That Enable Unruly and Disruptive Passengers to Avoid Prosecution and Encouraging Enforcement Action.

80   *See also* ICAO/37-WP/2-3 Appendix of the Working Paper of the Legal Committee – 37th Session. Montreal, 4-7 September 2018, Acts of Offences of Concern to the International Aviation Community and Not Covered by Existing Air Law Instruments, p. 2.

number of cases, the aircraft commander had to make an unscheduled stopover to disembark unruly or disruptive passenger(s) for safety reasons.[81]

In order to assist aircraft commanders in exercising their powers under Article 9 of the Tokyo Convention, it may be desirable to arrive at a common understanding of what constitutes a serious offence. The ICAO Secretariat Study Group was of the opinion that due to the need to provide enhanced legal protection for the aircraft crew and the type of risks involved as well as their potential consequences covered by Section 1 of the model legislation (in this case: Model Legislation on Certain Offences Committed on Board Aircraft), to be specific, assault and other acts of interference against a crew member on board a civil aircraft, should be considered as serious offences within the meaning of Article 9 of the Tokyo Convention.[82]

The heavy burden on the aircraft commander who was required to have reasonable grounds to believe that unruly behaviour constitutes a serious offence under the penal law of the State of registry, was thus taken away by the Montreal Protocol.

The Montreal Protocol represents a clear opportunity for governments to put in place an international legal instrument which gives them the means to deal with unruly and disruptive passengers more effectively, and to prevent future similar incidents.

Summarizing, the Montreal Protocol is an amendment to the Tokyo Convention which, unfortunately, failed to provide a suitable deterrent to unruly passengers, as under its conditions, the State of registry of the aircraft was considered the State with jurisdiction to judge the unruly behaviour of the passenger. The Montreal Protocol extends jurisdiction to the State in which the operator is located and also the State in which the destination of the flight is located.

The Montreal Protocol clarifies what constitutes unruly behaviour, which makes the aircraft commander's powers much clearer. Moreover, it strengthens the position of the civil airline industry by providing purposeful deterrents to be able to prevent such behaviour, or if such behaviour still occurs, it recognizes that airlines have a right to seek compensation for the significant costs incurred by those unruly passengers.

For the reference of the international community, IATA and IFALPA have worked as part of an ICAO Task Force to prepare guidance material and examples in respect of civil

---

81   ICAO Circular 288, 4.4.2. Section 1 provides that any person who commits on board a civil aircraft any of the following acts thereby commits an offence: assault, intimidation or threat, whether physical or verbal, against a crew member, if such act interferes with the performance of the duties of the crew member or lessens the ability of the crew member to perform those duties; refusal to follow a lawful instruction given by the aircraft commander, for the purpose of ensuring the safety of the aircraft or of any person or property on board or for the purpose of maintaining good order and discipline on board.

82   ICAO Doc. 10117, Appendix A, Section 1: Assault and Other Acts of Interference against a Crew Member on Board an Aircraft. *See also* Section 2 for assault and other acts endangering safety or jeopardizing good order and discipline on board an aircraft, and Section 3 for other offences committed on board an aircraft.

penalty systems, already in use by various governments as a deterrence element to acts of violence in aviation. New guidance material, created by IATA, is intended to help member airlines on the issue of unruly and disruptive passengers, which is a real challenge and continuing concern for airlines worldwide, by providing information and tools necessary to develop strong, effective and efficient policies.[83]

On 3 December 2021, IFALPA released a revised edition of its Position Paper on Unruly Passengers. The Federation observed the increasing number and severity of incidents involving unruly passengers on board an aircraft on a global scale. These unruly passenger incidents on board an aircraft that threaten safety and security unfortunately have become a significant and too common an issue faced by airlines, in particular their flight and cabin crews. Despite the complexity of the issue, there are practical steps that can be taken to prevent and manage unruly passenger incidents, and which can contribute to increased safety in the air.

One of the basic steps to be taken is to consider that safety in the air begins on the ground, thus unruly passenger incidents are best managed in a preventive manner by keeping unruly behaviour on the ground and off the aircraft. The primary goal should be to prevent potentially unruly passengers from boarding an aircraft and should consist of a clear 'zero tolerance' policy.[84]

With respect to this problem, ICAO Annex 9 – *Facilitation* – (16th Edition, July 2022) includes the following Standards in Chapter 6, International Airports – Facilities and Services for Traffic – Part E Unruly Passengers:

> 6.43 Each Contracting State shall, to deter and prevent unruly behaviour, promote passenger awareness of the unacceptability and possible consequences of unruly or disruptive behaviour in aviation facilities and on board aircraft.
> 6.44 Each Contracting State shall take measures to ensure that relevant personnel are provided training to identify and manage unruly passenger situations.[85]

Not only unruly passengers will put a responsibility on the pilot-in-command but also air traveller health issues such as communicable diseases. According to ICAO Annex 9 Chapter 8, Facilitation Provisions Covering Specific Subjects, E – Implementation of

---

83 IATA Guidance on Unruly Passenger Prevention and Management, December 2012. The objectives are to: evaluate safety and/or security risks; develop a zero-tolerance unruly passenger policy; develop unruly passenger prevention and management procedures; revaluate and possibly amend current operator standard operating procedures, if applicable; develop strategies to prevent unruly passenger incidents and the resulting impacts.

84 IFALPA Position Paper 23POS06, 13 March 2023, Unruly Passengers, p. 2.

85 *See also* ICAO Annex 17, 12th Edition, July 2022, Chapter 6 International Airports – Facilities and Services for Traffic, E Unruly Passengers, Paras. 6.45 and 6.46.

international health regulations and related provisions – Paragraph 8.15: the pilot-in-command of an aircraft shall ensure that a suspected communicable disease is reported promptly to ATC, in order to facilitate provision for the presence of any special medical personnel and equipment necessary for the management of public health risk on arrival.[86]

2.6   THE TOKYO CONVENTION: NECESSITY, FUNCTIONALITY AND FRAILTY

The Tokyo Convention was actually used as a starting point from which rules of international law, only occasionally referring to aircraft hijacking, could effectively be implemented. Basically, the Tokyo Convention obliges Contracting States to establish jurisdiction over serious offences or crimes only committed on board an aircraft of their own nationality. It is confined to a narrow range of human activity, and even within this range, its specific terms are the result of compromises among sovereign States. Nevertheless, the Tokyo Convention is considered a desirable and necessary addition to international air law. Its shortcomings, which have arisen over time, mainly due to a hardened global society, were translated into the strength of successive international legal instruments dealing with counter-terrorism.[87]

The Tokyo Convention made an attempt to provide solutions to the question which jurisdiction would be applicable to crimes committed on board an aircraft. It has provided for the jurisdiction of the national law of the aircraft, i.e. the State of registry, the law of the State flown over and a common jurisdiction of all the States Parties in case of hijacking of an aircraft. However, the term hijacking is not mentioned in the text.

The law of the State of registry applies as the general rule, while the State flown over is only able to exercise its jurisdiction if any of the conditions prescribed in Article 4 of the Tokyo Convention is fulfilled. Therefore, under all circumstances, the law of the flag State of the aircraft is practically always available which means that whenever an unlawful act is committed on board an aircraft which is registered in a State Party to the Tokyo Convention, there will be at least one State of competent jurisdiction, and the risk of such act going unpunished is therefore largely reduced.

The number of competent jurisdictions has been usefully reduced despite the right of all the States Parties to the Tokyo Convention to take appropriate measures against hijacking of civil aircraft, which is considered an exceptional case under the Tokyo Convention.

The primary purpose of a multilateral agreement such as the Tokyo Convention is to achieve worldwide uniformity of law which renders it a solid positive contribution to

---

86   *See also* Art. 14 of the Chicago Convention, Prevention of spread of disease.
87   Boyle, R.P., Pulsifer, R. (1964), p. 353.

international relationships among States, in particular by those States that are having substantive aviation interests. In addition to that, the Tokyo Convention is considered highly necessary to international air transportation and air law.

Important objectives of this need are the achievement of the normal functioning of international air transportation and the avoidance of the conflict of jurisdictions. It will promote civil aviation security and prevent impunity. The urgent need for the Tokyo Convention in the field of international air transportation is evidenced by the large number of ratifications, although the roadmap to this encouraging result took quite some time.

The rationale behind the creation of jurisdictional rules in the Tokyo Convention was to develop an internationally agreed legal system which would coordinate the exercise of national jurisdiction on offences committed on board a civil aircraft while in flight over sovereign territories and the high seas anywhere in the world.

The issues of jurisdiction over offences committed on board an aircraft, and the powers and duties of the aircraft commander over certain acts which jeopardize the safety of the aircraft or of persons or property therein or which jeopardize good order and discipline on board are considered two new fields of international law.

These given powers are in accordance with the aircraft commander's practical training and the safety of air navigation and entirely independent of any jurisdictional consideration which would seem to be beyond his capacity. After all, the aircraft commander is a technician and would, therefore, be unable to decide whether or not an act committed on board an aircraft is a penal offence. However, all that is required of the aircraft commander under the Tokyo Convention is that he should be familiar with his own laws, that is, the (penal) laws of the State of registry.

The shortcomings of the Tokyo Convention are identifiable in different fields. To start with, the determination of what 'in flight' means which limits the jurisdiction in time because of the fact that the definition states: an aircraft is considered to be in flight from the moment when power is applied for the purpose of take-off until the moment when the landing run ends. This provision does not take into account the possibility of a serious incident occurring while the aircraft is manoeuvring at the airport, which according to standard procedures means taxiing to the runway for take-off following embarkation, or taxiing after the landing roll to the terminal for disembarkation. Within these time frames, a person who attempts to commit an act or offence on board as described in Article 1, Paragraph 2, including unlawful seizure of control of an aircraft in flight, could possibly avoid punishment since such action would strictly speaking not be considered an offence under the Tokyo Convention.

Despite the strong sentiment within the Legal Committee that a system of priorities was essential, barring the intended priority of the State of registry, there has been no attempt whatsoever to establish such a priority system governing the order in which the potentially applicable jurisdictions can be exercised. In fact, support for a priority system, if present, weakened gradually, resulting in the absence of such a provision.

The issue of which laws should be applied to events occurring on an aircraft under lease, interchange or charter to a national of a State other than the State of registry could not be turned into a proper agreement in the meetings of the Tokyo Conference. Earlier, at its 14th Session in 1962, the ICAO Legal Committee established a new Subcommittee to study the legal problems affecting the regulation and enforcement of air safety which have been experienced by certain States when an aircraft registered in one State is operated by an operator belonging to another, and the legal problems concerning charter on a barehull basis in relation to the Draft Convention on Offences and Certain Other Acts Occurring on Board Aircraft. These problems were instigated by Resolution B of the 1961 Guadalajara Conference.[88]

Based on its two reports on the study's subject matter that contained three solutions in regard to the question of a chartered aircraft, the Subcommittee considered that:

> it will be competent for every State ratifying the Convention to exercise its jurisdiction, as declared in Article 2, paragraph 1 thereof, over offences committed on board aircraft of its registration wherever such aircraft may be, and that it would make no difference as a matter of law if such aircraft were leased without crew to a person who is not a national of such State.[89]

The Subcommittee interpreted the expression of a charter on a barehull basis as meaning an aircraft leased without a crew (dry lease).[90]

However, certain members of the Subcommittee were of the opinion that there was a problem concerning effective enforcement measures in respect of offences committed on

---

88   See also Mankiewicz, R.H. (Ed.), Yearbook of Air and Space Law 1967, Institute of Air and Space Law McGill University (Montreal: McGill-Queen's University Press, 1970), p. 148.

89   The terms of reference of the Subcommittee, established by the ICAO Legal Committee at its Fourteenth Session, were to study this subject, namely, legal problems affecting the regulation and enforcement of air safety which have been experienced by certain States when an aircraft registered in one State is operated by an operator belonging to another State (Part I). The Subcommittee should also study, in particular, the problems concerning charter on a barehull basis (Part II) in relation to the Draft Convention on Offences and Certain Other Acts Occurring on Board Aircraft (Source: Subcommittee on Resolution B of the Guadalajara Conference, (1963) 29 J. Air L. & Com. 241, p. 241 and concerning aircraft lease pp. 245-247.

90   Charter is a more restrictive and objective-focused contract for using an aircraft for a specific purpose defined in the contract. Leasing is a short/long-term rental, distinguishable in wet lease, mostly ACMI (Aircraft, Crew, Maintenance and Insurance, both hull and third-party liability), dry lease (only an aircraft), damp lease (an aircraft and cabin crew) or hybrid lease (the client's aircraft is dry leased to an operator, who then wet leases the aircraft back to the client with crew, maintenance and insurance). Under a wet lease, the lessor has operational control under its AOC (Source: IATA Guidance Material and Best Practices for Aircraft Leases, Fourth Edition, Effective May 2017, p. 132).

board a leased aircraft due to the possible inability of the State of registry to bring before its courts witnesses, evidence and when extradition is unavailable, the offender.

Lengthy discussions about possible solutions turned out to be unsuccessful. Ultimately, the Tokyo Conference decided that no provision was needed on this matter because the stated reason is that States will freely apply their laws to such an aircraft, if they wish, regardless of the Tokyo Convention. In fact, as indicated previously, that since a lease is an agreement in civil law, meaning a private law matter other than public law, such a matter should not determine the question of jurisdiction of a State.

There are two legal principles which were ultimately not or insufficiently included in the text of the Tokyo Convention. The first is the *ne bis in idem* principle, as used in criminal law. It should be noted that persons who are taken into custody or are subjected to trial or prosecution under the Tokyo Convention are given all the protections of the laws of the States in which such action occurs. This broad protection policy is based on the fact that prohibition against double jeopardy is enshrined almost everywhere in the national laws of States.[91]

The second principle is the legal obligation of States to extradite or prosecute, now traditionally described by the Latin expression *aut dedere aut judicare*. The rationale for this principle is to ensure that there are no jurisdictional gaps in the prosecution of internationally committed crimes. However, various reasons may prevent States in the territory of which a criminal is found from extraditing that person to the State in which territory the crime was committed or to any other State willing to prosecute the case.

The suspect is likely to escape prosecution and enjoy impunity if the authorities of the custodial State are not required to start proceedings against that person. The obligation to *aut dedere aut judicare* is an unwritten rule, which can also be described as a fairly specific obligation of persuasion, implying a legal obligation of States under public international law which is one of the most important means of collaboration designed by States to counter this phenomenon and, in particular, to deprive criminals, who in this particular case interfere with the safety of an aircraft in flight, of any safe haven. In 1970, The Hague Convention, dealing with terrorism on civil aircraft, provided the most recognized formulation, also known as The Hague formula of the obligation to extradite or prosecute (Art. 4, Para. 2 and Art. 7, The Hague Convention), which has been repeated in a large number of multilateral conventions.[92]

---

91   Rokutani, J., *Double Jeopardy, Self-Incrimination and Due Process of Law: The Fifth Amendment* (New York: Enslow Publishing, 2018), pp. 26-27.

92   Van Steenberghe, R., *Aut Dedere Aut Judicare*, Oxford Bibliographies. International Law (New York: Oxford University Press, 2013), Introduction.

Article 4, Paragraph 2 of The Hague Convention:

> Each Contracting State shall likewise take such measures as may be necessary to establish its jurisdiction over the offence in the case where the alleged offender is present in its territory and it does not extradite him pursuant to Article 8 to any of the States mentioned in paragraph 1 of this Article.

Article 7 of The Hague Convention:

> The Contracting State in the territory of which the alleged offender is found shall, if it does not extradite him, be obliged, without exception whatsoever and whether or not the offence was committed in its territory, to submit the case to its competent authorities for the purpose of prosecution. Those authorities shall take their decision in the same manner as in the case of any ordinary offence of a serious nature under the law of that State.

If this obligation is explicitly provided for within treaties, it possesses the features of a treaty, which means it only binds State Parties to the treaty. In relation to non-State Parties, it has no force of law. The validity of such an obligation is only *inter partes*.[93] However, this legal obligation of State Parties might be considered contradictory to the provision in Article 16, Paragraph 2 of the Tokyo Convention.[94]

The Tokyo Convention has drawn up detailed jurisdiction rules to ensure that certain offences and acts which jeopardize the safety as well as good order and discipline on board an aircraft, should not go unpunished because of a lack of applicable jurisdiction over those responsible. The scope of the Convention defines the nature of the acts to which it applies as including not only acts which are offences under penal law but also those acts which may or do jeopardize the safety of an aircraft, passengers and crew or property therein, or which jeopardize good order and discipline on board regardless of whether they are also offences.

---

93   Soler, C., *The Global Prosecution of Core Crimes under International Law* (The Hague: T.M.C. Asser Press, 2019), pp. 322-323.
94   Art. 16, Para. 2 states: Without prejudice to the provisions of the preceding paragraph, nothing in this Convention shall be deemed to create an obligation to grant extradition. *See also* Sopilko, I. (National Aviation University, Kyiv, Ukraine), Shevechuk, Y. (University of Cambridge), "Jurisdiction over Crimes Committed on Board Aircraft in Flight under the Tokyo Convention 1963" (Proceedings of the National Aviation University, 2016), 69.10.18372/2306-1472.69.11064, pp. 123-124.

Regarding this broad application, the Tokyo Convention limited the authority of the aircraft commander to take action in respect of those acts committed on board of his or her aircraft that directly affect the safety of the aircraft and jeopardize good order and discipline on board, thereby indicating that the jurisdiction of a State, in contrast to the authority of the aircraft commander, should not be limited.

It is significant to note that for the first time in the history of public international air law, the Tokyo Convention recognizes certain powers and immunities of the aircraft commander. The limitations, the extent, the period of operation and certain specific obligations of the aircraft commander's authority to deal with certain acts and offences involved in international flight are described in Chapter III of the Convention.

Article 5, Paragraph 2 of Chapter III constitutes an extension of the scope of the Tokyo Convention with respect to the aircraft commander's authority, deviating from the scope of the Convention with respect to jurisdiction (Art. 1, Para. 3).[95]

While the Tokyo Conference was dealing with the question of jurisdiction (Art. 1, Tokyo Convention), in the case of the powers and duties of the aircraft commander, the Conference extended the scope of the Draft Convention insofar as the authority of the aircraft commander is concerned. By defining a broader explanation regarding the movement of the aircraft, namely, both on the ground and in the air, the authority of the aircraft commander covers the entire movement of the aircraft. On the ground, from the moment when all external doors are closed following embarkation, followed by any push-back procedure while starting engines, taxiing on the apron and taxiways to the holding position, awaiting line up and take-off clearance, airborne for a flight to the destination where the landing is initiated and completed, on the ground taxiing to the terminal followed by a full stop and engines shut down until the moment when any external door is opened for disembarkation. Thus, for the purposes of Chapter III, the aircraft does not necessarily have to be in the air (with the addition of the take-off and landing segments) for the aircraft commander to take necessary measures to preserve the safety of the aircraft, its passengers and crew.

The delegates to the Tokyo Conference argued about the exact meaning of the words 'is about to commit', considered as a preparatory phase which embodied a purely subjective element. A misunderstanding of these words might cause serious damage to a passenger on board an aircraft. After all, in the opinion of the delegates, the aircraft commander was

---

95 Tokyo Convention, Art. 5, Para. 2: Notwithstanding the provisions of Art. 1, Para. 3, an aircraft shall for the purposes of this chapter, be considered to be in flight at any time from the moment when all its external doors are closed following embarkation until the moment when any such door is opened for disembarkation. In the case of a forced landing, the provisions of this chapter shall continue to apply with respect to offences and acts committed on board until competent authorities of a State take over the responsibility for the aircraft and for the persons and property on board.

not an expert in legal matters and might make a mistake with regard to the reasonable grounds that, at the time, he had for taking an action.

The question for consideration was whether the aircraft commander had to wait until the act had been committed before he or she could take action. It could well be that the aircraft commander might consider that he had reasonable grounds to believe, on the basis of a statement made to him, that another passenger was about to commit an offence and might then proceed to take an action in circumstances where there had been no acts. In a number of national legislations, a distinction was made between the repression of an offence and the police prevention of an offence and of other acts or disturbances which were not necessarily offences.

Carrying on board an aircraft a person who manifestly expresses the intention, for real or fake, to commit or is about to commit an offence, involves an obvious risk and a scary situation for other passengers. In cases of a tense atmosphere among passengers, it should always be possible to enable the aircraft commander to make a preliminary assessment of the situation. It is recognized that an act of unlawful interference could begin as seemingly unruly and disruptive behaviour such as agitation or an altercation. Preventing the escalation of such behaviour could therefore be an important factor in avoiding more serious threats to safety and security.

According to the considerations on the subject during the Tokyo Conference, it was reminded that in the purview of prevention which was concerned with maintaining general good order, legislations did not adopt very strict positions and it was neither necessary nor desirable to have something strict and rigid in that context. Hence, the Tokyo Conference could accept some vagueness in regard to the words 'is about to commit'. A proposal was adopted that these words be retained in the text of the Tokyo Convention.[96]

A person being the suspected offender, put under restraint by the aircraft commander, has the right (civil liberty protection) to be carried onwards beyond the first point of landing and might agree to continue to submit to restraint in order to do so if the first point of landing, whether in a Contracting or non-Contracting State to the Convention, was in a State in which he or she did not wish to be disembarked or delivered to competent authorities.

Article 9, Paragraph 1 of the Tokyo Convention states the terms and conditions under which an aircraft commander may deliver, as distinguished from disembark, persons on board his or her aircraft to the competent authorities. Such delivery must be accompanied by 'evidence and information' lawfully in the possession of the aircraft commander. In order to assure the individual so delivered of the civil liberty protection provided for in

---

96   ICAO Doc. 8565-LC/152-1, Tokyo 1963, Vol. I Minutes, 16th Meeting, Consideration of the draft Convention, pp. 177-179.

Articles 13, 14 and 15, Tokyo Convention, this authority to deliver is limited to Contracting States. In fact, the aircraft commander has no authority to deliver a person to the authorities of a non-Contracting State.

The act of delivery applies only to those persons whom an aircraft commander has reasonable grounds to believe have committed, on board an aircraft, an act which is a serious offence according to the penal law of the State of registry of the aircraft. The insertion of the words 'of the State of registry of the aircraft' would in fact involve a restriction to the scope of the Convention. However, regarding the expression 'serious offence', there was no general criterion which would enable the Tokyo Conference to reach an agreement on the meaning. Since the expression was undefined, one would require legal training in order to weigh an offence so as to determine whether it was serious.[97]

The Subcommittee was of the opinion that there were certain offences which were so universally considered to be of a serious nature, that no reference need be made to the laws of any particular State and that the elimination of the reference to the State of registry would give the aircraft commander, in the case of a serious offence, a greater flexibility for taking action in accordance with this Convention.[98]

Nonetheless, in the course of the Tokyo Conference, there was opposition to granting the aircraft commander certain powers regarding delivery in case of a serious offence. He could only execute such an action with great difficulty. By granting these specific powers, the Tokyo Conference would require of the aircraft commander to accept responsibilities that were well beyond his competence and his habitual work. The aircraft commander was considered, at the time, a reasonable person, a person of goodwill and one who was technically very proficient. However, all of the representatives to the Tokyo Conference would agree that the aircraft commander was quite ignorant of the law. Nevertheless, the Tokyo Conference proceeded to give the aircraft commander powers which were derived from juridical principles. In fact, this seemed contrary to the latter conclusion. At the same time, the Tokyo Conference was going to confer immunity from liability on the aircraft commander, a decision which contained certain contradictions.

It was not customary to establish in legislations the (absolute) immunity of a certain person in such an express manner, nor was it necessary to do it that way. The aircraft commander should not have a special immunity. Likewise, it was not right in the Tokyo Convention under consideration to confer an absolute immunity from liability to the aircraft commander and other persons. The measure that the aircraft commander decides to take must not only be subjectively reasonable, namely, based upon opinions of his own, but must also be objectively necessary to protect the safety of the aircraft, and to maintain

---

97   In Art. 9, Para. 1 of the Montreal Protocol, the phrase "according to the penal law of the State of registry" was deleted.
98   ICAO Doc. 8565-LC/152-1, Tokyo 1963 Vol. I Minutes, pp. 30-32.

good order and discipline on board, or in order to allow delivery or disembarkation, given the circumstances of the particular case.

The Tokyo Convention defined the powers of the aircraft commander and if he did what he was entitled to do and did so in a reasonable manner, then if his conduct was to be judged in a national jurisdiction, the aircraft commander might be able to state that, under the circumstances established by the Convention, there were no grounds for holding him liable. The proclamation of immunity was an extraordinary thing and quite dangerous.

The Tokyo Convention stated in several provisions that the aircraft commander could act upon rather subjective grounds, namely, based upon his own judgement. Thus, he should be open to censure by the judge if he did not act on good grounds. Hence, it was necessary that the aircraft commander's liability should be clearly declared. After extensive deliberations on the subject, the conclusion was that he should not have a special immunity.[99]

In respect of subjectivity, the aircraft commander, for example, may make an incorrect determination and deliver to the competent authorities a person whose act under the law of the State of registry of the aircraft may be only a minor offence. However, if in his opinion (reasonable grounds), it was a serious offence, and this subjective judgement had in fact some reasonable basis, and was not arbitrary and capricious, the aircraft commander would act within the scope of his powers granted under the provisions of the Convention. The immunity from civil action would be extended to the aircraft commander, crew members and the company only when action had been taken in accordance with the provisions of the Convention. That was exactly why the words 'reasonable' and 'necessary', the two-pronged objective/subjective tests by which these actions were to be measured, had been so gently put in the Convention.[100]

2.7   THE SIGNIFICANCE OF THE TOKYO CONVENTION

Before the adoption of the Tokyo Convention, there were no international rules in place addressing the status, powers and duties of the aircraft commander. Under the Tokyo Convention, the aircraft commander was given the authority to take reasonable measures which are necessary to restore order inside the aircraft in case of unruly and disruptive passenger behaviour during flight.

The Tokyo Conference has adopted a Convention which has the aims of securing international coordination in regard to the regime of penal law to be

---

99   Ibid., pp. 218-219.
100   Boyle, R.P., Pulsifer, R. (1964), p. 342. *See also* ICAO Doc 8565-LC/152-1, Tokyo 1963, Vol. I Minutes, pp. 181, 219 and 227.

applied to aircraft operating outside their national territories; of assuring cooperation amongst governments for the purpose of preventing the commission of dangerous acts on board aircraft and the apprehension of persons who may commit such acts or penal offences on board, with a view to their being dealt with according to law. The results of your work on the principles and rules relating to jurisdiction of States with respect to offences and other acts on board aircraft, relating to the powers of the aircraft commander, relating to the State in which the aircraft lands with the alleged offender on board, and with regard to ensuring that he receives, even though an accused person, the protection of the law designed to respect individual freedom, will now go to your governments and to other governments for approval. I belief that your arduous work of twenty-six days has been sufficiently fruitful so as to warrant the hope, which I entertain, that the Convention will receive wide approval by many States in accordance with their constitutional procedures.[101]

Unfortunately, the Tokyo Convention could not achieve perfection at the time of its adoption, all the more when this international legal instrument is considered in the current time frame. Nevertheless, the Convention can be regarded as a necessary addition to international air law. The scope is rather limited due to the fact that its focus is only on a small range of human activity. For years, States affiliated with ICAO have been busy establishing a legal instrument plausible in the opinion of as many States as possible to achieve ensuing ratification by these States, most of which have meaningful aviation interests.

Its creation was preceded by a substantial number of meetings of the ICAO Legal Committee and sessions of the Legal Status of the Aircraft Subcommittee and, finally, the Tokyo Conference. Obviously, the outcome of this process was achieved by the tremendous efforts of legal aviation experts through ongoing studies, deliberations, discussions, consultations, compromises, adjustments and, ultimately, consensus.

The Tokyo Convention, as the first global convention on aviation security, is widely regarded as an important component of the framework of international legislation which is necessary for dealing effectively with the issue of offences and other acts committed on board an aircraft. The purpose of the Tokyo Convention is to protect the safety of an aircraft and of the persons or property therein and to maintain good order and discipline on board. The main principle is to recognize the competence of the State of registry of an aircraft to exercise jurisdiction over all in-flight crimes. It is applicable to offences against

---

101 Address to all delegates and guests of honour at the Closing Meeting of the Tokyo Conference by President Mr. S. Saito. ICAO Doc. 8565-LC/152-1, Tokyo 1963, Vol. I Minutes, pp. 413-414.

penal law and to any acts jeopardizing the safety of persons or property on board civil aircraft while in flight and engaged in international air navigation. Although it was not primarily designed to meet the problem of aircraft hijacking, in other words, aerial piracy, it certainly deals with important aspects of this serious crime. More specifically, it attempted to fill the gap in criminal jurisdiction over hijacking that earlier existed under traditional international law.

Coverage includes, except as provided in Chapter III, offences committed or acts done by a person on board any aircraft registered in a Contracting State, while that aircraft is in flight or on the surface of the high seas or any other areas beyond the territory of any State in addition to the airspace belonging to any Contracting State. Chapter III, Article 5, Paragraph 1 states that the provisions of this chapter shall not apply to offences and acts committed or about to be committed by a person on board an aircraft in flight in the airspace of the State of registry or over the high seas or any other area outside the territory of any State unless the last point of take-off or the next point of intended landing is situated in a State other than the State of registry, or the aircraft subsequently flies in the airspace of a State other than the State of registry with such person still on board.

By way of derogation from the definition 'in flight' as stated in Article 1, Paragraph 3, an aircraft, for the purpose of Chapter III, shall be considered to be in flight at any time from the moment when all its external doors are closed following embarkation until the moment when any such door is opened for disembarkation. The provisions of Chapter III shall continue in the case of a forced landing until competent authorities take over all relevant responsibilities of the aircraft commander.

Criminal jurisdiction may be exercised by Contracting States other than the State of registry under limited conditions, when the exercise of jurisdiction is required under multilateral international obligations, in the interest of national security.

The rights and duties of the aircraft commander should be composed and integrated into a uniform, coherent and obligatory text established in an international instrument. For many years now, this appeal has predominated in almost every study about the legal status of the aircraft commander. Some juridical attempts have been made in the past like the 1947 Draft Convention on the Legal Status of the Aircraft Commander (ICAO Doc. 4006), however, with insignificant success. Existing regulations on the subject were scattered in various instruments, which, in particular, did not solve the question of the authority and responsibility of the aircraft commander prior to, during and after the flight, especially regarding unruly and disruptive passenger behaviour.

A further study on the subject made by an ICAO Panel of Legal Experts on the Legal Status of the Aircraft Commander which met at Montreal from 9 to 22 April 1980 was finally dropped in 1981, leaving international rules and regulations concerning the legal status of the aircraft commander relatively fragmented. While a number of States responded affirmatively to the need of a comprehensive international instrument on the subject, a majority of the Panel felt, however, after careful deliberation, that at the time, no further authority, other than the provisions of the Tokyo Convention, should be delegated to the aircraft commander, based on the view that a solution of certain issues would be closely related to matters of national sovereignty.[102]

Regarding the legal status of the aircraft commander, this means, apart from relevant ICAO documents and Annexes, a return to the Tokyo Convention and the Montreal Protocol. For the first time in international air law, these legal instruments recognized certain powers, duties and immunities of the aircraft commander.

The powers and duties of the aircraft commander are considered to be proportional which means that he cannot be given the status of a criminal investigation officer. Such far-reaching powers are of little practical value on board an aircraft, regardless of the fact that these kind of powers would undoubtedly meet objections from various quarters.

The provisions of the Tokyo Convention have shown that the aircraft commander holds a key position in civil aviation, as the safety of the flight, including the aircraft, persons and property on board often depends on his or her (nowadays) given powers, proficiency and judgement. The powers of the aircraft commander are aimed at the standards, provided for by the Tokyo Convention, for dealing with persons whose conduct threatens safety or good order and discipline on board.

From the point of view of the United States:

> Those provisions of Chapter III of the Tokyo Convention which describe the powers and duties of the aircraft commander in such a way as to minimize his role as a policeman are consistent with the aviation regulatory concepts prevailing in the United States. Articles 11 and 16, dealing respectively with hijacking and extradition, were advocated by the United States. The Tokyo Convention has resolved most major issues in accordance with the political and legal policies and traditions of the United States. At the same time the views of other States have been accommodated. An area of international relations has thus been regulated in a way not inconsistent with the law and practice of the world community of nations. Early ratification of the Convention by the United States and all of the States which participated in the Tokyo Conference would therefore be in the best interest of international aviation.[103]

---

102 Van Wijk, A.A. (1982), p. 334-335.
103 Boyle, R.P., Pulsifer, R. (1964), Partial conclusion of the authors at pp. 353-354.

2.8   ICAO AND THE LEGAL STATUS OF THE AIRCRAFT COMMANDER/PILOT-IN-COMMAND

Unruly and disruptive behaviour on board aircraft during flight increased significantly in the last decades of the 20th and early 21st centuries, despite the international legal framework provided by the Tokyo Convention of 1963 and ICAO Circular 288, updated, pursuant to the 2014 Montreal Protocol, by ICAO Doc. 10117, published in June 2019.[104] The terms 'unruly' and 'disruptive' passengers refer to passengers who fail to respect the rules of conduct on board an aircraft or to follow the instructions of crew members and thereby disturb the good order and discipline on board an aircraft and pose a threat to safety and security.

This condemnable behaviour which can be considered as offences and certain other acts committed on board, in many cases, may jeopardize the safety of the aircraft and its occupants, causing inconvenience and hindrance to other passengers as well as crew members, frequently resulting in operational disruption and associated rising airline costs. This kind of behaviour, in the aircraft cabin as well as in the airport terminal, is attributable to high rising irritation caused by too many people crowded together in a rather claustrophobic cabin with reduced seat pitch and recline, overloaded overhead luggage bins and limited movement space, not to mention the ban on smoking on board as well as the consumption of alcohol and drugs, resulting in intoxication, quite often leading to physical aggression to other passengers or damage to the aircraft.[105]

In the case that offences and certain other acts could pose a direct threat to the safety of the aircraft and its occupants, the aircraft commander is often forced to make a decision, without delay, to execute an unscheduled stopover at the nearest suitable airport to disembark unruly passengers for safety reasons.[106]

At the 33rd Session of the ICAO Assembly from 25 September to 5 October 2001 at Montreal, Resolution A33-4 was adopted setting forth model legislation as developed by the ICAO Secretariat Study Group on Unruly Passengers, mindful of the fact that until that time, the existing international law as well as national law and regulations in many States were not fully adequate to deal effectively with the growth of the number and gravity of reported incidents involving unruly or disruptive passengers on board civil aircraft jeopardizing the safety of the aircraft and its occupants.

---

104   The purpose of ICAO Circular 288 (and ICAO Doc. 10177), was to set out a model law on certain offences committed on board civil aircraft in flight.

105   Abeyratne, R.I.R., *Legal Priorities in Air Transport* (Cham: Springer, 2019), pp. 99-101. *See also* the meaning of seat pitch: the measurement of space between one point on an aircraft passenger seat to the exact same point on the seat in front or behind it. Recline is the seat backrest that can be tilted back.

106   ICAO Doc. 10117 maintains the use of "aircraft commander" which is the term used in the Tokyo Convention as amended by the 2014 Montreal Protocol. However, the term "pilot-in-command" is used in other ICAO publications, such as ICAO Annex 6 Part I, Twelfth Edition, July 2022.

The Assembly urged all Contracting States to enact as soon as possible national laws and regulations to effectively deal with the issue of unruly or disruptive passengers, incorporating so far as practical the model legislation set out in the Appendix to this Resolution, and called on all Contracting States to submit their competent authorities for consideration of prosecution all persons whom they have reasonable grounds to consider as having committed any of the offences set out in the national laws and regulations so enacted, and for which they have jurisdiction in accordance with these laws and regulations.[107]

ICAO Circular 288, published on 1 January 2002, can be regarded as a meaningful initial movement in establishing a national regime to deal with unruly and disruptive passengers which means that from that moment, the proposed model regulation was recommended for incorporation into national law or regulations.

The starting point of this specific guidance material is that a uniform list of offences was considered desirable for two specific reasons: firstly, in order to provide a common denominator for offences as a basis for national prosecution and, secondly, in order to offer uniform criteria for States to extend their respective jurisdiction. The list of offences, explained by ICAO Circular 288, serves as a guide for the purpose of facilitating States to deal with offences and other acts constituting unruly or disruptive passenger behaviour on board a civil aircraft.

The main purpose of ICAO Circular 288, consisting of guidance material actually deemed to be soft law, is to allow for flexibility and adaptability and to present a model law on certain offences committed on board a civil aircraft, in order to enable ICAO Member States to transpose or incorporate these particular offences into their national laws and regulations. The motivation for compiling this instrument is that the definition of acts of condemnable behaviour on board a civil aircraft and jurisdiction are quite often not recognized by many national legal regimes on a global scale.

In order to achieve uniformity in approaches by States in dealing with these unruly or disruptive passenger incidents, the adoption of an international instrument is the best method, given the international character of civil aviation. To address this method, an international instrument functioning as a supplement to national legal regimes, and as a legal fundament for the coordination between States in the event of an overlap of their jurisdictions, should be a reasonable solution. Implementing measures through national

---

107 *See* Resolutions adopted at the 33rd Session of the Assembly, pp. 11-12. Resolution A33-4 Adoption of national legislation on certain offences committed on board civil aircraft (unruly/disruptive passengers) and Appendix Model Legislation on Certain Offences Committed on Board Civil Aircraft. *See also* Resolution A39-11 Consolidated Statement of Continuing ICAO Policies in the Legal Field Appendix E Sections 1, 2 and 3 Model Legislation on Certain Offences Committed on Board Civil Aircraft. *See also* A32-WP/72 LE/7, 21 July 1998 Revised, 25 August 1998, Assembly – 32nd Session Legal Commission, Agenda Item 34: Working programme of the Organization in the legal field, Unruly Passengers (Presented by the International Air Transport Association – IATA).

or existing supranational organizations as the European Union, a geo-political entity, would prefer not to infringe State sovereignty.

IATA, a trade association of the world's airlines, proclaimed that national legislation concerning passenger behaviour on board an aircraft is often limited in scope to a narrow interpretation of the Tokyo Convention which covers actions jeopardizing the safety of the aircraft. It should, however, not be necessary to draft a new international treaty to deal with the issue of unruly passengers, according to IATA. Instead, since the airlines require urgent action, it would be more effective for the ICAO Assembly to urge States, as a matter of priority, to ensure that adequate legislation is in place that permits prompt and effective intervention at an arrival airport by law enforcement representatives following offensive behaviour by passengers during a flight. These actions should be taken on a consistent basis and regardless of the State of registry of the aircraft. In addition, for quite some time, IATA requests ICAO to assist States in meeting this need for adequate legislation.[108]

In this light, the airline industry as a whole recommends that States amend legislation to criminalize any action committed on board an aircraft, which is considered to be an offence in the State of landing, regardless of the State of registry or the State of the operator of that aircraft.

The manual that updated ICAO Circular 288 as a result of the adoption of the 2014 Montreal Protocol, ICAO Doc. 10117 – Manual on the Legal Aspects of Unruly and Disruptive Passengers, contains guidance on legislation relating to criminal offences and acts as well as elements of an administrative sanctions regime, which will assist States in implementing the appropriate legal measures to prevent and deal with unruly and disruptive passenger incidents.

If any person on board an aircraft is alleged to have committed an offence subject to an administrative sanction, according to common law systems referred to as defendant, the aircraft commander of the aircraft at the time of the alleged offence may, by any available means, notify, or cause to be notified, the appropriate regulatory authority or an authorized person.[109]

With respect to assault and other acts of interference against a crew member on board an aircraft (ICAO Doc. 10117, Section 1 of Appendix A, Model Legislation on Certain Offences Committed on Board Aircraft), the question what constitutes an offence, in this particular case, is defined as:

---

108   *See* ICAO A32-WP/72 LE/7, 21 July 1998 Revised, 25 August 1998.
109   ICAO Doc. 10117, Foreword and Appendix B Guidance for Introducing an Administrative Sanction Regime on Certain Offences Committed on Board Aircraft, Part B, (4) Procedure.

Any person who commits on board an aircraft any of the following acts thereby commits an offence:

1. physical assault or threat to commit such assault against a crew member;
2. intimidation or threat against a crew member if such act interferes with the performance of the duties of the crew member or lessens the ability of the crew member to perform those duties;
3. refusal to follow a lawful instruction given by or on behalf of the aircraft commander for the purpose of:
   a. protecting the safety of the aircraft or of persons or property therein;
   b. maintaining good order and discipline on board.[110]

As a remark: because of the type of risks and potential consequences involved, assault and other acts of interference against any crew member on board civil aircraft, covered by Section I, should be considered as serious offences within the meaning of Article 9 of the Tokyo Convention. However, this description of serious offences is rather not exhaustive. Especially in relation to assisting aircraft commanders, without in-depth legal knowledge, to exercise their powers under Article 9 of the Tokyo Convention, it is recommended in this respect to reach consensus about what constitutes a serious offence, except particularly unambiguous serious offences covered by international treaties, such as hijacking, sabotage and hostage-taking.[111]

Article 9, Paragraph 1 of the Tokyo Convention:

> The aircraft commander may deliver to the competent authorities of any Contracting State in the territory of which the aircraft lands any person whom he has reasonable grounds to believe has committed on board the aircraft an act which, in his opinion, is a serious offence according to the penal law of the State of registry of the aircraft.[112]

With respect to assault and other acts endangering safety or jeopardizing good order and discipline on board an aircraft (Appendix A, Section 2), the question what constitutes an offence in this particular case is defined as:

---

110 It should be understood that the authority to give instructions ultimately rests with the aircraft commander. However, unless there is contrary evidence, instructions from a crew member are deemed to be given on behalf of the aircraft commander. *See* ICAO Doc. 10117, Chapter 2 List of offences and other acts, 2.3.1.4.

111 Polkowska, M., "Unruly Passengers ICAO Cir. 288 Update," (2017) *Revista Europea de Derecho de la Navegación Marítima y Aeronáutica* 34, pp. 84-96.

112 The 2014 Montreal Protocol amended Art. 9 by deleting the phrase: according to the penal law of the State of registry of the aircraft.

1. Any person who commits on board an aircraft an act of physical violence against a person or of sexual assault or child molestation thereby commits an offence.
2. Any person who commits on board an aircraft any of the following acts thereby commits an offence if such act is likely to endanger the safety of the aircraft or of any person on board or if such act jeopardizes the good order and discipline on board the aircraft:
   a. assault, intimidation or threat, whether physical or verbal, against another person;
   b. intentionally causing damage to, or destruction of, property;
   c. consuming alcoholic beverages or drugs resulting in intoxication.

With respect to other offences committed on board an aircraft (Appendix A, Section 3), the question what constitutes an offence, in this particular case, is defined as:

Any person who commits on board an aircraft any of the following acts thereby commits an offence:
1. smoking in a lavatory, or smoking elsewhere when such act is prohibited;
2. tampering with a smoke detector or any other safety-related device on board the aircraft;
3. operating a portable electronic device when such act is prohibited.[113]

The list of offences in Sections 1 to 3, along with the jurisdiction clause in Section 4, is recommended for incorporation into national law or regulations. States are encouraged to incorporate the list into their criminal code and or their civil aviation legislation, for the sake of international uniformity.

Recognizing the need for a more effective deterrent regarding the increasing concern on the widespread presence, severity and frequency of numerous unruly and disruptive passenger incidents on international flights, a number of States adopted the Montreal Protocol that modernized the Tokyo Convention. The purpose of the Montreal Protocol is to expand the scope of the Tokyo Convention not just to allow States to exercise jurisdiction over unruly and disruptive passengers, but in addition to take appropriate criminal and other legal proceedings regarding this kind of behaviour.

The Montreal Protocol significantly improves the ability for States to prosecute unruly and disruptive passengers for offences and other acts committed on international flights

---

113 All the acts, included in Section 1, should be considered as serious offences within the meaning of Art. 9 of the 1963 Tokyo Convention. The term "refusal" includes intentional and express conduct of non-compliance but does not include inadvertent conduct. *See* ICAO Doc. 10117, Chapter 2 List of offences and other acts, 2.3.1.4. *See also* ICAO A40-WP/9 LE/1 Assembly – 40th Session Agenda item 39: Consolidated statement of continuing ICAO policies in the legal field, Attachment, Appendix E – Adoption of national legislation on certain offences committed on board aircraft (Unruly/Disruptive Passengers), A-5, A-6. For reference ICAO Circular 288, 2002, pp. 3-4. *See also* ICAO Doc. 10117, 2.2.2 Section 1, 2.2.3 Section 2 and 2.2.4 Section 3.

that land in their territory, even though in cases where the State of intended landing is different from the State of registry. Actually, the operational part of the Montreal Protocol, *inter alia*, Chapter II, Jurisdiction, recognizes, under certain conditions, the competence of both the State of landing and the State of the operator to exercise jurisdiction over offences and acts on board a civil aircraft.

The establishment of such jurisdiction over offences is mandatory if the criteria set out in the Montreal Protocol are met. The Montreal Protocol offers States a distinct opportunity to introduce an international legal instrument which provides them the tools to be able to deal more effectively with unruly passengers and strengthen their capacity to highly discourage future incidents.

Since 1962, a special covert law enforcement agent or IFSO, has been introduced in international air transportation, although not without controversy, to counter aircraft hijacking and to curb other unlawful interferences in order to restore or maintain good order and discipline on board an aircraft. Each Contracting State shall ensure that the pilot-in-command is notified as to the number of armed persons and their seat location on board the aircraft.

The Montreal Protocol extends legal recognition and certain protections like immunity to this IFSO, just as the aircraft commander, other members of the crew and passengers, for taking actions in accordance with the Tokyo Convention. Specifically, in this case, the Montreal Protocol amended the provisions of the Tokyo Convention through Articles 6 and 10. An IFSO deployed pursuant to a bilateral or multilateral agreement or some sort of arrangement between relevant Contracting States may take reasonable preventive measures on board, without the authorization of the aircraft commander, when this officer has reasonable grounds to believe that such action is immediately necessary to protect the safety of the aircraft or persons therein from an act of unlawful interference, and, if the agreement or arrangement so allows, from the commission of serious offences. In case of unruly or disruptive passengers, the aircraft commander may request or authorize, but not require, the assistance of in-flight security officers or passengers to restrain any person whom this officer is entitled to do so.[114]

ICAO Doc. 10117 has not updated the list of (serious) offences contained in the ICAO Circular 288. The rationale behind this omission is that the current list of offences is sufficiently comprehensive to cover most unruly and disruptive behaviour on board an aircraft. However, if any unruly and disruptive behaviour is not specifically listed, it is likely to fall within the scope of the provision concerning the refusal to obey the instruction of the aircraft commander.

---

114 Montreal Protocol 2014 (Protocol to Amend the Convention on Offences and Certain Other Acts Committed on Board Aircraft), Art. 6, Paras. 2, 3 and 4. *See also* ICAO Annex 17, Twelfth Edition, July 2022, Chapter 4 Preventive Security Measures.

On the other hand, behaviours left undefined might leave unregulated potential threats on board an aircraft. Definitions at an international level are problematic to draft, and can often only be discussed diplomatically, due to the fact that each State is concerned to avoid giving up (part of) their sovereignty to address disruptive behaviours and like to have their own characterization of objectionable behaviour. In addition, the current list of offences does not limit the power of a State to introduce into its national legislation any other offence or prohibited act in relation to unruly and disruptive behaviour on board an aircraft.

Where the seriousness of an unruly or a disruptive passenger incident, as mentioned above, is such that the aircraft commander decides to make a diversion to an airport in a State that is not the scheduled destination, that State has competence to assert and exercise jurisdiction. The Montreal Protocol will close the jurisdictional gaps that are not or inadequately covered by the Tokyo Convention, and will ensure that States have the indispensable right tools they need to deal with unruly and disruptive passengers that land in their territory, irrespective of where the aircraft is registered.

As one of the most complex man-made industries, international civil aviation involves a large number of procedures and systems that guide and monitor interaction between human beings and machines. This strict regime makes this mode of transport safe and provides a powerful impetus for progress in our modern global society.

In order to achieve an integral alignment in a world of different countries, cultures and languages, common understanding and a common language are indispensable, which means standardization in all sections of international air transportation.

The clock-work precision in procedures and systems to make international aviation safe, secure and efficient is made possible by the existence of universally accepted s-Standards. The SARPs in the Annexes to the Chicago Convention, alongside the tremendous technological progress achieved in the past, have enabled the realization of what must be recognized as one of mankind's greatest cooperative achievements and a crucial operating safety system of the modern international air transportation network which enhances global prosperity.[115] SARPs in the ICAO Annexes, however, do not have

---

115 Standard: Any specification for physical characteristics, configuration, matériel, performance, personnel or procedure, the uniform application of which is recognized as necessary for the safety or regularity of international air navigation and to which Contracting States will conform in accordance with the Convention; in the event of impossibility of compliance, notification to the Council is compulsory under Art. 38 of the Convention. Recommended Practice: Any specification for physical characteristics, configuration, matériel, performance, personnel or procedure, the uniform application of which is recognized as desirable in the interest of safety, regularity or efficiency of international air navigation, and to which Contracting States shall endeavour to conform in accordance with the Convention.

the legal status of the provisions of a widely ratified international treaty like the Chicago Convention.[116]

This is due to the fact that there is a discrepancy between States in favour considering SARPs are proportional to treaty rules and States which disagree. In this regard, the issue focuses on the distinction between self-executing and non-self-executing treaties and ICAO Annexes. The first method provides that the provisions of a treaty become judicially enforceable upon ratification and implementation into national law which means that the treaty provisions apply directly to individuals of a State and on which they can rely in legal proceedings. The second method only makes a treaty judicially enforceable by requiring legislative implementation. However, there is no general rule for legislative implementation of treaty provisions, or SARPs in national law.[117]

Wittingly, States do not consistently fulfil their obligations pertaining to notification in case of noncompliance, which practice does not really benefit the much needed uniformity of international aviation safety regulation. Yet, the core mandate of ICAO, in the past, now and in the future, was, is and will be to assist States to accomplish the highest possible degree of uniformity in aviation regulations, standards, procedures and organization. Enforcement of ICAO Standards is essential for the safe operation of international air transportation. Articles 33, 37 and 38 of the Chicago Convention play a crucial role in underpinning the legal force of ICAO Standards.

Almost all the Annexes to the Chicago Convention contain SARPs. Annex 2 is an all-Standards document. Seventeen out of 19 ICAO Annexes are of a technical nature, and, therefore, fall within the responsibilities of the Air Navigation Bureau and its sections. The remaining two annexes, Annex 9 – *Facilitation* and Annex 17 – *Aviation Security*, are under the purview of the Air Transport Bureau. ICAO Standards and other provisions are developed in the following forms:

–   Standards and Recommended Practices – SARPs;
–   Procedures for Air Navigation Services – PANS;
–   Regional Supplementary Procedures – SUPPs;
–   Guidance Material in several formats.

The Chicago Convention does not define the terms "Standard" or "Recommended Practice". Definitions were first adopted by the Assembly in 1947 (A1-31), later incorporated in the foreword of individual Annexes by way of Council Decision.

116   1969 Vienna Convention on the Law of Treaties (VCLT). *See also* Dempsey, P.S., "Compliance & Enforcement in International Law: Achieving Global Uniformity in Aviation Safety," (2004) 30 *N.C. J. INT'L.* 1, pp. 13-14.

117   *See* Mendes de Leon, P.M.J., "The Legal Force of ICAO SARPs in a Multilevel Jurisdictional Context" in Schnitker, R.M. (Ed.), *Journaal Luchtrecht* (The Hague: Sdu Publishers, June 2013), Special Edition, No. 2-3, pp. 11-13. *See also* Abeyratne, R.I.R., *Aviation Security: Legal and Regulatory Aspects* (Milton Park, Abingdon, Oxon: Routledge, 1998), pp. 10-11.

The Standards in Annex 2 – *Rules of the Air*, together with the SARPs of Annex 11 – *Air Traffic Services*, govern the application of the PANS – *Rules of the Air and Air Traffic Services* and the SUPPs – *Rules of the Air and Air Traffic Services*, in which latter document will be found subsidiary procedures of regional application.

Article 37 – Adoption *of international standards and procedures* – of the Chicago Convention mandates ICAO to draw up SARPs and procedures on the technical, mainly safety- and security-related subjects. To be precise, the vast majority of ICAO Annexes are related to technical issues. Annex 2 is special because it only contains s-Standards and forms the exclusive rulemaking for flying over the high seas. These rules apply without exception.

Article 38 – Departures from international standards and procedures – of the Chicago Convention states,

> Any State, which finds it impracticable to comply in all respects with any such international standard or procedure, or to bring its own regulations or practices into full accord with any international standard or procedure after amendment of the latter, or which deems it necessary to adopt regulations or practices differing in any particular respect from those established by an international standard, shall give immediate notification to ICAO of the differences between its own practice and that established by the international standard.

On the other hand, while Article 38 sets out obligations for the immediate notification of differences from standards, it is recognized that knowledge of differences from Recommended Practices may also be important. However, under the same article, this approach to understanding is not considered mandatory, as Recommended Practices are merely regarded desirable in the interest of safety, regularity and efficiency of air navigation. States are invited to inform the ICAO Council of noncompliance. All in all, the duty of States to comply with international standards remains the general rule, while the right to file differences is an exception to the rule. While lack of information on differences might create uncertainty and will pose a potential hazard to the safety, efficiency and regularity of air navigation, Articles 37 and 38 provide for important resources to standardize and contribute to ensuring the safe and orderly growth of international civil aviation at the global level.[118]

A disadvantage of this implementation method is that ICAO does not have a sanction mechanism at its disposal in case of noncompliance. In light of duty of notification and the

---

118 *See* ICAO Doc. 10055 AN/518, Manual on Notification and Publication of Difference, First Edition, 2018.

pursuit of uniformity of international aviation standards, it remains very important to keep ICAO informed of any differences. Notification of differences does not relieve a State of its obligations, according to the Chicago Convention, and may still result in an USOAP finding related to the specific standard or procedure.

Certainly, genuine enforcement powers on the side of ICAO do not meet the exalted objectives the Chicago Convention should serve. However, cooperation, consensus, compliance and the unwavering commitment to the continued implementation of SARPs have made it possible to develop a global aviation industry that has evolved into the safest mode of mass transportation in the world ever imagined. Flight crews of commercial aircraft can count on a standardized aviation infrastructure, achieved by ICAO and its Contracting States, wherever these pilots fly in the world, today and in the years to come.

The powers, duties and responsibilities of the aircraft commander within this integral aviation domain are collected and explained in a number of ICAO Annexes. While the term 'aircraft commander' is used in the 1963 Tokyo Convention as amended by the 2014 Montreal Protocol and earlier documentation within ICAO, the term 'pilot-in-command' is used in other ICAO publications such as a number of Annexes. The Chicago Convention Articles represent international law and contain basic principles which are the foundation of ICAO Annexes.

The ICAO definition of pilot-in-command, as it appears in a number of Annexes, is:

> The pilot designated by the operator, or in the case of general aviation, the owner, as being in command and charged with the safe conduct of a flight.[119]

The pilot-in-command, as a person, shall not act as a flight crew member of an aircraft unless a valid licence is held showing compliance with the specifications contained in Annex 1, and appropriate to the duties to be performed by that person.

Annex 1, Paragraph 1.2.1.2 states that from 22 November 2022, the flight crew member licence shall have been issued by the State of registry of that aircraft or by any other Contracting State and rendered valid by the State of registry of that aircraft. Annex 2 constitutes *Rules relating to the flight and manoeuvre of aircraft*, within the meaning of Article 12 – Rules of the Air, of the Chicago Convention. This Annex specifies international rules of the air, designated as Standards, agreed upon by ICAO Member States. The adoption and amendment of the international rules of the air is and remains a constitutional prerogative of the Council under Articles 37 and 54 (l) – *Mandatory functions of Council*

---

119 For comparison, according to U.S. Title 14 CFR § 1.1. General definitions: Pilot-in-command means: the person who: 1. has final authority and responsibility for the operation and the safety of the flight, 2. has been designated as pilot-in-command before or during the flight, and 3. holds the appropriate category, class, and type rating, if appropriate for the conduct of the flight.

and Article 90 – *Adoption and amendment of Annexes*, of the Chicago Convention. The Council is the only body with powers to enact the rules of the air over the high seas. Therefore, over these massive saltwater surfaces, the rules of the air apply without exception.[120] However, a State may take exception, in other words, does have different criteria, in its sovereign airspace only.

Regarding responsibility for compliance with the international rules of the air, the pilot-in-command of an aircraft shall, whether manipulating the controls or not, be responsible for the operation of the aircraft in accordance with these rules, except that the pilot-in-command may depart from these rules in circumstances that render such departure absolutely necessary in the interest of safety. Responsibility for the safety of the operation and the safety of the aircraft and of all persons on board during flight includes responsibility for obstacle clearance at all times, except when an IFR flight is being vectored by radar.[121]

If an ATC clearance, which is an authorization for an aircraft to proceed under conditions specified by an ATC unit, is not satisfactory to a pilot-in-command of an aircraft, he or she may request and, if safe and practicable, be issued an amended clearance.

To avoid collisions, nothing in the rules of the air shall relieve the pilot-in-command, in case of an imminent collision, from the responsibility of taking such evasive action, including avoidance manoeuvres, recommended to the pilots, primarily based on a traffic advisory (TA) which alerts the pilots to be ready for potential resolution advisories (RAs) provided by ACAS II/TCAS II equipment, in order to best avert a collision with the intruder aircraft.[122] The pilots are expected to comply with RAs promptly and accurately. Generally, nothing in the procedures with respect to the use of ACAS indicators shall prevent the pilot-in-command from exercising his or her best judgement and full authority

---

120 Art. 12 Rules of the air. Each Contracting State undertakes to adopt measures to insure that every aircraft flying or manoeuvring within its territory and that every aircraft carrying its nationality mark, wherever such aircraft may be, shall comply with the rules and regulations, relating to the flight and manoeuvre of aircraft there in force. Each Contracting State undertakes to keep its own regulations in these respects uniform, to the greatest possible extent, with those established from time to time under this Convention. Each Contracting State undertakes to insure the prosecution of all persons violating the regulations applicable. *See also* The high seas are defined in maritime law as all parts of the mass of saltwater surrounding the globe that are not part of the territorial sea or internal waters of a State.

121 ICAO Doc. 8168 OPS/611 Procedures for Air Navigation Services (PANS), Aircraft Operations Volume I Flight Procedures, Fifth Edition 2006, Part III Aircraft Operating Procedures, Section 1 Altimeter Setting Procedures, Chapter 4 Altimeter Corrections, Para. 4.1.1 Pilot's Responsibility.

122 ACAS II (Airborne Collision Avoidance System II), which is the standard and TCAS II (Traffic Alert and Collision Avoidance System II) is its implementation. This system, based on Secondary Surveillance Radar (SSR) transponder signals, was introduced in order to reduce the risk of mid-air collisions or near mid-air collisions between aircraft. In particular ACAS II provides RAs. *See also* ICAO Doc. 9863 AN/461 Airborne Collision Avoidance System (ACAS) Manual, pp. 1-3 1.4.5 ACAS Operation and 1.5 Design Intention of ACAS II.

in the choice of the best course of action to resolve a traffic conflict or avert a potential collision.[123]

When flying under control of an air traffic controller in a specific airspace block, it is the responsibility of the pilot-in-command to comply with ATC instructions, as long as they fall within the regulations, they are safe and the pilot-in-command is able to comply. If ATC instructions are contrary to regulations or would compromise flight safety, the pilot-in-command should exercise his or her authority to deviate from these instructions and communicate with ATC as soon as possible about the reason for deviation. This procedure applies in particular in case of an in-flight emergency or in response to a TCAS II resolution advisory, in the event that the pilot-in-command deviates from an ATC instruction or clearance.[124]

Flight information service is a service provided for the purpose of giving advice and information useful for the safe and efficient conduct of flights. This information shall, in particular, be provided to aircraft which are likely to be affected by the information. Normally all aircraft provided with ATC service or otherwise known to the relevant air traffic service (ATS) units will receive the information. However, flight information such as, for example, significant meteorological information (SIGMET) as volcanic ash clouds, or information on unmanned free balloons, does not relieve the pilot-in-command of an aircraft of any responsibilities and he or she has to make the final decision regarding any suggested alteration of flight plan.[125]

Generally, the pilot-in-command shall have final authority as to the disposition of the aircraft while in command, which means, *inter alia*, that in case an aircraft is subjected to unlawful interference during flight, the pilot-in-command shall attempt to select the onboard transponder to Mode A Code 7500 in order to indicate the situation (if circumstances so warrant, e.g. state of emergency, Code 7700 should be used instead), and shall attempt to land as soon as practicable at the nearest suitable aerodrome assigned by the appropriate authority unless considerations on board the aircraft dictate otherwise.[126]

If the pilot-in-command, in his or her opinion, is unable to proceed to the nearest possible aerodrome in the case as mentioned above, an attempt should be made to

---

123 ICAO Doc. 8168 OPS/611, Part III Aircraft Operating Procedures, Section 3 Secondary Surveillance Radar (SSR) Transponder Operating Procedures, Chapter 3 Operation of Airborne Collision Avoidance System (ACAS) Equipment, Para. 3.1.2. Procedures for the use of ACAS indicators are specified in Para. 3.2. *See also* ICAO Annex 10 – *Aeronautical Telecommunications* Volume IV *Surveillance and Collision Avoidance Systems*, Fifth Edition, July 2014, Chapter 4 Airborne Collision Avoidance System, Para. 4.3 General Provisions Relating to ACAS II and ACAS III.

124 *See* U.S. Title 14 CFR § 91.3 Responsibility and authority of the pilot-in-command. *See* U.S. Title 14 CFR § 91.123 Compliance with ATC clearances and instructions.

125 ICAO Annex 11 – *Air Traffic Services – Air Traffic Control Service – Flight Information Service – Alerting Service*, Fifteenth Edition, July 2018, Chapter 4 Flight Information Service, Para. 4.1.1 *Note*.

126 *See also* ICAO Annex 17, Twelfth Edition, July 2022, Attachment, 1.6 Unlawful Interference with Aircraft in Flight, 1.6.1, ATT-29.

continue flying on the last assigned track and at the assigned cruising level at least until able to notify an ATS unit or until within radar or ADS-B coverage. If there is no other choice than to depart from the assigned track or assigned cruising level in case of inability to establish radiotelephony contact with ATS, the pilot-in-command should, whenever possible, stick to the procedures as laid down in Annex 17, Attachment B, Paragraph 2.2.[127]

Interception of civil aircraft for the purpose of identification shall be governed by appropriate regulations and administrative directives issued by Contracting States in compliance with the Chicago Convention. The pilot-in-command of a civil aircraft, when intercepted, shall comply with the Standards in Appendix 2, Sections 2 and 3, interpreting and responding to visual signals as specified in Appendix 1, Section 2 of ICAO Annex 2.[128]

ICAO Annex 3, that deals with SARPs related to meteorology, states in Chapter 5, Aircraft Observations and Reports, Paragraph 5.6 Other non-routine aircraft observations: when other meteorological conditions not listed under Paragraph 5.5, e.g. wind shear, are encountered and which, in the opinion of the pilot-in-command, may affect the safety or markedly affect the efficiency of other aircraft operations, the pilot-in-command shall advise the appropriate air traffic services unit as soon as practicable.[129]

Annex 6 – *Operation of Aircraft* contains a number of Standards applicable to the function of pilot-in-command like compliance with laws, regulations and procedures as well as flight operations, duties of the pilot-in-command, aircraft performance operating limitations, flight documents, a check on secure stowage of baggage in the passenger cabin, flight crew qualifications and also dangerous goods, which, however, are discussed in detail in ICAO Annex 18.[130]

---

127 *See* ICAO Annex 2, Tenth Edition, July 2005, Chapter 2 Applicability of the Rules of the Air, Paras. 2.3 and 2.4, and Chapter 3 General Rules, Para. 3.7.2. *See also* ICAO Annex 17, Twelfth Edition, July 2022, ATT-1 Chapter 3 General Rules, Para. 3.7. Unlawful Interference and ATT-2 Attachment B Unlawful Interference, Para. 2. Procedures. *See also* ICAO Annex 17, Twelfth Edition, July 2022, ATT-24/25 Operation of Transponders.

128 *See* ICAO Annex 2, Tenth Edition, July 2005, Attachment A. Interception of Civil Aircraft, ATT A-1 to A-3.

129 Icing, turbulence and, to a large extent, wind shear are elements which, for the time being, cannot be satisfactorily observed from the ground and for which in most cases aircraft observations represent the only available evidence. Weather condition encountered or observed under Para. 5.5 are: moderate or severe turbulence, moderate or severe icing, severe mountain wave, thunderstorms with or without hail, that are obscured, embedded, wide spread or in squall lines, heavy dust storm or heavy sandstorm, volcanic ash cloud, pre-eruption volcanic activity or a volcanic eruption and runway braking action encountered is not as good as reported. In case of the latter condition, the pilot-in-command shall report the runway braking action special air-report (AIREP). Source: ICAO Annex 3 – *Meteorological Service for International Air Navigation*, Twentieth Edition, July 2018, Part I Core SARPs, p. 5-2 and ICAO Annex 6 Part I, Twelfth Edition, July 2022, p. 4-17.

130 *See* ICAO Annex 18 – *The Safe Transport of Dangerous Goods by Air*, Fourth Edition, July 2011, Chapter 9 Provisions of Information, Para. 9.5 Information from pilot-in-command to aerodrome authorities: If an in-flight emergency occurs, the pilot-in-command shall, as soon as the situation permits, inform the appropriate air traffic services unit, for the information of aerodrome authorities, of any dangerous goods on board the aircraft, as provided for in the Technical Instructions.

The operator shall ensure that all pilots are familiar with the laws, regulations and procedures, pertinent to the performance of their duties, prescribed for the areas to be traversed, the aerodromes to be used and the air navigation facilities relating thereto. Responsibility for operational control shall be delegated only to the pilot-in-command.

The pilot-in-command shall notify the appropriate local authority without delay if an emergency situation, which endangers the safety of the aircraft or persons, necessitates the taking of action which involves a violation of local regulations and procedures. If required by the State in which the incident occurs, the pilot-in-command shall as soon as possible submit a report on any such violation to the appropriate authority of such State and a copy of the report to the State of the operator.[131]

In order to be able to perform a safe flight, this flight shall not be commenced until flight preparation forms have been completed certifying that the pilot-in-command is satisfied that the aircraft is fully airworthy, the airworthiness certificates are on board, sufficient onboard instruments and equipment are operable, a maintenance release has been issued, the mass and balance of the aircraft are such that the flight, taking into account the flight conditions, can be conducted safely, any load on board is properly distributed and secured, a correct check has been completed indicating that operational limitations, as stated in Chapter 5 of Annex 6, can be complied with for the flight concerned, and an operational flight plan shall be completed, approved and signed by the pilot-in-command.[132]

Fuel planning and management is a responsibility of the pilot-in-command. First of all, before the flight, he or she takes care that the aircraft shall carry a sufficient amount of usable fuel to be able to complete the planned flight in a safe way and to allow for deviations from the planned operation. Depending on unanticipated variations from the planned flight operation, the pilot-in-command could take additional fuel at his or her discretion, so-called discretionary fuel, which shall be the extra amount of fuel to ensure that an adequate safety margin above the minimum fuel amount is maintained.

In the event of a low-fuel situation which may result in landing at the destination aerodrome with less than the final reserve fuel plus any fuel required to proceed to an alternate aerodrome or the fuel required to operate to an isolated aerodrome, the pilot-in-command shall request delay information from ATC, which actually means if a delay is expected, its approximate duration. If the fuel amount decreases to the state of minimum fuel, the pilot-in-command shall advise ATC by declaring – *minimum fuel* – leaving almost no alternative than land with less than the planned final reserve fuel. This is not an emergency situation but an indication that such a situation is possible should any additional delay occur.

---

131 ICAO Annex 6 Part I, Twelfth Edition, July 2022, Chapter 3 General, Para. 3.1.
132 Ibid., Chapter 4 Flight Operations, Paras. 4.3.1 and 4.3.3.

In a worst-case scenario, fuel wise, the pilot-in-command shall declare a situation of fuel emergency by broadcasting – *mayday mayday mayday fuel* – describing the nature of distress conditions, when the calculated usable fuel predicted to be available upon landing at the nearest aerodrome where a safe landing can be made is less than the planned final reserve fuel.[133]

Regarding duties to be performed, the pilot-in-command shall be responsible for the safety of all crew members, passengers and cargo on board when the aircraft doors are closed. The pilot-in-command shall also be responsible for the operation and safety of the aircraft from the moment the aircraft is ready to move for the purpose of taking-off until the moment it finally comes to rest at the end of the flight and the engine(s) used as primary propulsion units are shut down.

On the issue of flight crew members' physical fitness, the pilot-in-command shall be responsible for ensuring that a flight: (a) will not be commenced if any flight crew member is incapacitated from performing duties by any cause such as injury, sickness, fatigue, the effects of any psychoactive substance; and (b) will not be continued beyond the nearest suitable aerodrome when flight crew members' capacity to perform functions is significantly reduced by impairment of faculties from causes such as fatigue, sickness or lack of oxygen.[134]

The pilot-in-command shall ensure that the checklists used are complied with in detail. These checklists shall be used by flight crews prior to, during and after all phases of operations, and in emergency situations, to ensure compliance with SOPs contained in the Aircraft Operating Manual (AOM), also referred to as Flight Crew Operating Manual (FCOM) or documents pertaining to the Certificate of Airworthiness (CofA) and otherwise in the operations manual. Human factor principles are key elements in the design and utilization of checklists.

There are more circumstances, listed in Annex 6, where the pilot-in-command shall be responsible. Of utmost importance is the notification to the nearest appropriate authority by the quickest available means of any accident involving the aircraft, resulting in serious injury or death of any person or substantial damage to the aircraft or property. In view of safety, reporting of all known or suspected defects of the aircraft to the aircraft operator, at the termination of the flight, is mandatory. From an administrative point of view, a journey logbook and the General Declaration (GenDec) shall be updated and kept by the pilot-in-

---

133 ICAO Annex 6 Part I, Twelfth Edition, July 2022, Chapter 4 Flight Operations, Paras. 4.3.7.2.1-4.3.7.2.3. *See* for guidance ICAO Doc. 9976 Flight Planning and Fuel Management (FPFM) Manual.

134 ICAO Doc. 9966 Manual for the Oversight of Fatigue Management Approaches, Second Edition – 2016, App A-10 A2. ICAO Annex 6 – *Operation of Aircraft* Part II – *International General Aviation – Aeroplanes*, Eleventh Edition, July 2022, SARPs related to fatigue management in: Section 2, General Aviation Operations, Chapter 2.2 Flight Operations, Para. 2.2.5 Duties of the Pilot-in-command and Section 3 Large and Turbojet Aeroplanes, Chapter 3.4 Flight Operations, 3.4.2 – Operations Management.

command during flight operations. From a safety and security point of view, the pilot-in-command and/or the operator shall have the option, with respect to a deportee, to refuse the transport of such a person on a specific flight when reasonable concerns relating to the safety and security of the flight in question exist.[135]

If an aircraft, for reasons beyond the control of the pilot-in-command, has landed in a Contracting State, elsewhere than at one of its international airports, that State shall take steps to ensure that by its public authorities, all possible assistance is rendered to the aircraft and, to this end, shall keep control formalities and procedures, in such cases, to a minimum.

A report to these authorities about the unexpected landing shall be submitted as soon as practicable by the pilot-in-command or the next senior crew member available. If the aircraft will be substantially delayed or is unable to continue the flight, the pilot-in-command, while awaiting the instructions of these authorities concerned or in case all contact is lost with these authorities, shall be entitled to take such emergency measures as the pilot-in-command deems necessary for the health and safety of the passengers and crew and for avoiding or minimizing loss or destruction to the aircraft itself and its load.[136]

2.9   PROFICIENCY

The profession of a pilot, in particular, a pilot-in-command, appeals to the imagination of people all over the world. Undoubtedly, in the early days of civil aviation, pilots were considered adventurous and eccentric aviators. Handling big jets, flying passengers and freight between cities over great distances, is still an exciting and challenging but, above all, a fascinating job in a rather complex aviation industry that has transformed people's lives in so many magnificent ways. Pilots, especially pilots-in-command, are the crucial linchpin in the entire operation to give safe and structured direction to all processes that ultimately come together in the cockpit.

On the other hand, the operation done by pilots is subject to less glamorous issues, such as jetlag, irregular working hours and short recovery periods, to occasionally facing severe weather conditions and split-second decision making, to performing a low-visibility

---

135 ICAO Annex 6 Part I, Twelfth Edition, July 2022, Chapter 4 Flight Operations, Para. 4.5.5. Part III *International Operations – Helicopters*, Para. 2.5.5. General Declaration, *see* ICAO Annex 9 – *Facilitation*, Sixteenth Edition, July 2022, Chapter 2 Entry and Departure of Aircraft, B Documents – requirements and use, p. 2-2. Journey Logbook, *see* Art. 34 of the Chicago Convention. Serious injury, *see* ICAO Annex 13 – *Aircraft Accident and Incident Investigation*, Twelfth Edition, July 2020, Chapter 1, Definitions, p. 1-3. *See* for the transport of deportees ICAO Annex 9, Sixteenth Edition, July 2022, Chapter 5 Inadmissible persons and deportees, Para. 5.19.1.

136 ICAO Annex 9, Sixteenth Edition, July 2022, Chapter 7 Landing elsewhere than at International Airports, Paras. 7.1 to 7.4.

landing after a long demanding flight, to maintaining skills and knowledge through recurrent trainings and yearly proficiency checks being performed in a full-motion flight simulator, to passing recurring aeromedical examinations and, above all, dealing with the ever-present heavy burden of responsibility.

To the operator, the pilot-in-command shall demonstrate adequate knowledge of the route to be flown and the aerodromes which are to be used, including the terrain and minimum safe altitudes and seasonal meteorological conditions. He or she shall pay utmost attention to weather forecasts, communication and air traffic facilities, services and procedures, search and rescue procedures, navigational facilities and procedures, including any long-range navigation procedures, related to the route along which the flight will take place. Furthermore, the pilot-in-command must be familiar with procedures applicable to flight paths over heavily populated areas and areas of high air traffic density, obstructions, physical layout, lighting, approach aids and aerodrome arrival, departure, holding and instrument approach procedures and applicable operating minima.

The pilot-in-command and the co-pilot must be familiar with applicable procedures, rules and regulations but, most of all, qualified to operate the type of aircraft assigned to them by the operator. The qualification to operate at the flight controls of a type or variant of a type of aircraft during take-off and landing as a pilot-in-command or as a co-pilot requires that within the preceding 90 days that pilot has operated flight controls during at least three take-offs and landings on the same type of aircraft or in a full-motion flight simulator approved for the purpose.

The operator shall not continue to utilize a pilot as a pilot-in-command on a route or within an area specified by the operator and approved by the State of the operator unless, within the preceding 12 months, the pilot has made at least one trip as a pilot member of the flight crew, or as a check pilot, or as an observer in the flight crew compartment (cockpit), within that specified area, and if appropriate, on any route where procedures associated with that route or with any aerodromes intended to be used for take-off or landing require the application of special skills or knowledge.[137]

A Standard in Annex 6, related to security, states,

> With respect to the reporting of an act of unlawful interference during flight, the pilot-in-command shall, following such interference, submit, without delay, a report to the designated local authority.[138]

---

137 ICAO Annex 6 Part I, Twelfth Edition, July 2022, Chapter 9 Aeroplane Flight Crew, Para. 9.4.3 Pilot-in-command area, route and aerodrome qualification. A flight crew member is a licensed crew member charged with duties essential to the operation of an aircraft during a flight duty period.
138 ICAO Annex 6 Part I, Twelfth Edition, July 2022, Chapter 13 Security, Para. 13.5 Reporting acts of unlawful interference. *See also* ICAO Annex 2, Tenth Edition, 2005, Attachment B. Unlawful Interference.

In case of interception of a distress transmission or observation of another aircraft or a surface craft in distress, the pilot-in-command shall, if feasible in modern aviation, acknowledge the distress transmission, determine and record the position, if given, identification, type and condition of the aircraft and any survivors, record time of observation expressed in hours and minutes, Universal Time Coordinated (UTC) and actual weather conditions, to inform the appropriate rescue coordination centre (RCC) or the air traffic services unit by giving all available information.[139]

The rather limited freedom of movement on board a commercial aircraft, basically a small, isolated community, temporarily physically cut off from the rest of the world, leads to confirmation that the command of a commercial aircraft has a fundamentally different character from that of other forms of mass transportation. Clearly, in public international law, the pilot-in-command is subject to comprehensive international rules, regulations and procedures. Responsibility extends over many issues, from normal flight operation to abnormal phases of flight. In such situations, the pilot-in-command must have the authority to give all commands and take any appropriate actions for the purpose of securing the entire operation and the safety of the aircraft and persons and/or property carried therein. Especially in an emergency situation, which abruptly endangers the operation or the safety of the aircraft and/or persons on board, the pilot-in-command must take any action he or she considers necessary in the interest of safety. When such action involves a violation of local regulations or procedures, the pilot-in-command shall be responsible for notifying the appropriate local authority without delay.[140]

Occasionally, the pilot-in-command must deal with serious threats such as unlawful interference or seizure of aircraft in such a way as to prudently take all necessary measures to ensure the safe completion of the flight. From this point of view, if an aircraft is to be regarded as a vehicle *sui generis*, the pilot-in-command should unquestionably be accorded legal status appropriate to the specific features of civil aviation. Ultimately, it requires considerable time of convening, deliberations and laborious consensus before these specific powers are enshrined by codification in international law.

---

139 *See* ICAO Annex 12 – *Search and Rescue*, Eighth Edition, July 2004, Chapter 5 Operating procedures, Paras. 5.5 to 5.7.
140 Regulation (EU) 2018/1139 of the European Parliament and of the Council of 4 July 2018 on common rules in the field of civil aviation and establishing a European Union Aviation Safety Agency, L 212/1, 22 August 2018, Annex V Essential requirements for air operations, Paras. 7.2 and 7.3.

3 Human Factors and Decision Making in Flight Operations

3.1 Aeronautical Decision Making and Just Culture

FAA Order 9550.8A, 10/27/93 states: within the FAA, the term human factors entails a multidisciplinary effort to generate and compile information about human capabilities and limitations and apply that information to equipment, systems, facilities, procedures, jobs, environments, training, staffing, and personnel management for safe, comfortable, and effective human performance.

The aircraft commander, the decisive human element on board an air transport aircraft, is extremely essential for the safe, efficient and regular conduct of flight operations. As the principal of a small but relatively isolated community, the aircraft commander occupies a determinant position when it comes to aeronautical decision making (ADM), in other words, good pilot judgement carried out in a dynamic and complex environment is important. ADM builds upon the foundation of conventional or traditional human decision making but will enhance the process to diminish the probability of pilot error.[1]

The need for a decision is triggered by the recognition that something has changed or an expected change did not occur. Human traditional (everyday) decision making is a complex process which is strongly dependent on the environment in which the decision must be made. In the 1980s, researchers started to study how experienced people actually make decisions in demanding real-world settings, especially their natural environments. This kind of decision making, naturalistic decision making (NDM) is the way people use their experience to make decisions in these settings. Decision making in an aeronautical environment involves any pertinent decision a pilot must make during the conduct of a flight. This particular domain of aviation is considered a dynamic and complex, but above all, safety-critical endeavour where making decisions can affect the lives of hundreds of people and have extraordinary economic and social consequences.[2]

---

1   Aeronautical decision making is decision making in a unique environment – aviation. It is a systematic approach to the mental process used by pilots to consistently determine the best course of action in response to a given set of circumstances. It is what a pilot intends to do based on the latest information he or she has (Source: FAA Advisory Circular AC 60-22, 13 December 91).

2   Zsambok, C.E. & Klein, G. (Eds.), *Naturalistic Decision Making* (New York, NY: Psychology Press, 1997), pp. 4-5.

A seemingly successful decision made in a dynamic and complex environment like commercial aviation, characterized by, among other things, ill-structured problems, uncertainty, high stakes with high levels of risk and time constraints, might not necessarily be the optimal or most rational decision. It is the decision which the human in question understands and knows how to effectively apply in the context of the situation.

The process of ADM consists of gathering and reviewing all available information, analysing and rating the applicable options, selecting a course of action, and evaluating that course of action for correctness. It addresses all aspects of decision making in the cockpit and identifies the steps involved in good decision making. ADM is strongly dependent on the flight crew's situational awareness that determines the solutions that will be considered, and the available alternatives known to the flight crew. Moreover, in complex operational environments, situational awareness is considered with the flight crew member's knowledge of particular task-related events and phenomena.[3]

While some situations, such as an engine failure during take-off, require immediate pilot action by using established procedures, there is usually ample time during the flight to analyse any changes that might occur, and to systematically assess risks before the aircraft commander makes a solution-oriented decision. However, in all such abnormal situations, a number of factors, including human factors and external conditions might influence the aircraft commander's decision making.

The decisive human element, in particular the aircraft commander, who explicitly makes essential decisions in the interest of aviation safety, is the most flexible, adaptable, interpretable and valuable individual throughout the aviation industry. At the same time, he or she is the most vulnerable professional to influences which can adversely affect its attitude and performance in general, and decision making in particular. Proper handling of various circumstances on board the aircraft mainly depends on acquired qualities such as leadership, knowledge, experience, skills and rational judgement of the aircraft commander.

The leadership role of the aircraft commander is essential with regard to optimal interaction between crew members, which means motivated crew coordination and teamwork resulting in more effective crew performance. The quality of the leader depends on the leader's attitude within the crew. However, especially under stress because of, for

---

3   Decision making is the cognitive process resulting in the selection of a belief or a course of action among several alternative possibilities. *See* Ostroumov, I.V. & Kuzmenko, N.S., *Applications of Artificial Intelligence in Flight Management Systems,* and Sikirda, Y., Kasatkin, M. & Tkachenko, D., "Intelligent Automated System for Supporting the Collaborative Decision Making by Operators of the Air Navigation System During Flight Emergencies" in Shmelova, T., Sikirda, Y. & Sterenharz, A. (Eds.), *Handbook of Research on Artificial Intelligence Applications in the Aviation and Aerospace Industries* (Hersley, PA: IGI Global, 2020). *See also* SKYbrary Decision Making (Operational Guide to Human Factors in Aviation), ICAO, Flight Safety Foundation, EUROCONTROL.

instance, high workload, time constraints, technical difficulties or rapid deterioration of weather conditions, there is a high risk that crew coordination will diminish to a level that entails wrong decisions or lack of corrective actions.

Especially during high workload conditions, usually in demanding circumstances, despite the previously mentioned acquired qualities, the aircraft pilot, especially the aircraft commander with far-reaching responsibilities, is most vulnerable to the risk of making (fatal) errors and, as a consequence, the rather controversial possibility of prosecution and punishment and civil liability in the (individual) capacity of the employee, who may have legal protection from such liability when acting, in good faith and without gross negligence, in an official capacity.

Safety in international air transportation is at a significantly high level, *inter alia*, thanks to voluntary, though confidential, reporting of occurrences, including errors, unsafe situations or serious incidents. In the current thinking about civil aviation safety management, reporting of safety-related occurrences together with incident and accident investigation reports is exceptionally essential, in particular to further enhance protection against any recurrence through adequate recommendations and subsequent actions.[4]

For the aviation frontline workers, such as flight crew members, to step forward to report human errors or safety occurrences without fear of trial and the threat of possible punishment and reprisal, an organizational sphere to encourage reporting of such incidents must be established, a so-called just culture. Reporting should be done without fear of incrimination, let alone self-incrimination.

Unfortunately, reality still shows that threat of criminal proceedings tends to deter incident reporters from submitting valuable safety information that, however, could potentially be used against them. There is still widespread concern among flight crew members about what is seen as an increased focus on legal issues in aviation safety occurrences. This perception is a cause of fear to provide information in the context of safety occurrences investigations and reports, even in cases where tasks are perceived to be exercised in a responsible and professional way. This restraint can have an impact on the flow of important safety data and consequently aviation safety. Mandatory reporting can result in crucial safety data being withheld. It is known that there is a need to learn from aircraft accidents and incidents through safety investigation to be able to take appropriate action to prevent recurrence of such events. Just culture should create an environment in which reporting and sharing of information is encouraged and facilitated,

---

4   For mandatory reporting of occurrences in civil aviation, in particular regarding air operations, a list is included in Annex 1 Occurrences related to the operation of the aircraft in Commission Implementing Regulation (EU) 2015/1018 of 29 June 2015 laying down a list classifying occurrences in civil aviation to be mandatorily reported according to Regulation (EU) No. 376/2014 of the European Parliament and of the Council, L 163/1, 30 June 2015.

although not frustrated by indiscriminate actions of the judicial authorities. A just culture reporting milieu, sincere and humane, within aviation organizations, regulators and investigation authorities has to make the difference.

A balance between the roles and responsibilities of the judicial authorities and the civil aviation safety system, or in other words, mutual respect for each other's expertise in concurrent judicial and technical accident and incident investigations, is needed to achieve a defined atmosphere of trust in which people are encouraged, even rewarded, for providing essential safety-related information, but in which they are also clear about where the line must be drawn between acceptable and unacceptable behaviour, in other words, between unintended errors and wilful violations.[5]

> A culture in which frontline operators or others are not punished for actions, omissions or decisions taken by them which are commensurate with their experience and training, but where gross negligence, willful violations and destructive acts are not tolerated.[6]

Protection has to come from the creation of a non-punitive environment. In the first place, this medium could be accomplished by developing and implementing non-punitive safety information reporting systems, and secondly through the adoption of appropriate legislation ensuring the protection of information and data, critical to flight safety. The customary legal process for activities such as air transportation should be entirely separate from accident investigation. That means that entirely open and honest safety reporting during civil aircraft operations must be feasible to reach a desired point that 'lessons are learnt' and action taken to mitigate the risk of future accidents.

The ICAO Technical Commission stated in a Working Paper the following:

> Just culture means openly reporting and discussing safety issues and mistakes, without punitive response, while also accepting and consistently enforcing the principle that individuals must be held to account for malicious actions. A just culture recognizes that an employee's intent is critical to properly evaluating safety performance. A healthy just culture plays a vital role in a successful

---

5   Schnitker, R.M. & van het Kaar, D., *Aviation Accident and Incident Investigation, Concurrence of Technical and Judicial Inquiries in The Netherlands*, Essential Air and Space Law, Vol. 9, Series Editor Benkö, M.E. (The Hague: Eleven International Publishing, 2010), pp. 188-189. *See also* Reason, J.T., *Managing the Risks of Organizational Accidents* (Milton Park, Abingdon, Oxon: Routledge Taylor & Francis Group, 2016), pp. 195-196.

6   36th Session of the ICAO Assembly, Montreal on 18-28 September 2007. Implementation of a just culture concept. Working Paper presented by Portugal, on behalf of the EU and its member States, by the other States, members of the European Civil Aviation Conference (ECAC) and by EUROCONTROL. *See also* Regulation (EU) No. 376/2014, Art. 2 Definitions under (12).

safety culture by encouraging employees to report safety incidents and hazardous conditions.[7]

The concept of a just culture has already become a broadly accepted, although not universally defined, phrase to express the intercourse with safety provisions which has become common practice within different organizations. These safety-related practices in international civil aviation include elaborated organizational processes and procedures like safety and hazard reporting systems as well as applied policies with respect to responsible treatment and adequate protection of reporters.

Most civil aviation incidents and accidents have resulted from significantly less than optimal human performance, commonly classified as human errors. These, albeit debatable, human errors cannot be helpful in the prevention of civil aviation accidents. However, they may give an indication of where a fault in the system occurs although they do not provide any guidance why such a breakdown occurs. In civil aviation, human factors are dedicated to better understanding in what way humans can most safely and efficiently be integrated with the technology.[8]

Multiple human factors and external conditions may influence the manifestation of human errors in any organization, but especially in the civil aviation industry. This sector uses advanced technologies on a large scale because the transport of people and goods by air is considered a high-risk/high-hazard activity. With respect to this kind of transportation activity, it is undeniably characteristic that the consequences of safety breakdowns in organizations within sociotechnical systems, which are large-scale high technology systems as the civil aviation industry, are catastrophic in terms of loss of life and property.

Human factors in aviation is about people in their working situations, about their interaction at every human-machine interface or hardware interface, in which the human individual is the principal component, including ergonomics, displays and proper location and movement of cockpit controls, but also their interface with nonphysical aspects of the aircraft systems (liveware-software), defined as procedures, computer programmes, rules, manuals and symbology. Moreover, purely human, their relationship with environmental aspects, the liveware-environment interface, which means human-related biological, bodily rhythms, disturbances induced by external and internal environmental effects, and also of utmost importance, their relationship with other people, the liveware-liveware interface, which is about the process of interaction between people affecting crew effectiveness and can be distinguished in people aspects concerned with physical

---

7   ICAO A39-WP/193 TE/73, 25 August 2016, Assembly 39th Session, Technical Commission, Agenda item 36: Aviation safety and air navigation implementation support, Para. 2.2.1.

8   ICAO Doc. 9683-AN/950 Human Factors Training Manual, First Edition – 1998, Chapter I Fundamental Human Factors Concept, 1.2.2.

knowledge, attitudes and cultures, and in-flight crew aspects dealing with crew teamwork, leadership and command, coordination and communication as well as personality interactions.[9]

The term 'human factors' is considered to optimize the relationship between people and their activities by the systematic application of human sciences (human factor technologies), integrated within the framework of systems engineering. Human factors is defined as a multidisciplinary effort to generate and compile information about human capabilities and limitations and apply that information to equipment, systems, facilities, manuals, procedures, jobs, environments, training, staffing and management of personnel for safe, comfortable and effective human activity.[10]

The entire aviation industry, as a standardized system, benefits greatly from human factors research and development as it helps to better understand how humans can most safely and efficiently perform their jobs. In particular with regard to flight crew members, the actual concept of human factors encompasses conditions based on professional specializations to generate specific information related to human performance capabilities and limitations in a cockpit setting.

Physiological factors such as, for instance, workload, stress, vigilance, pressure and sensory limitations could affect decision making which in itself is a decisive factor. It may cause normal situations to turn into abnormal events and if human errors are not recognized at an early stage, events could just turn into an accident. However, human errors and their possible adverse consequences in the cockpit can be quite effectively controlled by human factor technologies, which is all about a profound understanding of human factors. Decision making is normally intended to achieve a positive solution-oriented goal. However, in exceptional cases, unfortunately, the aircraft commander can no longer be the deciding element on board an aircraft.

In very few cases, it has been demonstrated that apparently normal, sensible acting and interacting passengers or, paradoxically, even flight crew members, carefully screened for mental health and cognitive abilities, yet with malicious intent, have deprived aircraft commanders and/or their first officers of any opportunity, through overwhelm or cunning, to make decisions to maintain order and discipline on board or even to remain in control of the aircraft, with fatal consequences, as shown in the past.[11]

---

9   The SHELL concept (Software, Hardware, Environment and Liveware/Liveware), the relationship of human factors and the aviation environment was first developed by Professor E. Edwards in 1972, modified by KLM Captain F.H. Hawkins in 1975. *See also* Five-Factor Model (FFM) Personality includes extraversion, agreeableness, conscientiousness, emotional stability and openness to experience. Martinussen, M. & Hunter, D.R., *Aviation Psychology and Human Factors*, Second Edition (Boca Raton, FL: CRC Press Taylor & Francis Group, 2018), p. 217.

10   U.S. Department of Transportation FAA Order 9550.8 Human Factors Policy, 27 October 1993, p. 2.

11   The September 11 attacks were four coordinated suicide terrorist attacks against the United States on 11 September 2001 by the militant Islamic extremist network al-Qaeda.

3.2   Factors Influencing In-Flight Decision Making

Human errors in general are the result of actions that fail to generate the intended outcomes. Human errors in air transportation are due to carelessness, negligence, failure to apply standard operating procedures according to the manner they are intended, poor tactical judgements and other mainly technical imperfections like poor equipment or procedure design. There are basic concepts associated with the nature of human error. Human errors could have fundamentally different origins while identical human errors could have consequences which in turn are also considered significantly different. Making human errors is all about the capabilities and limitations of the human information processing system. Information must be sensed in an accurate manner before processing. However, especially in stressful situations, causing mental or emotional stress, the sensing function will narrow, which may imply a cause to the potential of error.

Remarkably enough, even apparently healthy, determined, type proficient and duly certificated professional air transport pilots are subject to human errors. In the cockpit, human performance, the functioning of the human body, may be degraded by high altitude, even in a soundproof, pressurized and air conditioned jet aircraft.

Controlling, in fact reducing, human errors on board an aircraft in flight, travelling at high speeds, cruising at high flight levels and over ultra-long distances, while being exposed to ozone concentrations, radiation hazards and insidious performance degradation by circadian dysrhythmia (more commonly known as jet lag), sleep disturbance and deprivation, stress, fatigue, medication, tranquillizers, nutritional state and drugs or any other factors affecting physiological as well as psychological human well-being, human performance or fitness, is a harsh challenge.[12]

Especially long-haul night flights (extended time awake) and transmeridian flights (time-zone changes) and lengthy duty times as well as short recuperation periods, but also short-haul flights (couriers and freight) on irregular or night schedules can lead to potentially unsafe situations through deterioration in efficiency and mental alertness. Objective evidence showed slowed reaction and decision making times, inaccurate or even loss of memory of recent events, errors in computation and a tendency to wearily

---

In 2015, on 24 March, an Airbus A320-211 crashed 100 km northwest of Nice in the French Alps. The crash, in which all 144 passengers and 6 crew members were killed, was deliberately caused by the first officer, Andreas Lubitz, who had previously been treated for suicidal tendencies. At cruising altitude, while the aircraft commander was out of the cockpit, Lubitz locked the cockpit door and initiated a controlled descent until the aircraft collided with a mountainside. Other crashes that were possibly caused by intentional manoeuvres (deliberate flight-control inputs) by one of the flight crew members: EgyptAir Flight 990, Boeing 767-300ER crashed into the Atlantic Ocean approximately 100 kilometres south of Nantucket Island, Massachusetts, USA in 1999. SilkAir Flight 185 crashed into the Musi River near Palembang, Sumatra, Indonesia in 1997.

12   ICAO Doc. 9683-AN/950, Chapter I, 1.4.

tolerate lower standards of operational performance. Efficiency in decision making is defined as performing a given task as best as possible in relation to some predefined performance criterion.[13]

Researchers concluded, after assessing the impact of fatigue-mitigation guidance on pilot's sleepiness during non-stop ultra-long-haul flights, also known as ultra-long-range (ULR) operations that analyses revealed a pattern of gradually increasing sleepiness and fatigue across the entire flight, with slight decreases in sleepiness and fatigue following each scheduled short in-flight sleep period, with a general pattern of slower performance of flight crew members across the flight, with the exception of primary crew on the outbound flight. Furthermore, the study showed that westbound ULR operations can be safely managed using a range of mitigation strategies, and that resulting fatigue levels are no worse than, and in fact, in many instances, better than the return non-ULR flight.[14]

As part of the decision making process, various external pressures put time-related pressure on the aircraft commander, which is the one risk factor category that can cause him or her to ignore all the other risk factors. As a general rule, the aircraft commander's objective is to manage risk, not to create hazards. Some risks can be eliminated, some can be accepted or can be reduced to the level where they are accepted.

The main point in managing external pressure is to be ready for and accept delays. External pressures, such as the irrepressible urge to complete the inbound leg of a delayed return flight within the maximum legal duty time, in order to get home in time for a special meeting or celebration day, or waiting for late arriving transfer passengers who have to catch a scheduled flight, although, with a real chance of missing the air traffic flow management (ATFM) slot time, are influences external to the flight that create a sense of pressure to complete a flight on time, often at the expense of flight safety.

In aviation, the essential goal of risk management is to proactively identify safety-related hazards and mitigate the associated risks. Safety-related hazards are real or perceived conditions, events or circumstances encountered by pilots. When facing hazards, accurate assessment of those hazards will be paramount because otherwise decisions will be made on the basis of most likely incomplete information. If the aircraft commander follows good decision making practices, which is based on education, skill and direct or indirect experience, the inherent risk of a flight is reduced or even eliminated. However, it must be realized that different pilots see hazards differently.[15]

---

13   Ibid., 1.3.5-1.3.20.
14   Werfelman, L., "In It for the Ultra-Long-Haul," (2015) *AeroSafety World*, April 2015, Flight Safety Foundation. This article is based on "Mitigating and Monitoring Flight Crew Fatigue on Westward Ultra-Long-Range Flights," written by T.L. Signal, *et al.*, and published in *Aviat. Space Environ. Med.* Vol. 85 (December 2014): 1199-1208.
15   www.faa.gov/sites/faa.gov/files/04_phak_ch2.pdf, pp. 2-3 and 2-9.

Considerations regarding environmental phenomena, such as rapidly deteriorating weather conditions, posing a potential hazard, may contribute to stress. Since stress is related to a person's ability to pay attention to cues in the environment, it could therefore significantly decrease human performance in a rather complex situation with many cues at the risk of ignoring the most crucial signals, which eventually can lead to pilot errors. Pilot errors and wrong or erroneous decision making during flight might potentially result in non-reversible actions with adverse consequences, relatively different from making errors while working with both feet on the ground with a plethora of available resources, tools, time, assistance and alternatives to be able to make an assessment and to take corrective actions.

The best guideline to optimal performance by the aircraft commander includes, in addition to his or her operational and technical expertise as well as knowledge of all flight conditions such as unsafe situations that he or she has experienced before, being prepared for unanticipated but alarming situations that suddenly may arise. However, no flight is exactly the same as another in a way that decision making in critical stress situations, especially in an environment like parts of Earth's atmosphere with less oxygen, inherently unforgiving to humans, could potentially have adverse implications. The troposphere is the lowest layer of the atmosphere and envelopes Earth's entire surface. Within the troposphere, barometric pressure falls as altitude increases. Commercial jet aircraft are normally cruising in the troposphere and the stratosphere, located above the tropopause border that demarcates the beginning of the temperature inversion, at high altitudes where the effects of (acute) altitude sickness (*hypobaric hypoxia*) might occur, even in a pressurized aircraft cabin. Modern commercial aircraft are pressurized to a typical cabin altitude of approximately 6,000 feet. The concentration of oxygen in the air (21%) remains constant with the result that, as the barometric pressure decreases, the partial pressure of oxygen (PaO_2) decreases proportionately. At 18,000 feet, the partial pressure of oxygen is approximately one-half of the normal sea level value.

Pressurization becomes increasingly necessary at altitudes above 10,000 feet above mean sea level (MSL) to protect crew members, passengers and animals from the risk of a number of physiological problems. Nonetheless, frequent prolonged flying at high altitudes (long-term exposure to *hypobaric hypoxia*) may lead, apart from other altitude sickness-related symptoms, to creeping performance degradation.

Especially in an emergency situation, for example, in the event of sudden loss of cabin pressure, considered as a stressful occurrence associated with uncomfortable and sometimes far-reaching consequences, adequate crew performance is crucial.

As an essential countermeasure, flight crew members who recognize performance degradation associated with particular stressful situations should more willingly embrace human factors training. Identifying and understanding of human factors and their effects on air transportation, as well as adherence to international safety standards, are essential prerequisites for those aviation professionals.

ICAO has drawn up a large number of international standards to which the aircraft commander or, in terms of ICAO, pilot-in-command of a commercially operated air transport aircraft must adhere to before commencing a flight. From the point of responsibility, a flight shall not be commenced until flight preparation forms have been completed certifying that the pilot-in-command is satisfied that the aircraft in question is airworthy and the appropriate certificates are on board the aircraft.

Furthermore, a flight shall not be commenced unless the necessary instruments and equipment are properly installed and a maintenance release has been issued in respect of the aircraft. Mass and balance calculations, as stated on the load sheet, must be such that the flight can be conducted safely under the anticipated flight conditions, that any load carried, in particular dangerous goods, is properly distributed and safely secured.[16]

Next to the flight technical preparation, data entry in the computers and setting instruments for the anticipated departure procedure, an administrative procedure must be completed such as routinely checking and re-checking the load sheet, the operational flight plan, the fuel quantity and performance requirements in case of indefinite delay or rerouting, if applicable the dangerous goods list and boarding and/or loading progress.

It should, however, be clear that in a contemporary highly specialized world of civil aviation, the aircraft commander by no means personally will be able to carry out an in-depth inspection or examination of all aspects of the flight preparation phase. He or she will check at random if everything is in good order, relying on the preparatory work of the company flight dispatch office. However, due to the fact that the aircraft commander is charged with the safe conduct of the flight, he or she is therefore entitled not to commence the flight if he or she considers that the flight cannot be conducted in a safe manner.

In other words, in case of safety deficiencies before commencing the flight, the right to refuse or delay the flight by the aircraft commander is linked to his or her ultimate responsibility laid down in law. In an abnormal flight phase or a worst-case emergency in the air or on the ground, directly endangering the safety of the aircraft and its occupants, the aircraft commander must take appropriate action necessary in the interest of safety, even when such action involves violation of local regulations or departure from the international rules of the air.[17]

---

16   ICAO Annex 6 Part I, Twelfth Edition, July 2022, Chapter 4.3 Flight Preparation.
17   ICAO Annex 2, Tenth Edition, July 2005, Chapter 2 Applicability of the Rules of the Air, section 2.3.1 Responsibility of pilot-in-command.

> The pivot of an aircraft is the captain and round him rotates everything else. Before he has come on board, he has signed for his weather forecast, signed for his freight and his passengers on the load sheet, signed for his fuel, signed his flight plan, signed the serviceability sheets for his aircraft. In fact, he has signed for everything and everybody on board. Once he leaves the ramp, he has absolved all those he leaves behind. The aircraft, the passengers, the crew, the freight are his total responsibility. (David Beaty, Senior Captain British Airways)[18]

The unprecedented growth of air transportation and aviation technology in the years following World War II will demand a much higher degree of airmanship, a more complicated knowledge, skill, professional training and flight management capacity of today's air transport pilot in comparison with its predecessor in the glorious early stages of the aviation era.

In human endeavours involving complicated enterprises such as civil aviation, the vulnerability to making errors is considerably high, despite the ability to eliminate such errors by focusing on safety issues. Modern aircraft are increasingly reliant on automation, the single most important advance in aviation technologies, but this innovative technique of controlling an aircraft in flight unfortunately has also the potential to cause serious incidents or even fatal accidents. In view of that, there are concerns about the effects of automation on air transport pilots. Therefore, future cockpits should be designed to provide automation that is human-centred rather than technology driven. Aircraft manufacturer Boeing explains with respect to this vital safety aspect that cockpits are designed to provide automation to assist, but not replace, flight crew members responsible for the safe operation of an aircraft.

Nevertheless, advanced application of automation on cockpit displays and controls may breed complacency and excessive reliance on automated systems. A study revealed that flight crew members can become confused concerning the state of automation, a condition often referred to as decreased mode awareness. Cockpit design has always been recognized as a factor in preventing and mitigating human error. Flight crew errors typically occur when the crew does not perceive a problem and fails to correct the error in time to prevent the situation from deteriorating.

> Flying for the airlines is not supposed to be an adventure. From takeoff to landing, the autopilots handle the controls. This is routine. In a Boeing as much as an Airbus. And they make better work of it than any pilot can. You're not supposed to be the blue-eyed hero here. Your job is to make decisions, to

---

18   Beaty, D., *The Human Factor in Aircraft Accidents* (New York, NY: Stein and Day Publishers, 1969).

stay awake, and to know which buttons to push and when. Your job is to manage the systems.

(Bernard Ziegler, former Airbus Senior Vice President for Engineering)[19]

To avoid human-machine coordination breakdown in the cockpit, pilots have to maintain situational awareness of the automatic system's status. Mode awareness is a critical ingredient for avoiding automation-related problems. In this respect, eye tracking methodology, monitoring flight mode annunciators (FMA) and calling out mode transitions seen via the FMAs is considered important for ensuring more mode awareness in the cockpit.[20]

High technology sophisticated systems such as engine indicating and crew alerting system (EICAS), multifunction flight display (MFD), integrated flight management computers (FMC), GBAS landing systems (GLS), as well as enhanced ground proximity warning systems (EGPWS) and traffic alert and collision avoidance systems (TCAS II) are human-assisted technologies which undoubtedly have made civil aviation very safe and efficient.[21]

However, the pilots' full involvement in flying the aircraft is more or less degraded to a monitoring role. To a certain extent, this passive role will generally make the pilot more complacent. As a side effect, this automation-related complacency could easily lead to flight safety concerns such as insidious neglect of knowledge of basic aerodynamics and flying skills, in particular traditional hand-flying techniques. It is mainly the loss of these techniques that can lead to fatal human errors. Therefore, automation, in fact the technology-centred approach to automatic flight, may create an entirely new set of pilot errors, unless human factors are skilfully identified and properly addressed.[22]

In practice, crew resource management (CRM) and balanced recurrent training could remedy these deficiencies. CRM courses are specifically designed to teach aviation professionals such as flight crew members, cabin staff and maintenance personnel about cognitive and inter-personnel (teamwork) skills that are quite essential for optimum human performance with the aim of safely and effectively executing flight operations.

---

19   www.aviationquotations.com/pilotquotes.html. Interview in William Langewiesch's Fly by Wire: The Geese, the Glide, the Miracle on the Hudson, 2009.

20   See Li, W.-C., et al., "The Evaluation of Pilot's Situational Awareness during Mode Changes on Flight Mode Annunciators" in Harris, D. (Ed.), Engineering Psychology and Cognitive Ergonomics. EPCE 2016. Lecture Notes in Computer Science, Vol. 9736 (Cham: Springer, 2016), p. 410.

21   GBAS landing system (GLS) is a global navigation satellite system (GNSS)-dependent alternative to instrument landing system (ILS) which uses a single ground based augmentation system station to transmit corrected GNSS data to suitably-equipped aircraft to enable them to fly a precision approach with much greater flexibility (Source: Skybrary).

22   ICAO Doc. 9683-AN/950, Chapter I, 1.4.38.

A common definition of human factors: The discipline that deals with human-machine interface. It deals with the psychological, social, physical, biological, and safety characteristics of individuals and groups at the sharp end of organizations and the environmental context in which they perform.[23]

A dramatic example of flawed human factors related to the complicated human-machine interface, influenced by internal factors and environmental conditions is the following accident:

Air France Flight AF 447, a scheduled international flight from Rio de Janeiro-Galeão International Airport, Brazil to Paris-Charles de Gaulle Airport, France, crashed on 1 June 2009 into the Atlantic Ocean due to a catastrophic chain of events. About 228 passengers and the crew were killed. En route, the aircraft, an Airbus A330-203, was about to cross a convective zone linked to the inter-tropical convergence zone (ITCZ), characterized by convective activity which generates often vigorous thunderstorms and moderate to severe turbulence.

A few minutes later, the aircraft encountered icing conditions. Apparently, because of ice built up on the pitot tubes the autopilot disengaged, seconds later followed by the autothrottle systems, causing loss of alternate law protection, erroneous airspeed indications, incomprehension of the actual situation (failure of situational awareness) and sensitivity on the aircraft pitch and roll, resulting in inappropriate, high amplitude pilot-induced manual control inputs.

Erratic flight manoeuvres followed until seconds later, the aircraft, due to crossed control input cancellations, entered into a full aerodynamic stall condition with an extraordinary high angle of attack until the impact with the ocean.

On 5 July 2012, the French Bureau of Enquiry and Analysis for civil aviation safety or *Bureau d'Enquêtes et d'Analyses pour la sécurité de l'aviation civile* (BEA), Le Bourget Airport, released its final report of the accident, in which some flight crew-related failures were included:

– The crew's lack in practical training in manually handling the aircraft both at high altitude and in the event of anomalies of speed indication.
– The weakening of the active flight crew member's task sharing (two first officers, designated by the pilot-in-command as pilot flying (PF) and pilot monitoring (PM) and one of them as relief pilot-in-command), both by incomprehension of the situation

---

23   Salas, E. & Maurino, D. (Eds.), *Human Factors in Aviation*, Second Edition (Burlington, MA: Academic Press, 2010), p. xi Foreword by Helmreich, R.L.

at the time the autopilot disconnected and by poor management of the so-called startle effect that generated a highly charged emotional factor for both pilots (for clarity, both first officers were on duty in the cockpit, while the aircraft commander, according to the work and rest regulations for long-haul flights, was taking a break in the crew rest cabin).

– The crew's lack of response to the stall warning, whether due to a failure to identify the aural warning, to the transience of the stall warnings that could have been considered spurious, to the absence of any visual indication that could confirm that the aircraft was approaching the stall after losing the characteristic speeds, to confusing stall-related buffet for overspeed-related buffet, to the indications by the flight director that might have confirmed the crew's mistaken view of their actions, or to difficulty in identifying and understanding the implications of the switch to alternate law (which is a reconfiguration mode), which does not protect the angle of attack.

– The lack of any link by the flight crew between the loss of indicated speeds called out and the appropriate procedure.

An internal safety report that was undertaken by Air France after some events and accidents, revealed the following:

– Situational awareness, decision making and CRM causal factors were inseparable and were by far the most significant contributing factors in many events
– The piloting abilities of long-haul and/or *ab-initio* pilots were sometimes poor
– A notable loss of good sense and general aeronautical knowledge
– Weaknesses in terms of representation and awareness of the situation during system failures (reality, severity, danger level, induced effects…).[24]

Especially in this accident, it has become clear that the term situational awareness is knowledge relevant to the task being performed. For the airline pilot, situational awareness means having a mental picture of the existing inter-relationship of location, flight conditions, configuration and energy state of the aircraft as well as any other factors that could affect its safety such as obstacle clearance, conflicting air traffic and weather systems. With respect to meteorological factors, at all times during flight, airline pilots must know the state of their aircraft and the environment through which they are flying. In addition, they should be aware of relationships between aircraft and environmental phenomena, *in casu* atmospheric features such as thunderstorms that can be associated with conditions conducive to icing and turbulence. Situational awareness is a crucial factor in effective decision making, especially in the dynamic flight environment, and has been included in

---

24   Final Report on the accident on 1 June 2009 to Airbus A330-203, registered F-GZCP, operated by Air France, Flight AF 447, Rio de Janeiro-Paris, published July 2012, pp. 167-178, 192 and 199-201.

several models of effective decision making. Generally, effectiveness involves identifying what should be done and ensuring that the chosen criterion is the relevant one.

With regard to situational awareness in aviation, researchers assumed that errors induced by situational awareness were classified into one of three major categories: level 1, failure to correctly perceive the information; level 2, failure to comprehend the current situation; and level 3, failure to project the situation into the future. Errors occurred due to inability to detect or discriminate relevant data, failure to monitor or misperceive data, loss of memory, overreliance on default values and automation-induced complacency, which may result in non-vigilance based on unjustified assumption of satisfactory system state.[25]

Today, it is more crucial than ever before to be able to understand what makes the increasingly important international aviation industry vulnerable. The term 'human factors' has become more and more popular as the aviation industry realized that human error, rather than mechanical failure, underlies the majority of aviation incidents and accidents. Fortunately, aviation accidents, especially at airlines, are extremely rare events, but in the wake of deregulation, public concern has risen over safety matters in the international aviation industry. Yet, the level of flight safety, accomplished by major airlines in most countries worldwide, is one of the greatest success stories of today's digitized aviation industry.

Flight execution, the result of interaction between man and machine is, however, not only dependent on computer systems but still largely on human performance of highly skilled, competent aviation professionals. Despite rapid gains in technology, humans are ultimately responsible for ensuring the success, profit and safety of the aviation industry. This special human performance is driven by the influence of a vast number of factors. However, things can go wrong at this point.

Factors like carelessness, negligence, poor judgement or fatigue, to name a few, can contribute to making errors. Human errors, unintentional actions or decisions, where the cognitive functions like the human processing ability are physically deteriorated (fatigue), whether or not in conjunction with external influences, are the primary contributors to more than 70% of air transport aircraft hull-loss accidents.[26]

It is a proven fact that with a steady increase in technological reliability, there is a tendency that human factors in flight should be considered as a dominant cause of air transportation accidents, which should seriously be regarded as a wake-up call. But the

---

25   Gawron, V., "Nothing Can Go Wrong-A Review of Automation-Induced Complacency Research," (2019) *MITRE* Technical Report, January 2019. *See also* Jones, D.G. & Endsley, M.R., "Sources of Situational Awareness Errors in Aviation" (1996) 67 *Aviat. Space Environ. Med.* 6, pp. 507-512.

26   *See* www.boeing.com/commercial/aeromagazine/aero_08/human_textonly.html. The Role of Human Factors in Improving Aviation Safety – Human Factors.

term 'human factors', in fact, the study of the principles concerning human-machine interaction and the functional interrelation between humans operating that machine, is more complex in civil air transportation than in most other industries.

Obviously, as mentioned before, it cannot just be neglected that human factors are significantly contributing to the cause of aviation accidents. In other words, human factors, today and in the future, will be exceptionally important for aviation safety. It has been said that the greatest impact on flight safety in the near future does not come from improving aviation technology, but it will be from basic human factors education of airline pilots to recognize and prevent human error in the cockpit.[27]

> The study of human factors is about understanding human behaviour and performance. When applied to aviation operations, human factors knowledge is used to optimize the fit between people and the systems in which they work in order to improve safety and performance.[28]

Numerous causative factors are involved in an aircraft incident or accident such as human factors in aircraft design and manufacturing, computer technology and software, aircraft maintenance, airline management and in-flight operation as well as environmental conditions purely affecting the human. Since humans still have the ultimate responsibility when at the controls of an aircraft, human factors are the most pervasive.

Human factor accidents are mostly associated with flight operation. However, more and more aviation professionals such as engineers, pilots, mechanics, designers and air traffic controllers all have to do with the interaction of human factors, especially when aviation accidents occur. The application of human factors knowledge of interaction between distinct cooperating aviation disciplines will finally enhance safety and efficiency in their daily operations. Knowledge involves gathering research data specific to certain situations in these different aviation domains about human abilities, usage, limitations and other characteristics, making it a kind of science or human factors technologies.

Human factors technologies is a multidisciplinary field incorporating contributions from psychology, engineering, industrial design, statistics, operations research and anthropometry, the scientific study of the measurements and proportions of the human

---

27   The original meaning of the term cockpit is diverse. It is generally used as nautical term referring to the location in the rear from which a sailing vessel is steered. Cockpit in aviation is used since 1914. In a commercial aircraft, the cockpit is usually referred to as the flight deck. This term is derived from its use by the Royal Air Force to designate the upper platform of large flying boats where the commander and first officer were seated (Source: Wikipedia).

28   *See* Mirpuri Foundation for a Better World. Aerospace Research: Research on Human Performance and Limitation Focusing on Crew Fatigue.

body. Despite all the changes in technology to enhance flight safety, one factor remains the same, the human factor in the chain which can lead to errors.[29]

The role of humans in the aviation system is quite complicated. As a consequence, the nature of human errors, from pure mental to physical, in this system, varies widely in terms of aviation incidents and accidents. Cognitive errors may include improper judgement or poor, eventually incorrect, decision making while physical errors may originate from motor skill insufficiencies or equipment design. Human factors, including all contributing factors, can give rise to non-technical as well as technical skill-based errors, decision making errors and perceptual errors, which means inaccurate perception of sensory information.

Non-technical skills include cooperation which deals with the issue how people function as a working group, for example a flight crew, with regard to leadership and managerial skills of the aircraft commander which cover all aspects of goal-directed initiatives qua coordination and teamwork in relation to all crew members, essential for greater effective performance and responsibility. Both cooperation, leadership, managerial skills, situational awareness and decision making are also defined as social skills.

Situational awareness deals with the person's ability to accurately perceive what in fact is going on within and outside the cockpit, in particular all aircraft systems and crew members, in fact monitoring all relevant operational factors, or in other words 'staying in the loop'.

Decision making is the cognitive process of selecting a course of action consisting of defining the problem (problem definition and diagnosis), considering the options (option generation), risk assessment and selecting and implementing an option while balancing the pros and cons of the probable outcome (risk assessment and option selection).

It involves pilot judgement, the process of reaching a judgement, choosing an appropriate option, preferably the appropriate option for a particular circumstance, following a situation assessment, choice among available and usable alternatives and assessment of risk.[30] Decision making, a biological, sociological and economic need for survival, often consists of different types of decisions made at different times depending

---

29   www.faa.gov/regulations_policies/handbooks_manuals/aviation/phak/media/04_phak_ch2.pdf, pp. 2-10 and 2-11.

30   Flin, R., *et al.*, Position Paper "Development of the NOTECHS (non-technical skills) system for assessing pilot's CRM skills" in Harris, D. & Muir, H.C. (Editors-in-Chief), *Human Factors and Aerospace Safety, an International Journal* (Milton Park, Abingdon, Oxon: Routledge, 2018), Vol. 3, No. 2, pp. 101-102. *See also* Hörmann, H.J., *FOR-DEC – A Prescriptive Model for Aeronautical Decision Making* in Fuller, R., Johnston, N. & McDonald, N. (Eds.), *Human factors in aviation operations. Proceedings of the 21ˢᵗ Conference of the European Association for Aviation Psychology (EAAP)*, (Andershot, UK: Avebury Aviation, 1995), Vol. 3, pp. 17-23. FOR-DEC: Facts, Options, Risks & Benefits, Decisions, Execution and Check was developed in the 1990s by Lufthansa and the German Aerospace Center.

on the complexity of the situation. Both situational awareness and decision making are cognitive skills.

From a flight tactical standpoint, disruptive advanced technologies like innovative artificial intelligence/machine learning (AI/ML), in particular model-driven and data-driven or statistical AI combined applications (so-called hybrid AI), are very well capable of assisting the aircraft commander in the decision making process. AI has evolved along with advanced technology and is defined in the EASA *Artificial Intelligence Roadmap 1.0* (2020) as any technology that appears to emulate the performance of a human. AI is a fast-emerging technology and is widely adopted, also within the aviation domains, although it still raises major ethical issues. Only if AI is developed and used in a way that respects widely shared ethical values, it can be considered trustworthy. Therefore, there is a need for ethical guidelines that build on the existing regulatory framework.[31]

These advanced technologies can provide advice on routine tasks, for example, to optimize the flight profile, or can conduce enhanced advice on aircraft management issues or flight tactical nature, to assist the flight crew (human-AI interface) to take decisions particularly under high workload conditions (e.g. go-around or aborted landing, diversion to an alternate airport or technical failures), or in a supporting role by anticipating and preventing some critical situations depending on the flight operational context and the flight crew health situation, for example in stressful situations or fatigue.

This application, one of many, which may change the human-machine interface, should not, however, lead to neglect of basic human decision making. To meet AI safety risk mitigation, among other things, some kind of supervision of AI functions must be present at all times such as to keep a human in command (HIC) or a human in the loop (HITL). However, in this respect, the future limits of AI are truly amazing, if not a bit scary, taking into account the scientific and technological advancements.[32]

Nevertheless, with regard to this kind of advanced technology capable of flying an aircraft remotely or fully autonomously, there are experts who are for or against. Many experts believe commercial aircraft will never be pilotless, in other words, the future pilot is still to be needed, but he or she, in the capacity of a remote pilot, will sit in an office flying and managing the aircraft from the ground.

---

31 EASA (European Union Aviation Safety Agency) Artificial Intelligence Roadmap: A human-centric approach to AI in aviation, February 2020, Version 1.0, Chapter D The EU AI Strategy, p. 5. *See also* Ethics Guidelines for Trustworthy AI. Independent High-Level Experts Group on Artificial Intelligence, set up by the European Commission, published on 8 April 2019, A. Introduction and B. A Framework for Trustworthy AI.

32 EASA Artificial Intelligence Roadmap, Version 1.0, Chapter C. What is AI? Chapter D. The EU AI Strategy and Chapter H. AI Trustworthiness building blocks, 1. Trustworthiness analysis (including human-AI interface).

The pilot is still the pilot, whether he is at a remote console or on the flight deck. With the potential for thousands of these unmanned aircraft in use years from now, the standards for pilot training need to be set high to ensure that those on the ground and other users of the airspace are not put in jeopardy. (Mark Rosenker, National Transportation Safety Board (NTSB) Chairman, verbal comments following the release of the NTSB's first report on an unmanned aerial vehicle (UAV) accident, 16 October 2007).

Other experts are convinced that a pilotless commercial aircraft is going to come, but it is just a matter of when. A Boeing chief technology officer stated that there is no doubt in our minds that we can solve the problem of autonomous flight, which includes autonomous taxiing and flight control technology, machine learning and high-integrity systems. Focused on practice, it is just a question of certification procedures, regulatory requirements and, even more importantly, public perception.

"By the time they are ready to retire, around 2060, pilot jobs as we currently know them will start to become obsolete," according to Richard de Crespigny, the Qantas aircraft commander who led a five-pilot team that safely landed a crippled Airbus A380-842 in Singapore in 2010. Pilotless commercial aircraft will eventually be built, he predicted, perhaps in production by 2040. Innovative airlines will buy them and adventurous passengers will fly them.

However, what happens if the computers that fly the aircraft fail? Moreover, AI, when it is functioning, would merely follow 'by the book' rules-based judgement and might not be able to make human-type 'generative intelligence' decisions as was the case with the Airbus A320-214 emergency ditching in the Hudson River in 2009. Humans are particularly good at adaptive problem solving and discovery, areas where there has been little machine intelligence progress so far. However, AI is developing at a breakneck pace.

With respect to the Hudson River emergency ditching, the aircraft commander's effortful attention was narrowed due to the fact that he was not only intensely being focused on maintaining a successful flight path but also distracted by aural alerts, ATC communication, CRM and adherence to SOPs in a very, very compressed time frame. The decision to ditch was most probably made by engaging in both controlled thinking and automatic thinking, an instinctive, highly efficient cognitive process to rapidly solve, in this case, a life-threatening problem. The aircraft commander's experience, rule-based mental process and intuition told him that the only survivable option left, however extremely dangerous, was to ditch on an obstacle-free section of the icy river.

Worst-case scenarios like cascading aircraft system failures occur many times and those are the kind of abnormal situations when you really need a pilot on board, the aircraft commander, with the assessment and experience to make decisions. In particular, the training and timing around handling emergencies such as engine failure(s) at rotation speed (V_r) in take-off, under any conditions, are not going to be easily transferrable to autopilots and machines.[33]

Although, in the distant future, a new scenario will most probably emerge in which artificial intelligence machines not only are capable of learning to accomplish complex tasks on their own but will most likely be able to repair or replicate themselves, seek their own fuel source and can make decisions contrary to their original intended design. This might be the incentive of autonomous pilotless aircraft.[34]

The phenomenon of fatigue, as an insidious human factor, has been defined as a condition reflecting inadequate rest. Fatigue is also considered to be a collection of symptoms associated with displaced or disturbed biological rhythms. A short nap during a period of work, for example during a long duty period in the cockpit, can improve alertness and performance and is a valuable mitigation strategy in fatigue management. Fatigue can be divided into different types. Acute fatigue is induced by long duty periods or by a sequence of particularly demanding tasks performed within a short period of time. Chronic fatigue is induced by the cumulative effects of fatigue over the longer term while mental fatigue may result from emotional stress, even with normal physical rest. Hypoxia and environmental noise are contributing factors. Just like the disturbance of body rhythms, fatigue may lead to potentially unsafe situations and a deterioration in efficiency and well-being of, in particular, but not limited to, airmen.[35]

> Fatigue is the inability to function at the desired level due to incomplete recovery from the demands of prior work and other waking activities. Acute fatigue can occur when there is inadequate time to rest and recover from a work period. Cumulative (chronic) fatigue occurs when there is insufficient recovery from acute fatigue overtime. Recovery from fatigue, i.e. restoration of function (particularly of cognitive function), requires sufficient good quality sleep.[36]

The human body is not designed to work around the clock. It has a vital need to sleep because sleep has a restorative function (sleep loss and recovery) which is essential for mental performance. Reducing the amount or the quality of sleep, even for a single night,

---

33   Adams, R., "The Future of Flight," (2019) *Uniting Aviation – News and Features by ICAO*, 5 July 2019.

34   EASA Artificial Intelligence Roadmap, Version 1.0, Chapter E. Impact of Machine Learning (ML) on aviation, 1. Aircraft design and operation and Chapter H. Trustworthiness building blocks, 4. AI safety risk mitigation. *See also* Barnhart, R.K., *et al.*, *Introduction to Unmanned Aircraft Systems* (Boca Raton, FL: CRC Press, 2012), p. 191.

35   ICAO Doc. 9683-AN/950, Chapter I, 1.3.10.

36   Gander, P., *et al.*, "Fatigue Risk Management: Organizational Factors at the Regulatory and Industry/Company Level," (2011) 43 *Accid. Anal. Prev.* 2, pp. 573-90. doi:10.1016/j.aap.2009.11.007.

decreases the ability to function and increases sleepiness the next day. Two other of the many human factors which may affect the health or well-being of international air transport pilots are body rhythm disturbance (shift in the day/night cycle) and sleep deprivation or disturbance.[37]

High workload, stress, mental illness (psychiatric disorder), frustration, shift work as well as long duty times, ultra-long-haul flights in relation to monotony and jet lag, adverse time-zone changes and short rest or recuperation periods causing circadian rhythm disruption or de-synchronization, meaning sleep-wake disorders, misperceptions and a reduced alertness level are contributors and symptoms of acute fatigue. In terms of workload, which is recognized as a complex concept potentially causing fatigue, there is, however, no universal definition or agreed way of measuring it.[38]

Apart from possible influencing factors like temperature, humidity, vibration, light, hypoxia and seat comfort in the cockpit, fatigue is recognized as a contributing factor for serious incidents and fatal accidents. Errors made by air transport pilots as a result of lack of situational awareness, poor crew communication and distraction or attention deficit disorder may have fatigue as an underlying factor. On the other hand, a wide variety of fatigue symptoms may directly influence the performance of an air transport pilot, which may entail potentially unsafe situations and deterioration in efficiency. ICAO has defined fatigue as:

> A physiological state of reduced mental or physical performance capability resulting from sleep loss, extended wakefulness, circadian phase, and/or workload (mental and/or physical activity) that can impair a person's alertness and ability to adequately perform safety-related operational duties.[39]

3.3   FLIGHT CREW COORDINATION

Communication (verbal and non-verbal) in the aviation community is seemingly one of the most critical human factor elements. Aviation accident investigation reports have shown that poor communication performance may have significantly contributed to a number of fatal aircraft accidents since the commencement of modern civil air transportation.

Most errors in aviation communication, especially between crew members, can be related to misunderstanding, which can be found in both native and non-English speakers.

37   ICAO Doc. 9683-AN/950, Chapter I, 1.3.11-1.3.13. *See also* ICAO Doc. 9966, Manual for the Oversight of Fatigue Management Approaches, Second Edition, 2016, p. 2-12.
38   ICAO Doc. 9683-AN/950, Chapter I, 1.3.16-1.3.17. ICAO Doc. 9966, p. 2-29.
39   ICAO Doc. 9966, p. 2-1.

Results support that errors in communication, defined by incidents of pilots not understanding, occur significantly more often when speakers are both non-native English, messages are more complex and when numerical information is involved. Other hazards are language problems, unclear or ambiguous messages, the medium of transmission, background noises or distortion of the information, wrong interpretation of a message or even its disregard and or physical problems in listening or speaking.[40]

ICAO has adopted English as the official language of international civil aviation. However, there are States like, for example, Russia (or the former USSR), China, France and Spain that allow the use of the native language for communication between their national airline pilots and air traffic control on domestic flights. This divergence in language use can lead to potentially hazardous air traffic conflicts.

In the cockpit, crew coordination is a powerful tool to prevent errors, especially when it comes to communication either between crew members or in radio contact with ATC. What follows is a short description of an aircraft accident due to poor communication and accumulation of errors. Human factors played a major role in the cause of the crash of Avianca Airlines flight 52 at Cove Neck, Long Island on 25 January 1990. The aircraft ran out of fuel after a failed attempt to land at JFK International Airport. At the time the flight became critically low on fuel during the second attempt, the flight crew failed to declare an emergency, hence ATC did not recognize the situation as an emergency.

External factors as adverse weather and visibility conditions, human factors as poor radio communication between the Avianca Airlines pilots and ATC, due to lack of standardized understandable aviation terminology for these pilots to indicate or recognize minimum and emergency fuel states of the aircraft, inadequate traffic flow management by ATC as well as inadequate aircraft management and decision making by the aircraft commander, in particular with regard to the critical low fuel state and associated imminent emergency situation were the cause of the crash.[41]

Exchanging information is seen as a key factor in flight crew coordination ensuring the primary task of safely flying the aircraft, monitoring the performance of each flight crew

---

40 See Study at Bangkok International Airport Approach Control by Tiewtrakul, T. & Fletcher, S.R., "The Challenge of Regional Accents for Aviation English Language Proficiency Standards: A Study of Difficulties in Understanding in Air Traffic Control-Pilot Communications," (2010) 53 *Ergonomics* 2, pp. 229-239. doi:10.1080/00140130903470033. *See also* ICAO Doc. 9683-AN/950, Chapter I, 1.4.22-1.4.23.

41 Avianca Airlines Flight 52 (IATA flight number AV052/Call sign Avianca 052) was a regularly scheduled flight from El Dorado International Airport in Bogotá, Colombia, to the John F. Kennedy International Airport in Queens, New York City, with an intermediate stop at José María Córdova International Airport near Medellin, Colombia. The aircraft that crashed on 25 January 1990 was a Boeing 707-321B with an aircraft commander, first officer and flight engineer in the cockpit. The crew never made clear to ATC how desperate their situation (delays due to bad weather conditions in the northeastern United States, holding patterns, missed approach and associated rapidly decreasing fuel load etc.) had become.

member and enabling the aircraft commander to have utmost decision making ability under both normal and abnormal conditions.

Purely functional communication in the aviation industry, including all transfer of information, is essential for the safe operation of flight. However, despite the use of standard operating procedures and typical aviation phraseology in aviation English, which is slightly different from Standard English (SE), considered as the universal language (lingua franca), human factors like body language, hierarchy, stress, difference in attitude among crew members, distinct personalities, nationalities, cultures and even native languages in the cockpit could all impair teamwork and thus could be detrimental to flight safety.[42]

Especially under stress (physical, emotional or managerial), there is a high risk that coordination will break down. The results are a decrease in communication to a situation of marginal or no exchange of information (because of communication barriers), an increase in errors, for example poor or wrong decision making, and a lower chance of correcting deviations either from standard operating procedures or the desired flight path.[43]

Effective communication needs inquiry: seeking information and clarification from crew members, use of visual scan and tolerance, advocacy: ability to tell what one knows or is convinced of having a forthright position, sticking to a point of view (belief bias) until it is proven by facts, not by authority, that it is wrong, listening: the art of active listening in today's fast-paced world requiring active attention is key to communication and, finally, conflict resolution: arguments regarding issues of disagreement in the cockpit having a serious effect on the quality of decision making. Recognizing and defining the problems, fact finding and formulation of solutions, which are items of a problem solving process as well as fair discussion, acceptability, coordination and mutual respect of feelings can solve communication problems.[44]

Cockpit teamwork, responsibility and, in particular, leadership are key performance factors. Leadership is one aspect of teamwork or cooperation in the cockpit. The success of the leading person, in hoc casu the aircraft commander, depends on the quality of his/her relationship with the team. Coordinated cooperation, which is a social skill, requires team building so that cooperative actions are based on mutual agreement by flight crew members, which in fact are highly skilled individuals. The cockpit is the workplace where these individuals perform to their full potential, leading to an increase in safety through redundancy to detect and correct individual errors, often through situational awareness,

---

42   Cockpit standard operating procedures (SOPs) identify and describe the standard tasks and duties of a flight crew for each flight phase, including what to do and when to do it in a given situation (Source: Skybrary: Adherence to SOPs (OGHFA) Operators Guide to Human Factors in Aviation).

43   ICAO Doc. 9683-AN/950, Chapter I, 1.4.26.

44   See Human Factors in Aviation by P.S. Ganapathy, Consultant (Flight Ops.) Jet Airways (India) Ltd.

and in efficiency through the organized use of all existing resources which improves in-flight management.[45]

On the other hand, lack of open and active communication between flight crew members could result in crew cooperation being far from optimal. This could mean that team building would be insufficient, in the sense that suggestions for solutions or assistance from flight crew members in demanding situations can be considered imperfect or even be ignored. In particular, authoritarian, narcissistic or antisocial behaviour and substandard or even completely failing CRM are unfortunately perfidious variables that can lead to operational errors.

The aviation system includes product and service providers and regulators as well as oversight officials, which are State institutions. It is a rather complex system that requires an assessment of the contribution to aviation safety done by humans and a concept of how human performance can be affected by its multiple and interrelated components. Components such as software, hardware, environment and liveware are of great influence on human performance. In particular the interface liveware-liveware, which is all about leadership, teamwork, personality interactions and crew cooperation, thus the relationship between flight crew members in the work environment, for long hours in a relatively small compartment like the cockpit, is considered quite important to recognize that communication and interpersonal skills play a significant role in determining human performance. Coherent and effective communication, which includes all transfer of information is essential for safe flight management.

Inadequate communications between flight crew members could lead to loss of situational awareness, a breakdown in teamwork in the cockpit, and, ultimately, to wrong decision making which might result in a serious incident or fatal accident. The quality and effectiveness of communication within the cockpit is determined by its intelligibility. This form of understanding and inter-human communication is reflected in flight crew briefings.[46]

Briefings are an essential part of every air transportation flight. From a safety point of view, this is an extremely important statement. Even so, Flight Safety and Human Factors experts of Alaska Airlines and the Royal Aeronautical Society's Human Factors Group have found, after extensive research and review of aviation safety action programmes and line operations safety audits (LOSA), that flight crew briefings are already for a long time completely overloaded with data.

Furthermore, these briefings consist more or less of a unilateral explanation and finalization, and are definitely not adapted to the next-generation digital cockpit systems

---

45   ICAO Doc. 9683-AN/950, Chapter I, 1.4.25-1.4.27.
46   *See* ICAO Doc. 9859-AN/474, Safety Management Manual (SMM), Third Edition-2013, pp. 2-7 to 2-9.

layout and associated recent breakthroughs in cognitive patterns and functioning with respect to problem solving and decision making in pilot-proven challenging environments.

As long-standing standard operating procedures briefings are not really adapted to the typical contemporary glass-cockpit and corresponding modification in human learning and understanding, the adapted crew briefing format is subdivided into three main elements, namely threats, plan of action and considerations (T-P-C). Studies revealed that advanced cognitive theories regarding decision making, for example automated assistance for human tasks in the cockpit, are requiring a different order of objectives for a modern approach to cockpit preparation and briefing format.

An efficacious briefing methodology, encouraging open and interactive flight crew communication between the PF and the PM, identifying the potential threats, determining appropriate mitigation strategies, and delineating an appropriate plan of action, can significantly enhance flight safety. For reasons of clarity, the aircraft commander and first officer can alternately hold the position of PF or PM.[47]

The cockpit preparation process for departures and arrivals starts with a review of the weather conditions, airport automatic terminal information service (ATIS) data and notices to airmen (NOTAM) information, a final check on aircraft performance calculations and aircraft systems, the set-up of the electronic (paperless) flight bags (EFBs), glass-cockpit instrument panels, navigational guidance and suitable cross-checks on the programmed or automatically uploaded departure or arrival waypoints in the FMC and/or other relevant data as well as additional tasks. This preparation process is done by the pilots in an independent and silent way, which means only to discuss relevant items that may affect safety. Once they have completed their respective set-up tasks, both pilots are ready for the particular phase of flight, except for the operational briefing whose format has been adapted to modern reliable aircraft performance.

The first element 'threats' will trigger the PF to ask the PM to review any threats that might be relevant to the departure or arrival flight profile that will be flown. To first address the relevant threats to the respective flight profile (threat forward) and applicable specific countermeasures to be taken for each identified threat degrading safety margins will not only more thoroughly retain the method of approach but also encourage team building and leadership, in fact social, non-technical skills, through 'interactivity', the second element.

Especially, with respect to complex, high-risk departure and arrival procedures, the threat discussion can be lengthy but will make the plan of action more compact. This plan

---

47   Loudon, R. & Moriarty, D., "Rethinking the Briefing: Alaska Airlines Revamps Approach and Departure Briefings to Focus on Flight-Specific Threats," (2017) *AeroSafety World* July-August 2017. (Capt. Ritch Loudon is an instructor evaluator and leads the Human Factors Working Group for Alaska Airlines. Capt. David Moriarty is the author of Practical Human Factors for Pilots and a member of the Royal Aeronautical Society).

of action, manifestly outlined by the PF, should be 'scalable', the third element, which means a lean explanation covering important items both based on and depending on subjects as flight crew member proficiency, experience, recent familiarity with the arrival and departure profiles, procedural complexity, dense air traffic and adverse weather conditions.

The final part of the briefing format covers the considerations portion. From a 'cognitive' perspective, the fourth element, the principle of the recency effect refers to the finding that humans tend to have a better memory for information they were told more recently. According to that effect, considerations should include a recap of any specific duties of the PM for each particular departure or arrival procedure and agreed-upon countermeasures to be taken in the event of critical threats, responding in accordance with a mentally primed pattern briefed or learnt earlier.

However, the thinking underlying the method of recapitulation in this portion gives some kind of discrepancy. A number of research studies suggest that the recency effect might involve short-term memory (STM), while other studies indicate that the recency effect in itself may be more complicated due to more than just STM processing of information transferred from the sensory memory (selective perception). Not all sensory memory is being transferred to STM. Only when sensory memory is enjoying conscious appreciation, does it become STM.[48]

3.4   PILOT ERROR

Cuiusvis hominis est errare; nullius, nisi insipientis, in errore perseverare.[49]

Human error tends to continue to be at the forefront of aviation accident statistics. However, the human element in the cockpit, the pilot at the controls of the aircraft, is not the only factor but rather part of an extensive domain consisting of vital links that together significantly contribute to the success of airline operations, *in casu* the final product, the safety of flight while offering operational efficiency. In the chain of the vital links such as design, manufacturing, testing, training, maintenance and operational use of commercial aircraft, humans are ultimately responsible to ensure the success and safety of the aviation industry.

Human beings are by nature intelligent, creative, flexible, dedicated and efficient. However, these creatures are to some extent vulnerable to making errors, not only during

---

48   Baddeley, A.D., *Essentials of Human Memory*, Classic Edition (Hove, East Sussex: Psychology Press, 2014), Short-term Memory Store. *See also* Dharani, K., *The Biology of Thought, A Neural Mechanism in the Generation of Thought – A New Molecular Model* (London: Academic Press, Elsevier, 2015), pp. 57-59.

49   Anyone can err; but nobody but the fool persists in error (*Cicero, Orationes Philippicae* 12, 2, 5.).

the entire aircraft production process but also in the cockpit during flight operations. With respect to cockpit design, one of the preliminary phases of the production process, a lot of progress has been made in reducing the accident rate and increasing efficiency by analysing human factors design requirements. Cockpit layout in particular has always been recognized as an essential factor in minimizing but above all preventing human errors.

Human factors design requirements are defined by operational experience in the past, operational objectives and scientific knowledge. Moreover, practical methods such as mock-up or simulator evaluations are used to assess how various design elements meet these design requirements. Human-centred design philosophy is the underlying factor that has been validated by experience and empirical research data as well as observations systematically gathered during a multitude of flights.[50]

Human factors design of cockpits ultimately focuses on effectively reducing human errors caused by this specific design. It includes five main aspects: layout, control device, information display, alerting and automation. Today, cockpits are designed to provide an appropriate degree of automation.

Automation is defined as the use of machines and computers to do work that was previously done by people (*Oxford Dictionary*). Automation has been gradually introduced in the entire aviation system, especially in aircraft. Cockpit automation has the potential to make aircraft operations safer and more efficient by ensuring more precise flight manoeuvres, providing display flexibility and optimizing cockpit space and ergonomics. The purpose of the introduction of automation is to assist rather than replace flight crew members and not least to eliminate pilot error.

The benefits of automation far outweigh the actual and potential problems that are causal to automation. Although there is still no international consensus regarding the proper use of automation, there is no question that the reduction in incidents and accidents related to human error can, in part, be explained by the introduction of automation in the cockpit. However, the record also shows that failures of automatic equipment, and, more frequent, mismatches at the interface between human and certain equipment (liveware-hardware/software) remain crucial links in the causative chain of aircraft incidents and accidents.

Although ultra-high levels of aircraft flight automation (advanced automation) are extremely useful, particularly under conditions of high workload, they just allow distraction that may cause loss of flight crew monitoring performance or may cause confusion leading to declining situational awareness.

---

50   *See* www.boeing.com/commercial/aeromagazine/aero_08/human_textonly.html. The Role of Human Factors in Improving Aviation Safety – Human Factors 1. Flight Deck Design.

It has been demonstrated that the application of automation to cockpit displays and controls may induce complacency or create overreliance on the automated system. Pilot errors typically occur when flight crew members do not perceive a problem and thus fail to correct the error in time to prevent the resulting situation from getting worse, which eventually may lead to accidents and incidents. If, however, human factors-related issues, such as limited performance of the human as monitor and effects on motivation, are addressed in a correct way, there may be adequate justification for automation. Somehow, automation may relieve the flight crew of certain tasks in such a way as to reduce the work load in specific phases of flight where it reaches the limit of operational acceptability.

The cockpit systems layout is considered the most important example of human-machine interface (liveware-hardware) on board aircraft. Cockpit designers must at all times be alert about potential hazards in the field of human-machine interface being a frequent source of human error. Naturally, in the interest of aviation safety and ultimate responsibility, the human should remain (for now) the central focus point in cockpit design.[51]

Pilot error because of cockpit design factors has become extremely worrying for the airworthiness authorities, especially in highly automated next-generation air transport aircraft. During apparently hectic phases of flight such as take-off and final approach to land or likewise abnormal or emergency situations, standard operating procedures are normally applied by the flight crew. Yet, in these busy phases of flight and even during the preparatory actions on the ground, flight crew members could make unintentional errors in monitoring, controlling or proper setting of aircraft systems in the cockpit. Misinterpretation and mode confusion are, to a significant extent, considered design-induced errors.

Standardization of cockpit panels layout relates to flight safety, unlike inconsistent panel layouts which might involve inadvertent reversion to an operating practice appropriate to an aircraft previously flown. Even the smallest modifications made to original instruments of aircraft of the same type caused layout differences that induced pilot errors. This problem also applies to the installation and certification of modern cockpit alerting systems in variants of the Boeing 737 MAX-7 and MAX-8 needed to comply with new safety standards.[52]

It turned out that pilot error by design and layout factors on the one hand do not follow predictable patterns, while on the other hand, many other types of human errors are systematic, amazingly following certain predictable trends.

---

51 See www.boeing.com/commercial/aeromagazine/aero_08/human_textonly.html – Flight Deck Design – Appropriate Degree of Automation.

52 See Giacomo Amati, "Boeing's CEO Believes The 737 MAX Will Get a Certification Extension," (2022) Simple Flying News, 26 September 2022.

> Pilot error may, and often does, exist without legal responsibility of the pilot for the accident, because every act of the pilot contributing to the accident although unavoidable or completely justifiable, is called pilot error. The accident analyst must attribute the accident to aircraft structure, power plant, pilot, other personnel, etc., and he is not concerned with whether the pilot's action was justified or wrong in either moral or legal sense.[53]

Adverse weather conditions, time pressures to meet departure/arrival slots, delays, aircraft malfunctions and intricate security measures are conditions external to the cockpit, originating outside the influence of the flight crew which, individually or in combination, may increase the complexity of the operational environment and thus can potentially lead to making errors.

Other serious external factors comprise commercial interests. For airline operators, not only aviation safety comes first, but also punctuality from an explicit economic point of view. Increasing time pressure, annoying last-minute changes and associated baggage up- or download, deteriorating weather conditions and imminent delay regarding an allocated slot time, considered decision whether or not to de-ice and if so to meet de-icing hold-over times and lack of knowledge from experience to name a few effects on decision making, all of which turn out to be treacherous opponents in the aircraft commander's mindset when it comes to flight safety. In such situations, humans tend to make minor mistakes, which easily can lead to a potentially dangerous situation, especially when trying to depart with an aircraft while ignoring, among other things, reapplication of de-icing in a situation of hold-over time exceedance, flight manual recommendations for icing situations and unreal instrument panel readings during the take-off run.[54]

---

53   Kamminga, M.S. (1953), p. 101 (Original source: Flight Safety Foundation, Accident Prevention Bulletin 50-20, 28 August 1950).

54   Air Florida Flight 90 was a scheduled domestic passenger flight from Washington National Airport (today: Ronald Reagan Washington National Airport) to Fort Lauderdale-Hollywood International Airport with an intermediate stopover at Tampa International Airport. On 13 January 1982, the Boeing 737-222 crashed shortly after take-off in winter weather conditions into the 14th Street Bridge over the Potomac River. The NTSB determined that the cause of the accident was pilot error. The pilots failed to inspect the aircraft to see if it was free of ice and snow, failed to switch on both engine nacelle anti-ice systems (the captain responded on the checklist item with 'Off'), used reverse thrust in a snowstorm prior to take-off, tried to use the jet exhaust blast of a plane in front of them to melt the ice build-up that had accumulated on Flight 90's wings, and failed to abort the takeoff run on a slushy runway even after detecting engine power problems due to the failure to switch on the engine anti-ice systems which caused the engine pressure ratio (EPR) thrust indicators to provide false readings. Both pilots had limited experience in jet air transportation winter operations.

In encountering severe or adverse weather conditions during flight, pilots could experience false impressions leading to misinterpretation, in the worst case causing a potentially disastrous situation at times beyond a so-called point of no return.[55]

Over the years, safety of the civil aviation system has been the major objective of ICAO. The ICAO Assembly recognized that considerable progress has been made, but additional improvements are still needed and can be achieved. It has long been known that some three out of four accidents result from less than optimum human performance, indicating that any advance in this domain can be expected to have a significant impact on the improvement of flight safety. For that reason, in 1986, the ICAO Assembly adopted Resolution A26-9 on Flight Safety and Human Factors. The Air Navigation Commission formulated the following objective for the task:

> To improve safety in aviation by making States more aware and responsive to the importance of human factors in civil aviation operations through the provision of practical human factors material and measures developed on the basis of experience in States, and by developing and recommending appropriate amendments to existing materials in Annexes and other documents with regard to the role of human factors in the present and future operational environments. Special emphasis will be directed to the human factors issues that may influence the design, transition and in-service use of the (future) ICAO/ATM systems.[56]

As a result of Resolution A26-9, ICAO implemented the Flight Safety and Human Factors programme, with the objective of improving aviation safety by making States more aware and responsive to the importance of human factors in civil aviation. ICAO is primarily obtaining human factors data with regard to flight crew errors derived from technical reports of incident and accident investigations conducted by Contracting States.

International provisions which deal with the technical investigation and reporting of aviation occurrences are included in ICAO Annex 13 – *Aircraft Accident and Incident Investigation*, and in the ICAO Manual of Aircraft Accident Investigation and the Accident/ Incident Data Reporting (ADREP) System.[57]

Aviation occurrences, including aircraft accidents and incidents, may not only be subjected to a technical investigation, but also to some form of judicial, regulatory,

---

55 *See also* Air France Flight AF 447 Final Report on the accident on 1 June 2009, published July 2012.
56 *See also* ICAO Doc. 9495, A26-RES Assembly 26th Session, Montreal, 23 September-10 October 1986, Resolutions Adopted by the Assembly and Index to Documentation, p. 69.
57 ICAO Doc. 9756-AN/965 Manual of Aircraft Accident Investigation, First Edition, 2011 – Part III Investigation and Second Edition, 2014 – Part IV Reporting, Chapter 2 ADREP Reporting System.

administrative and/or disciplinary inquiry. The role of the professional human in the aviation system is rather complicated, especially if that person is involved in an aircraft accident. The causes of human error can be complex and any investigation, but most of all technical and judicial, must include the entire scenario in which the error occurred. Was the accident due to an unintentional act, an incorrect action or omission? Its opposite can also mean malicious intent or wilful misconduct, gross negligence, careless or reckless conduct during the execution of the flight. Or else, another option is to find out whether the accident was due to conditions beyond human control.

In the event of injury or death to persons or damage to property due to pilot error, there will always be the pressing question: is the aircraft commander, apart from anyone else such as the airline or aircraft manufacturer, legally to blame? In other words, who is considered liable, and from a criminal point of view, is there cause for prosecution in respect of a criminal charge?

While recent statistics indicate that the majority of aviation accidents are caused by human error, human factors in aircraft accidents and serious incidents are often less tangible and detectable than technical causes.

To err is human, even or maybe especially, in a computerized digital environment like modern aviation. Though very rarely, highly experienced professional pilots do make errors, in the worst scenario, fatal to themselves, to passengers and other crew members as well as to third parties on the surface. A human error is defined as an inappropriate or undesirable and often unintentional human decision or behaviour that reduces, or respectively has the potential to reduce, effectiveness, flight safety or system performance. Human error in flight operation, *in casu* pilot error, reflects that anyone acting in a support capacity during a flight can contribute to the error chain.

In other words, the term 'pilot error' generally refers to an aircraft accident in which an action or decision made by the pilot, usually the aircraft commander, was the cause or the contributing factor that led to the accident. This definition also includes the aircraft commander's failure to make a correct decision or take proper action. Regarding operations such as flight operations, a human error is defined as an action or inaction by a person that leads to deviations from organizational or the operational person's intentions or expectations. Another, more general definition of an error is a failure to exercise due diligence that results in the intended outcome not being achieved. Only, a single decision or event does not normally lead to an accident, but a series of events and the resultant decisions together form a chain of events which might lead to a potentially catastrophic outcome. The description of these actions or omissions should however be separated from deliberate pilot error or wilful misconduct.[58]

---

58   *See* ICAO Doc. 9859-AN/474, p. xii, Definitions, pp. 2-8 and 2-9.

With respect to flight crew operations, adherence to standard operating procedures is extremely important since noncompliance is a serious threat to aviation safety. To effectively control a high-quality mechanism like an aircraft in an exceptionally complex, sometimes unforgiving environment, air transport pilots must strive to be compliant. Unfortunately, procedures are not always followed. Human factors such as fatigue or distraction can easily lead to mistakes while the flight crew's intention is to be compliant with the written procedures, whether these standard operating procedures are manufacturer-provided or customized developed by the operator.

Deviating from these procedures can be divided into two opposite acts, procedural intentional or unintentional noncompliance (PINC/PUNC) acts, in other words, the difference between more risky intentional noncompliant acts and unintentional acts where the sole purpose is to be compliant with standard operating procedures. Intentional noncompliance errors are wilful deviations from regulations and/or operator procedures.

Intentional noncompliance with standard operating procedures such as omitted altitude callouts, checklists conducted from memory, failure to respond to TCAS alerts, failure to execute a mandatory missed approach, violations of the law and lack of vigilance are defined as active failures or pilot errors having an immediate adverse effect. A computer-implemented method that makes it possible to alert for intentional noncompliance with standard operating procedures to mitigate these direct pilot errors.

Latent (passive) failures or pilot errors like distraction, complacency, overreliance, misunderstanding, obliviousness, lack of knowledge and aircraft handling errors, which are proficiency-based errors and operational decision errors, which means ignorance of more conservative options, giving no information to other flight crew members about decision making, lack of resource management, misjudgement, and the aircraft commander's manifested marginal leadership are considered activities and or omissions, the consequences of which could remain dormant for some time. These pilot errors become evident when triggered by active, efficacious human failures, technically-basedfailures or adverse system conditions, breaking through system defences any time during flight crew operations.[59]

When dubious flight crews exacerbate errors or fail to respond to errors, the outcome could be an undesired aircraft state (airspeed or altitude deviation), an accident or incident. Analyses of LOSA observations during scheduled flights have found that flight crews that are rated poor/marginal in their monitoring and cross-checking skills or intentionally noncompliant with cockpit standard operating procedures are during these flights two to three times more likely to commit other, unintentional errors or to mismanage threats to flight safety. The best flight crews are those that not only manage the operational complexity of their flights but also anticipate threats and errors, and manage

---

59   ICAO Doc. 9683-AN/950, Chapter II, Human Factors, Management and Organization, 2.4.3.

those too. They use threat and error management (TEM) defences that include monitoring/ cross-checking, policies and procedures, checklists use, CRM, deviation callouts, aircraft hardware, airmanship and some good fortune.[60]

3.5   HUMAN FACTORS IN FUTURE PERSPECTIVES

If human error is the cause of most aviation accidents, then should we not take the human out of the cockpit? An interesting but also a controversial question! Modern advanced automation is well capable of performing almost all of the functions envisaged in the aircraft cockpit. However, even with the assist of highly advanced technologies, the human-centred automation principles will remain the focal point with regard to flight operations. These essential principles should ideally minimize the likelihood of errors. In practice, it is a decisive rule that humans will retain responsibility for the safety of aircraft operations, whether the pilot is remotely controlling the aircraft or is physically present and working in the cockpit.[61]

In a study, The National Aeronautics and Space Administration (NASA) cited a number of aircraft accidents that substantiate both the pros and cons of the earlier question. The following are the names of a few of these accidents and their human factors involved:

First of all, Eastern Air Lines Flight EA401, a Lockheed L 1011-1 Tristar that crashed in 1972 into the Florida Everglades, 18.7 NM of Miami International Airport following a missed approach because of a suspected nose gear malfunction. The aircraft climbed to 2,000 feet and proceeded on a westerly heading. The four flight crew members became preoccupied with a malfunction of the nose landing gear indicating system that distracted the crew's attention from the instruments. They failed to notice the autopilot had inadvertently been disconnected.[62]

Resultantly, the flight gradually lost altitude and eventually crashed while the flight crew was still distracted with the indicator problem. The NTSB determined that the probable cause was the failure of the flight crew to monitor the flight instruments in the final four minutes of flight.[63]

---

60   Werfelman, L., "Intentionally Noncompliant: LOSA Data Show that Purposely Skipping a Checklist or Ducking Under a Glideslope Can Lead to Bigger Problems," (11 December 2013) *AeroSafety World*, Flight Safety Foundation, December 2013-January 2014.

61   *See* NASA-Ames Research Center, Jay Shively.

62   The listed flight numbers of Eastern Air Lines, Varig, Helios Airways, British Airways, US Airways and Qantas are IATA flight numbers.

63   NTSB File No. 1-0016, 14 June 1973, Report No. NTSB-AAR-73-14, Aircraft Accident Report Eastern Air Lines Inc, L-1011, N310EA, Miami, Florida, 29 December 1972.

The following human factors involved successively were lack of recognition and mitigation of threats, lack of situational awareness, non-adherence to standard operating procedures in case of a malfunction, distraction and lack of attention in order to detect an unexpected descent soon enough to prevent impact with the ground. The crash of the aircraft that was on a scheduled flight from New York JFK International Airport to Miami International Airport caused 101 total fatalities.

Secondly, Varig Flight RG254: on 29 September 1989, prior to take-off from Marabá Airport, the flight crew of the Boeing 737-241 of the Brazilian airline performing a scheduled domestic flight from São Pualo Guarulhos International Airport to Belém/Val de Cans/Júlio Cezar Ribeiro International Airport with six stopovers, the last one being Marabá, the aircraft commander inserted a wrong heading (heading select knob) into the horizontal situation indicator (HSI), clearly inconsistent with a route from Marabá to Belém.

The 737 was only equipped with basic navigation systems such as VOR (very high frequency omnidirectional range) and ADF (automatic direction finding) and an uncomplicated aircraft performance management system (PMS). The magnetic heading notation in the flight plan was recently changed by the company from 3 to 4 digits which was not known to the aircraft commander due to holidays at the time. The aircraft flew due west instead of a northeasterly heading ending up over a remote area of the Amazon jungle without positive radio or radar contact with Belém ATC.

Negligence (incorrect heading insertion and no supervision of cockpit activities), confusion, misinterpretation in radio communication, misleading perception about geographical landmarks, predisposition, failure to cross-check the flight plan data, boredom with this routine flight and inattention causing the aircraft commander to engage the autopilot to steer the wrong heading, poor flight crew coordination and fixation of attention were all human factors involved.

Thirdly, Helios Airways Flight ZU552: on 14 August 2005, a Boeing 737-31S crashed into the hills near Grammatiko, north of Marathon, Greece, due to human error. When climbing out of Larnaca International Airport, Cyprus, the aircraft's cabin altitude warning horn sounded while passing an altitude of 12,000 feet. The flight crew disregarded the warning, believing it to be the (identical sound) of the take-off configuration warning instead, which, however, was quite odd at this altitude.

The flight crew continued the climb without noticing cabin pressure loss currently occurring on board. At last, they reported an air-conditioning problem. Soon after this call, the aircraft commander and the first officer were beginning to experience symptoms of hypoxia which incapacitated them, leading to the aircraft's eventual crash after flameout of both engines due to fuel exhaustion. At that moment, flight attendant Andreas Prodromou, who had managed to remain conscious by using a portable oxygen supply bottle, entered the cockpit but was unable to take control of the aircraft due to lack of experience.

The accident was caused by human error. The flight crew did not recognize that the pressurization system was set to the manual mode instead of the automatic mode because of a pre-departure maintenance leak check on the system. Direct causes were non-recognition that the cabin pressurization mode selector was in the manual position during the performance of the cockpit pre-flight procedure, the before start checklist and the after take-off checklist. Non-identification of the warnings and the reasons for the activation of several warnings (cabin altitude warning horn, passenger oxygen masks deployment indication and the master caution), and the continuation of the climb eventually resulting in incapacitation of the flight crew due to hypoxia, resulting in semi-automatic continuation of the flight via the FMC and the autopilot, depletion of the fuel followed by dual engine flameout, and impact of the aircraft with the ground were the findings of the air accident investigation team.[64]

Human factors involved in the accident were non-recognition by the flight crew that the pressurization system was set to the manual mode, lack of knowledge, non-identification by the flight crew of the true nature of the problem which was the reason for not taking corrective action, which then resulted in incapacitation of the flight crew due to hypoxia. Before the flight, the ground engineer on duty failed to reset the pressurization system to the auto mode on completion of the test.

The three accidents described can be seen as a paradigm of human errors that could have been prevented by advanced technologies and automation in a supporting role, which means that automation is highly paramount but not to the extent of removing the human out of the cockpit. Automation, which entails a multitude of safeguards into the aircraft systems, shall mean the replacement of a human function only, either manual or cognitive, with a machine function. However, keeping the pilots in the loop is a mandatory requirement for any automated function. With regard to all functions, application of CRM principles by the flight crew must be observed.

That professional pilots in the cockpit, with all their knowledge, skills, experience, training, resource management, teamwork and creativity, are still paramount, has been confirmed by the following incidents and accidents.

First of all, British Airways Flight BA009 (call sign Speedbird 9), a Boeing 747-236B en route from London Heathrow Airport to Auckland Airport, New Zealand, with stopovers in Bombay, Kuala Lumpur, Perth and Melbourne, flew into a cloud of volcanic ash thrown

---

64   The Hellenic Air Accident Investigation and Aviation Safety Board (AAIASB) is the air accident investigation agency of Greece (EAAAII).

up by the eruption of Mount Galunggung 180 km southeast of Jakarta, Indonesia, resulting in the failure of all four engines.

The event occurred at night obscuring the ash cloud which was the reason that it was not immediately clear to the flight crew what caused the engines to flame out. While descending, a high Indonesian mountain range needed to be crossed safely to land at Jakarta. The flight crew initially decided that if the aircraft was unable to maintain altitude by the time they reached 12,000 feet, they would make a turn to the sea and attempt to ditch into the Indian Ocean. Fortunately, after gliding out of the ash cloud, all engines were restarted only after several attempts, although one engine failed again. Notwithstanding that, the flight crew managed to make a safe landing at Halim Perdanakusuma International Airport in Jakarta.

Secondly, talking about an imminent ditching, a remarkable, even astonishing accident took place on 15 January 2009 when US Airways Flight US1549 (call sign Cactus 1549), an Airbus A320-214, ditched in the Hudson River of Midtown Manhattan. After take-off to the northeast from New York City La Guardia Airport bound for Charlotte Douglas International Airport with a direct onward service to Seattle-Tacoma International Airport, the aircraft struck a formation of Canada geese at an altitude of approximately 2,800 feet. Passengers and crew members heard very loud bangs and saw flames coming out of both engines, followed by a strange awkward silence. What remained was the smell of burning birds and fuel fumes that filled the passenger's cabin.

The aircraft commander assumed control, realizing that both engines had shut down, while the first officer immediately worked the checklist for engine restart. During the engines-out glide, the aircraft commander informed ATC about the loss of thrust on both engines. An immediate turn to La Guardia for landing, given the low altitude, was not considered, from that position, to be feasible. The second landing option, Teterboro Airport in nearby New Jersey, was out of range due to decreasing altitude while gliding at less than 900 feet near the George Washington Bridge. The third and final option was a smooth unpowered ditching on the Hudson River which turned out to be a successful crash landing, roughly opposite West 50th Street near the Intrepid Sea, Air & Space Museum.[65]

While gliding at low altitude to the ditching area, despite being unable to complete the so-called engine dual failure checklist, the aircraft commander started the auxiliary power unit, which improved the outcome of the ditching by ensuring that a primary source of electric power was available to the aircraft and that the aircraft remained in normal law and maintained the flight envelope protections, one of which protects against a stall. The

---

65   FAA Memorandum, 2 February 2009, Aircraft Accident File N90-TRACON-0122. New York Terminal Radar Approach Control Facility. Full Transcript Aircraft Accident AWE 1549, New York City, 15 January 2009.

aircraft commander's decision to ditch on the Hudson River rather than attempting to land at the nearest runway provided the highest probability that the accident would be survivable. It was clear early on that the only place that was large enough, wide enough, smooth enough to land a jet airliner was the Hudson River.[66] After the ditching, the decision turned out to be successful.

> There can't be a checklist for everything. Procedural compliance is a necessary but not sufficient condition for safety.[67]

Furthermore, the professionalism of the flight crew members and their excellent CRM during the accident sequence contributed to their ability to maintain control of the aircraft, configure it to the extent possible under the circumstances and fly an approach that increased the survivability of the impact.[68]

Documents released by the NTSB revealed that according to Airbus, the aircraft manufacturer, simulator trials under the same conditions showed that if the aircraft commander had immediately attempted to make a turn to La Guardia Airport after ingesting geese into both engines, the Airbus A320 would have made it, although, barely. In that scenario, the aircraft commander would have to make an immediate decision while little or no time was left to assess the situation.

Moreover, he could not have known that he would be successful, and therefore would have risked the possibility of a catastrophic crash in a densely populated area of the city, the Bronx. Although an emergency return to La Guardia runway 13 was technically feasible from an aircraft performance point of view, the emergency landing on the ice-cold Hudson River tidal estuary seemed the most appropriate decision according to Airbus.

The NTSB determined that the probable cause of this accident was the ingestion of large birds into each engine, which resulted in an almost total loss of thrust in both engines and the subsequent ditching on the Hudson River. Everyone on board survived the crash landing. Nearby ferry boats rescued all 155 people on board. Contributing to the survivability of the accident was the decision making of the flight crew members and their CRM during the accident sequence.[69]

Thirdly, a dramatic accident of British Airways Flight BA38 (call sign Speedbird 38), a Boeing 777-236ER, occurred at London Heathrow Airport on 17 January 2008. While on

---

66   Testimony of Captain C.B. Sullenberger III (born 23 January 1951) during the Hearing on US Airways Flight 1549 accident, Tuesday, 24 February 2009.

67   Captain Chesley Burnett "Sully" Sullenberger III, interview with Roger Rapoport and Shem Malmquist, April 2021.

68   NTSB.2010. Loss of Thrust in Both Engines After Encountering a Flock of Birds and Subsequent Ditching on the Hudson River, US Airways Flight 1549, Airbus A320-214, N106US, Weehawken, NJ, 15 January 2009. Aircraft Accident Report NTSB/AAR-10/03, Washington, DC.

69   Documents released by the NTSB. CBS News, 4 May 2010.

approach to Heathrow from Beijing Capital International Airport, China, at 720 feet above ground level (AGL), the right engine ceased responding to autothrottle commands for increased engine power, and instead the power reduced considerably. Seven seconds later, the left engine power reduced as well. The total thrust reduction led to a loss of airspeed.

In attempting to maintain the glideslope of the instrument landing system (ILS), the autopilot sacrificed more and more airspeed to a critical point, the stalling speed. The autopilot disconnected at 150 feet, as the first officer took manual control. Meanwhile, the aircraft commander reduced the flap setting from 30° to 25° to reduce the drag on the aircraft and stretch the glide. This rapid decision and action, based on aerodynamic knowledge, allowed the aircraft to clear the A30 Great South-West Road and the Airport Southern Perimeter Road and to barely miss the ILS beacon within the airport perimeter, thus avoiding more substantial damage. Ten seconds before touchdown, the stick shaker operated, indicating that the aircraft was nearing a stall, and in response, the first officer pushed the control column forward reducing the aircraft's nose-high pitch attitude before the aircraft crashlanded on the grass some 300 metres short of the paved surface of runway 27L. Three seconds before touchdown, the aircraft commander transmitted a 'mayday' call. The cause of the accident was purely technical, *in casu*, the recorded fuel flows showed that both engines had suffered restrictions in the fuel delivery system to the engine.[70]

Finally, an impressive piece of airmanship of the flight crew of a Qantas Airbus A380-842 with registration number VH-OQA, who ensured that all passengers and the crew survived an unprecedented in-flight complex multiple system failure. On 4 November 2010, Qantas Flight 32 (call sign Qantas 32) sustained an uncontained engine rotor failure (UERF) of the no. 2 engine, a Rolls-Royce Trent 900, while climbing through 7,000 feet AGL, four minutes after departure from Singapore's Changi International Airport on its way to Sydney Kingsford Smith International Airport, New South Wales. The disintegration was accompanied by a very rare uncontained explosion. Debris of the liberated Intermediate Pressure (IP) turbine disc penetrated the left wing and the left wing-to-fuselage fairing, affected control systems and heavily punctured two main wing fuel tanks, resulting in significant structural and systems damage to the aircraft, and losing the ability to transfer fuel between different fuel tanks for balancing purposes.

Against all odds, the flight crew members, expertly assisted by supernumerary A380 Qantas flight crew members on board, a paradigm of impressive leadership and successful collaborative decision making, facing life-threatening and extremely complex system failures, managed to land the aircraft safely at Changi Airport after nearly two hours of continuous monitoring of a multitude of electronic centralized aircraft monitor (ECAM)

---

70   Aircraft Accident Report 1/2010. Report on the Accident to Boeing 777-236ER, G-MMM, at London Heathrow Airport on 17 January 2008. Air Accidents Investigation Branch of the Department for Transport (EW/C2008/01/01).

messages and checklists reading, assessments, analysing systems interaction, sharing aerodynamic as well as technical knowledge, flight performance calculations, logic and experience, restore actions required for most of the major system failures and emergency landing procedures preparation (heavy weight, high approach and landing airspeed due to wing slats failure, unavailable engines reverse thrust and badly degraded brakes) while flying a holding pattern close to the airport.[71]

The last four accidents all came to a successful end by what is called in aviation: airmanship. It proves again that humans, professional pilots in the aircraft cockpit, are capable of making the right decision usually within a very short time often under extremely difficult circumstances. Although humans are far from being perfect sensors, it must be known that aircraft commanders in particular, as professional decision-makers, possess a number of invaluable attributes, the most significant of which are their ability to reason effectively in the face of uncertainty and also their capacity for abstract and conceptual analysis of an emergency situation. Humans, considered as intelligent creatures, who are facing a new situation, will swiftly and, as a rule, successfully respond to this unusual situation, thus providing a degree of flexibility that cannot now and may never be attained by computational systems.

The thinking pattern of humans is still hard to emulate or imitate by these systems. The most advanced interactive computer systems including AI are able to store and process huge amount of data covering static information about a particular aircraft and its systems, technical characteristics, flight plan data, layout information about numerous suitable airports, approach and departure procedures, aircraft technical manuals, meteorological conditions, aircraft normal and emergency procedures, applicable background statistics, registration of practical experiences, information assessment processes, models and procedures for data and knowledge processing, sequences of problem solutions or alternatives.

Interactive computer systems, intelligent decision support systems (IDSSs), based on AI technology and methods, are designed to support various activities of the flight crew. Special support will be given to the pilots, in particular the aircraft commander, during the decision making process on ill-structured and unstructured problems.

AI can help in the reduction of aircraft accidents. Deep learning (DL), a subset of machine learning, is an advanced technique based on AI that emulates the human brain working to process data and generate patterns to decision making on a particular problem. Computer vision and natural language processing are among a wide range of DL

---

71   *See* ATSB Australian Transport Safety Bureau. Aviation Safety Investigations & Reports. Investigation Number: AO-2010-089 In flight uncontained engine failure Airbus A380-842, VH-OQA, overhead Batam Island, Indonesia, 4 November 2010.

applications that could benefit aviation. Machine learning, which is the use of data to train algorithms to improve their performance, assists in data and pattern analysis through AI data mining by making use of enormous data sets (big data) to identify trends and patterns, and is able to bring the learning capability a bit closer to the function of the human brain, for example decision making with or without human intervention.[72]

This kind of automation, a technique in which processing is carried out without any or minimal human intervention, should be considered fourth generation of aircraft automation. From a technological point of view, automation, to almost any degree, has been gradually introduced in aircraft cockpits over time.

In the early years of aviation, automation was initially aimed at stabilizing aircraft attitude through the control of aerodynamic surfaces. This requirement was met with gyroscopic devices which were used to maintain the attitude of the aircraft for all (three-dimensional) spatial axes for a long time. During World War II, vacuum-driven gyroscopes were used intensively providing information about the heading and attitude in the cockpit resulting in a reduction of manual control requirements, which in turn alleviated fatigue. Noteworthy, in 5 years, the war gave to electronics an impetus and boost that some 15 years of peaceful development might not have given.

Electrical systems and amplifiers replaced the old-fashioned gyros. In the 1950s, rapid technological development came about. Especially the introduction of the ILS permitted the coupling of autopilots to the output signals of this system's localizer and glideslope beams.

The increase in speed and altitude capability of commercial air transport jet aircraft required more accurate and trustworthy aircraft systems and precise flight instruments. Examples of automatic devices without any pilot intervention are yaw dampers, to dampen (aileron-rudder synchronization) undesirable tendencies such as oscillating in a repetitive roll and yaw motion of the aircraft, a well-known phenomenon called Dutch roll, and a Mach trim to counteract the tendency to pitch down at high Mach numbers (tuck-under effect or Mach tuck).

Flight director systems, which integrated attitude and navigational information into a single instrument as well as basic autothrottle systems found their way into the cockpit. From the 1960s, advances in solid-state electronics made it possible to make automatic landings using autopilots, flight directors, radio altimeters and autothrottle integrated in an autoland system, often applied in a threefold structure to incorporate a high degree of redundancy and, therefore, safety.

In the 1970s, the so-called glass-cockpit was introduced. This type of cockpit is equipped with electronic displays, called an electronic (digital) flight instrument system

---

72   EASA Artificial Intelligence Roadmap, Version 1.0, Chapter E Impact of Machine Learning (ML) on aviation, 1. Aircraft design and operation.

(EFIS), linked to computers which allow data from multiple sources to be processed. In this type of cockpit, flight data is shown on electronic flight displays (EFDs) like the primary flight display (PFD) which combines data from several instruments and is the pilot's primary source of flight information and the multifunction flight display which allows data to be presented to the flight crew on multiple pages.

These displays (LCD) are driven by flight management systems (FMSs) that can be adjusted to display flight information as needed. In case of EFIS failure, standby analog flight instruments will still provide basic flight information. Another feature introduced was the electronic sidestick controller, located on the side console of the pilot in aircraft equipped with fly-by-wire control systems.

With respect to advanced automation, fully autonomous aircraft flight management controlling the entire flight has proved feasible. In 2018, Airbus started its A350-1000 test aircraft fully automatic taxi, take-off and landing (ATTOL) project, one of the technological flight demonstrators being tested in order to understand the impact of autonomy on aircraft. The project was successfully performed in 2020 by demonstrating fully automated, vision-based take-offs and landings controlled by onboard image recognition technology. Findings indicate that it certainly assists air transport flight crews to focus less on aircraft operations and more on strategic ADM as well as mission management. An additional drawback of this advanced technology seems to be the flight crew's mind numbing monitoring function.

Except in predefined situations, automation should never assume command and, in those situations, it must be able to be discontinued easily. Automation must remain subordinate to the human supervisor. However, the fully automated and autonomous flight operation of conventional aircraft systems is from a technological point of view feasible. In the quest for autonomous flights, EASA conditionally predicts the following time frame: from approximately 2022 to 2025, assistance and augmentation of the flight crew, a scenario encompassing a gradual transition trajectory to single-pilot operations in the context of the concept of reduced crew operations (RCO) by using a virtual pilot assistant (VPA) system instead of the second pilot disappearing completely from the cockpit.

This concept is being introduced to compensate for a so-called expected shortage of pilots, which, incidentally, is an unconvincing argument. Meanwhile, initiatives are being developed to reduce the safety risks associated with this kind of flight operation. Up to this time (2023), most commercial air traffic is required by law to be operated by not less than two pilots in the cockpit (multiple pilot operations), especially above certain weight classes. This kind of operation is legally enshrined in both European and American regulations, but there are plans for change.

Another concept that falls within RCO is called extended minimum crew operations (eMCOs). With this particular method, it is researched whether it is possible to carry out the take-off and landing phases with a normal crew, but that at cruising level only one pilot will perform all actions while the other pilot is resting, either in the cockpit or in a flight crew rest area.

In Europe, EASA is considering approval of limited single-pilot operation for parts of the flight as early as 2027. The objective is that two pilots would be in the cockpit for the more demanding parts of the flight, such as take-off and landing, but solo flying would be possible in the less demanding cruise phase of the flight. This kind of operation is only reserved for the most advanced aircraft, equipped with a higher level of safety than required by minimum certification standards. The VPA performs a real-time assessment of the single pilot's cognitive states and provides useful and timely alerts based on predictions on the performance levels of the pilot in control. In case of an emergency or pilot incapacitation, the pilot taking rest will be alerted to resume control of the aircraft. However, to safeguard this time-consuming action and possible pilot incapacitation in case of loss of cabin pressure, an advanced control function will automatically initiate an emergency descent, unless one of the flight crew members is able to respond immediately to this emergency according to applicable memory items. An autonomous automatic landing at the nearest suitable aerodrome based on new technologies is very well possible. Yet, the challenges with respect to full-flight single-pilot operations are considered substantial because even during crucial flight phases, only one pilot is controlling the aircraft. In that case, there is no longer any possibility to correct or alert each other, which means that all cockpit procedures, including the underlying philosophy and current CRM principles, must be rewritten. The total absence of interaction between colleagues can lead to mental problems, the loss of sharing knowledge, experience, just culture mentality and reduced protection against any criminal action.

A transition to single-pilot operation in less demanding phases of flight will need approval of ICAO, airlines, IATA, national pilot associations, IFALPA and other regulatory bodies as well as public acceptance. PF experience and medical condition will also be limiting factors. The full transition, which means single-pilot operation throughout the flight has been positively ruled out by EASA before 2030. Full-flight single-pilot operations could impact areas such as crew training, medical requirements as well as mental health and job satisfaction. EASA predicts from 2025 human-machine collaboration, which means semi-autonomous flights with human supervision and from 2035+ autonomous commercial air transport operations, all under certain conditions.[73]

The rapid development of unmanned aircraft systems (UAS), a general term, shows the possibilities of remotely piloted aircraft systems, a subset of UAS, that will be piloted from

---

73   EASA Artificial Intelligence Roadmap, Version 1.0, Chapter F, Timeframe.

one of many possible remote human-operated stations usually located on the ground, on a ship, on board another airborne platform or in space.

The regulatory framework, so far developed by ICAO, is formed within the context of Article 8 of the Chicago Convention, amended by the ICAO Assembly (Doc. 7300). Article 8 states:

> Pilotless aircraft.
> No aircraft capable of being flown without a pilot shall be flown without a pilot over the territory of a contracting State without special authorization by that State and in accordance with the terms of such authorization. Each contracting State and in accordance with the terms of flight of such aircraft without a pilot in regions open to civil aircraft shall be so controlled as to obviate danger to civil aircraft.

It means that all unmanned aircraft, whether remotely piloted, fully autonomous or a combination thereof, are subject to the provisions of Article 8. Only remotely piloted aircraft will be able to integrate into the international civil aviation system, which means a safe and seamless integration into non-segregated airspace and aerodromes, albeit after special authorizations. However, RPAS cannot include fully autonomous systems according to ICAO because autonomous aircraft do not allow pilot intervention in the management of the flight. Remote pilots, however, must be able to override automated functions, except where such actions cannot be executed safely due to immediacy of the situation, for example, in case of imminent collision avoidance manoeuvres or where the complexity of a task makes human intervention unreasonable.[74]

In order to meet the authorization requirements of Contracting States, UAS must comply with identified minimum requirements, like certificates of airworthiness, licensed personnel, and documents carried in aircraft, needed to fly within the airspace open to traditional manned aircraft. However, the requirement that any aircraft, including unmanned aerial vehicles, the flying elements of UAS, must carry such documents on board is practically impossible for very small UAVs or drones.

The commercial UAS market is expected to develop significantly. The use, with a variety of options, will increase as public confidence in safety and reliance grows, and new regulations and technical specifications are developed for flights initially intended for the

---

74   ICAO Remotely Piloted Aircraft System (RPAS) Concept of Operations (CONOPS) for International IFR Operations, 2.6.2 Automation and Human Intervention.

lower parts of civil airspace. UAS operation in very low level airspace is supported by unmanned traffic management (UTM) airspace or U-space.[75]

U-space, a European project, is a set of specific services and procedures designed to ensure safe and efficient access to airspace for a large number of UAS based on high levels of digitalization and automation entailing greater complexity.

The purpose of U-space is therefore to achieve automated UAS management and integration, allowing for a comprehensive series of operations, many of them even simultaneous and, all of this, in harmonious coexistence with the current air traffic management (ATM) system. The principal objective of the international U-space regulatory framework is to achieve and maintain the highest possible uniform level of safety.[76]

While UAS are well suited to dull, dirty, dangerous or difficult civil applications that otherwise can have an adverse effect on human health, there is a much wider potential scope for pilotless aircraft. Within segregated airspace, urban air mobility, battery-powered air parcel delivery, air metros and air taxis between and within cities are not only feasible but are about to be introduced (from 2024 to 2025). To support these new applications of unmanned air transport, the need for a specific infrastructure will increase to make the future UAS landscape look very different from the simple UAS activities of today. In this context, one can think of so-called vertiports with multiple take-off and landing pads for people and package air transportation by cutting edge electrically powered unmanned autonomous electric vertical take-off and landing (eVTOL) aircraft, service centres where such UAS can be stored, inspected, maintained and repaired, battery-charging stations and distribution hubs to store and (off)load goods for last-mile delivery.[77]

There are also critical assessment points regarding the feasibility of UAS activities such as urban parcel delivery and air taxi services. In an urban context with a well-developed conventional transport system, especially in the metropolises of Europe, travel time of air taxis flying the shortest possible route to its inner city destinations often does not make a big difference. Moreover, intensive urban air mobility needs an extensive ATM capacity to meet safety requirements. Another point of attention is how and where to implement the necessary physical infrastructure in a densely populated area.

In the foreseeable future, the parcel delivery and air taxi mode will be followed by RPA operations to include transportation of cargo and ultimately passengers, only if appropriate

---

75   See ICAO Circular 328-AN/190 Unmanned Aircraft Systems (UAS), 2011. Chapter 3 Overview of UAS, pp. 7-9.

76   See ECAC UASBulletin #02, December 2021, What is U-space? The new EU regulatory framework for U-space.

77   Cohn, P., et al., "Commercial Drones Are Here: The Future of Unmanned Aerial Systems," (2017) McKinsey & Company, December 2017, pp. 7-9.

regulatory frameworks are in place and moral, ethical, cyber security barriers as well as societal acceptance will have to be overcome. Regarding the last point, the level of acceptance of UAS operations among the general public remains consistently low according to the latest representative survey about this topic, held in Germany.[78]

The results of another survey with regard to the question on participants' comfort level with fully autonomous flights showed that the majority of the participants were uncomfortable with fully autonomous aircraft operations. This technology is not perceived with a positive connotation, in other words, the emotions associated with this technology had a largely negative connotation, according to the results. Even participants who were uncomfortable with single-pilot aircraft operations responded the same way to fully autonomous aircraft operations.[79]

According to industry forecasts, UAS operations will increase exponentially once they are fully integrated into non-segregated airspace. Expert discussions about the question regarding the future of unmanned air cargo operations revealed that there are opportunities to initially create niche unmanned aircraft transport operations. These operations would provide more information on whether this kind of transport would be economically viable, competitive, safe and secure. Moreover, a stumbling block could be the considerable time required for the regulatory process to allow for these on-demand mobility operations.

Seen from this point of view, together with the current and future strong expansion of conventional full freighters and passenger aircraft with spare belly hold capacity, largely because of global e-commerce, it is quite unlikely that intercontinental IFR UAS heavy cargo operations would be developed over a short term. For this special branch of intercontinental cargo transport operations, it is most probably hard to offer a more cost-effective solution. However, some more profitable opportunities may arise for regional cargo operations to hard-to-reach destinations or areas with substandard or heavily congested infrastructure, in particular for the so-called last-mile deliveries.[80]

The absence of an onboard pilot introduces new considerations with respect to the fulfilment of safety-related responsibilities such as incorporation of technologies for detect and avoid, command and control, communications with air traffic control stations and prevention of onboard or remote unintended or unlawful interference.

---

78   Dannenberger, N., *et al.*, "Traffic Solution or Technical hype? Representative Population Survey on Delivery Drones and Air Taxis in Germany," Unpublished.doi:10.13140/RG.2.2.17542.40003. Project: The Sky is the Limit: Future use of urban airspace (*Sky Limits*) by Kellermann, R., *et al.* (January 2019-December 2020).

79   Wollert, M., *Public Perception of Autonomous Aircraft*, A Thesis Presented in Partial Fulfillment of the Requirements for the Degree Master of Science in Technology (Arizona State University, May 2018), pp. 45-46.

80   *See* "Is There a Future for Unmanned Air Cargo Operations?", *Air Cargo News*, 23 May 2016.

In this regard, ICAO deems a legally mandatory human responsibility for, and with authority over, the flight of UAS, taking into account that the responsible remote-aircraft commander can override the flight mode at any time when necessary.

Technologies are continuously evolving in a way that humans will play a minor role in managing the aircraft while automation will take an ever-increasing share in aircraft operations, both manned and unmanned, and will reduce and maintain the possibility of harm to persons or damage to property at or below an acceptable level. This is done by means of a continuous process of hazard identification and safety risk management.

However, the era of fully autonomous passenger airliners, performed according to a pre-planned flight path profile, including ground movement, take-off, climb, cruise flight, approach and landing, within controlled non-segregated airspace and aerodromes, is still far from reality. To ensure a safe flight, autonomous aircraft will inevitably rely on systems to enable complex decision making. At the current state of technology, AI will enable full autonomy in this field. Very powerful algorithms will be necessary to cope with the huge amount of data, generated by sensors and machine-to-machine communications.

AI-based computer vision and machine-learning technologies are crucial to make this kind of air transportation practical. Hitherto, typical human skills, feelings, creativity and mindsets cannot be matched by robotics, despite ongoing machine learning. Moreover, like any digital network, the connection from the robot-sensing unit through its data link to the cloud service can be attacked and manipulated by cyberattacks. Therefore, risk mitigation must be assured through integrated security systems.[81]

Another meaningful issue, which must be taken into account, is the absence of a pilot, more specifically the aircraft commander, on board an autonomous or remotely controlled air transport aircraft and the associated consequences, apart from the above-mentioned social barriers, with regard to authority and responsibility for the safe conduct of flight.

The Tokyo Convention regime, and in particular the 1963 Tokyo Convention, is playing an important international role regarding safety and security in aviation. For the first time in the history of international air law, it is the Tokyo Convention that recognized certain powers and immunities of the aircraft commander.[82]

---

81 Rosteck, T., "Robots Need More Human Skills: Connected and Equipped with Sensors and AI Capabilities, Machines Can Cooperatively Work With People. Together, They Can Increase Productivity and Sustainability," (2022) *IoT World Today*, 13 May 2022.

82 The Tokyo Convention regime comprises of the 1963 Tokyo Convention, the 1970 The Hague Convention (Convention for the Suppression of Unlawful Seizure of Aircraft), the 1971 Montreal Convention (Convention for the Suppression of Unlawful Acts against the Safety of Civil Aviation), the 1988 Montreal Protocol (Protocol for the Suppression of Unlawful Acts of Violence at Airports Serving International Civil Aviation), the 2010 Beijing Convention (Convention on the Suppression of Unlawful Acts Relating to International Civil Aviation), the 2010 Beijing Protocol (Protocol Supplementary to the Convention for the Suppression of Unlawful Seizure of Aircraft) and the 2014 Montreal Protocol (Protocol to Amend the

However, pilotless aircraft lack the authority, powers and immunities of the aircraft commander laid down in Chapter III of the Tokyo Convention. The aircraft commander is authorized, under certain conditions, to impose reasonable measures including restraint upon a person who has committed or is about to commit, on board the aircraft in flight, an offence against penal law or act which, whether or not it is an offence, may or do jeopardize the safety of the aircraft or of persons or property therein or which jeopardizes good order and discipline on board.

Furthermore, the aircraft commander may disembark and deliver such a person, under certain conditions, to the competent authorities of any Contracting State in the territory of which the aircraft makes a landing. A pilotless aircraft, however, is only controlled by a human remote pilot from any remote station or is controlled by a robotic system that fully replaces the human capacities, such as sense organs, including vision, and human powers. In other words, the resultant is that physical presence in the aircraft cockpit or cabin of a human, vested with certain powers, has ceased to exist. Unmistakably, both capacities having control over the aircraft, *in casu* the remote pilot as well as the robotic pilot, lack these on the spot powers and sensing capabilities as conferred on the traditional aircraft commander.

In the near future, robotic controlled aircraft can have different sizes and capacities, ranging from an autonomous eVTOL air taxi carrying 5 passengers to, for instance, a fully autonomous Airbus A350-1000 capable of carrying around 400 passengers or, in freight configuration, a payload of approximately 110 tonnes.

This futuristic approach will have far-reaching consequences for the enforceability of a number of provisions laid down in the Tokyo Convention, certain supplements and amendments to this international legal instrument. It remains indisputably of paramount importance that pilotless passenger aircraft, whether it is an autonomous urban air taxi or a passenger carrying aircraft like the Airbus A350, needs a kind of protection or security mode, a person, an experienced aviator invested with powers, as is the case with conventional passenger aircraft, for reasons of potential criminal conduct on board.

It will be a trade-off between the rapid pace of development of pilotless aircraft technology and lengthy negotiations, in particular on international regulations and treaties involving multiple States with different proposals, interests, ideologies and cultures. Technologies supporting capabilities of fully autonomous aircraft, such as intelligent self-adaptive behaviour for dynamic learning and autonomous decision making, largely through the integration of increasingly powerful microprocessors, specific

---

Convention on Offences and Certain Other Acts Committed on Board Aircraft). Significant private international instruments related to civil aviation, which may well be applicable to UAS, include the 1929 Warsaw Convention (Convention for the Unification of Certain Rules Relating to International Carriage by Air) and the 1952 Rome Convention (Convention on Damage Caused by Foreign Aircraft to Third Parties on the Surface).

types of algorithms, also known as artificial neural networks (ANNs), or simulated neural networks (SNNs) and DL neural networks (DLNNs), but also the introduction and use of next-generation all-solid-state batteries (SSBs) that advanced more rapidly than any innovation in history, in fact have outpaced the anthropocentric law.

It means that for the time being, these novices are inadequately supported by a dedicated and enforceable regime of rules, regulations and standards with regard to their safe integration into non-segregated airspace and aerodromes. Despite legal uncertainties, ICAO, as a coordinating global organization, will play an important role in keeping up the principal objectives of the Chicago Convention that stand for the promotion of safety and the orderly development of international civil aviation, both conventional manned aircraft and unmanned (pilotless) aircraft operations.[83]

The answer to this practical issue are a set of guiding principles, a non-binding source of international aviation law principles and best practices, intended as a preliminary step to conclude international treaties. The advantages of guiding principles are their efficiency, cost effectiveness and uncomplicated amendment procedure while the disadvantages are the lack of a legally binding force and compliance by States.[84]

In addition to the guiding principles, the ICAO Council adopted new and amended SARPs in a number of Annexes to the Chicago Convention pertaining to the unique characteristics of unmanned aircraft, in particular RPA, about licensing, safety, interoperability, certification, communication and rules of the air with the objective of sharing existing airspace with conventional aircraft.

Certification of RPAS is intended for international cargo operations. Furthermore, advanced capabilities are anticipated for future UAS. The ICAO Council expects that all 19 Annexes will eventually require either significant or minor modification to achieve a safe, secure and efficient integration of RPAS into the current global aviation framework.[85] In line with this, it will be a matter of time for international legal instruments like civil aviation conventions to be adapted for the purpose of flight safety during fully autonomous unmanned aircraft operations, carrying cargo and ultimately passengers.

Yet, human barriers as public perception, distrust and criticism still cling to those state-of-the-art operations. Improving reliability is the key to gaining the confidence of the general public. Today and for the time being, in the near future, it will be very reassuring to the public's confidence to know that a skilled and experienced onboard aircraft commander is flying the aircraft. Most potential, even stouthearted airline passengers are quite reluctant to give full control to a three-dimensional moving robotic

---

83   *See* ICAO Doc. A40-WP/268, EX/111, 1/8/19, Artificial Intelligence and Digitalization in Aviation.

84   Hodgkinson, D. & Johnston, R., *Aviation Law and Drones: Unmanned Aircraft and the Future of Aviation* (Milton Park, Abingdon, Oxon: Routledge, 2018), pp. 97-98.

85   *See* ICAO Council makes progress on new remotely piloted aircraft system (RPAS) standards, Montreal, 1 March 2021.

air machine that theoretically could kill them. These apprehensions are much less common in contemporary two-dimensional road or rail-bound fully autonomous public transportation.[86]

Nevertheless, in the reasonably near future, fully autonomous aircraft operations, carrying cargo and/or passengers are technically feasible. From a scientific point of view, advanced technology is about to be capable of realizing operations of this transport mode without human supervision or intervention. Multiple sensors like computer vision cameras, forward-looking infrared sensors (FLIRs), light detection and ranging or laser imaging detection and ranging (LIDAR) radar, detect and avoid systems, combined with current maps and GPS-aided navigation, computers able to process huge amounts of real-time data together with software, including AI-based systems, coupled with aircraft FMSs and external systems such as ATC/ATM as well as Internet of Things (IoT) via direct data link, all allow for fully autonomous, rather than just highly automated, commercial air transportation.[87] The incorporation of systems based on AI and IoT in autonomous aircraft will not only drastically reduce the accidents and damages to such aircraft, but will increase the precision and efficiency in the autonomous operation.

> With autonomy, the machine can say no to the human. It's capable of making authoritative decisions and being independent. (Prof. Ella Atkins, Aerospace and Engineering at the University of Michigan)

Selected computer models and algorithms, expanding the capabilities of aircraft by augmenting onboard decision making systems, are able to address complex problems or worst-case scenarios, because of unexpected or unusual events, by means of instantaneous emergency flight planning within milliseconds, which is potentially life-saving. Obviously, ultra-high technology emergency flight planning eliminates precious loss of time inherent to the human startle effect, the physical and mental responses to a sudden unexpected stimulus. In aviation, the startle effect can be defined as an uncontrollable, automatic reflex that is elicited by exposure to sudden, intense events that violate a pilot's expectations. The mental responses, the ability to consciously process the sensory information to evaluate the situation and then take appropriate action, can be much slower than the purely automatic and almost instantaneous physical responses.

---

86   *See* Pakusch, C. & Bossauer, P., "User Acceptance of Fully Autonomous Public Transport." *Department of Management Sciences, Bonn-Rhein-Sieg University*, Sankt Augustin, Germany, ICE-B 2017 14th International Conference on e-Bussiness, 4.2 Intention to Use Fully Autonomous Transport, 5. Conclusion and Implications.

87   Atkins, E., Director of U-M's Autonomous Aerospace Systems (A2SYS) Lab, "The Future of Autonomous Aircraft," (2020) *College of Engineering*, University of Michigan, 1 December 2020.

The human processing of sensory information can be severely hampered or even overwhelmed through intense physiological responses, resulting in deteriorating processing performance. Thereby, if human tasks become more complex, the duration of such degradation could have disastrous consequences for decision making and the safety of flight. Airline pilots may be exposed to a variety of stimuli such as explosive decompression, bird strike, lightning strike or multiple engine failure that have the potential to elicit the startle reflex, sometimes causing disorientation and confusion for a brief period accompanied by task interruption, requiring immediate cognitive recovery, reorientation and task resumption. As opposed to human flaws, algorithms lack these specific shortcomings or emotional influences. In essence, an algorithm is a set of instructions for achieving a desired goal, and is used for data processing, to perform automated reasoning and decision making.

Stringent regulations, preferably on an international level, have to be followed by manufacturers for safety and security purposes regarding autonomous operations. Overall safety must be guaranteed under extremely harsh environmental conditions, especially the effects of adverse weather phenomena like snow, dust or sandstorms, extreme heat, night or low visibility, even IFR, conditions. Passengers' safety and security in fully autonomous (pilotless) aircraft operations are decidedly crucial issues: not only flight safety in non-segregated airspace and aerodromes but also liability to third parties on the surface (1952 Rome Convention) or a security issue as the threat from cyber attacks.

With respect to autonomy, accident prevention in autonomous flight operations needs systems and architecture convincingly capable of avoiding operational risks such as physical security and cyber risks. Essential safety requirements are, for example algorithm-based collision avoidance, recognition of hazards and threats, combined traffic management, robotic monitored self-diagnostic reparation and maintenance, early failure detection, meteorological real-time information, up-to-date database and historical data in a reference base.

For safety reasons, the use of monitoring devices and ultra-high accuracy sensors in autonomous aircraft operations will be indispensable and of vital importance. The design of groundbreaking redundant, fail-safe sensory technology and state-of-the-art monitoring equipment is therefore paramount.

Data link communication and natural language processing (NLP) technology and automatic speech recognition (ASR) by artificial intelligence and machine learning, for ATC and pilot communications, if accurate enough, are key items when it comes to improve safety in a critical environment as non-segregated airspace.

With today's advanced computer technology, a modern aircraft is perfectly able to perform a fully autonomous flight profile, from the departure terminal gate to the assigned arrival terminal gate at the destination airport. This entire fully autonomous flight operation includes cockpit pre-flight checks, automatic checklists completion, ATC data link communications, engines start up, ground manoeuvring and take-off, climb, cruise, descent, approach and landing, taxiing in, engines shut down, as well as all other actions required to solve any emerging problem.

Fully autonomous unmanned aircraft must be able to comply with the requirements of the class of airspace in which they operate. It can be expected that these aircraft transit all classes of airspace, cross international borders, and operate to and from both controlled and uncontrolled aerodromes. To operate under IFR, these aircraft should be capable of flying the published instrument departure and arrival procedures along with conventional manned aircraft. Obviously, fully autonomous unmanned aircraft need to be equipped in conformity with standing rules and have the required operational approvals in terms of required performance for navigation, communication and surveillance, which is mandatory in the airspace class within which they plan to operate. For ground manoeuvring, apart from radar and sensor guidance, they need the ability to detect and respond to visual signs and markings.

To summarize, a number of most important requirements are necessary to validly, safely, securely and responsibly integrate fully autonomous unmanned aircraft operations into non-segregated airspace and aerodromes. Such integration requires extensive legislative challenges to be addressed. Drafting of rules and regulations, preferably on an international level, and the availability of spectrum for innovative and flexible commercial use, are fundamental to the success of this advanced mode of air transportation. After all, the development of this emerging air transportation market will largely depend on the successful implementation of an up-to-date comprehensive regulatory framework.

Moreover, a complex set of most highly advanced technologies need to be mature enough to ensure full integration into the conventional aviation system. However, implementation of state-of-the-art technologies and expected benefits would evolve over a period of time depending on the present aviation infrastructures in various States and regions, and the overall requirements of the aviation stakeholders. With regard to the issue of overall safety versus state-of-the-art technologies, the task is to balance technological innovations with safety concerns.

A review about modern conventional aircraft cockpits shows that various technical systems take over tasks that were previously carried out by the flight crew. The new concept has made the pilot to move further away from actually flying the aircraft to the tasks of programming and monitoring aircraft automation. But the irony of automation is that psychological effects, such as decreased attention, boredom, automated control induced complacency and overreliance, of the passive role of the monitoring pilot may cause multiple safety problems.

However, if the human factors-related issues, such as the limited performance of the human as monitor and effects on motivation, are properly addressed, there may be a justification for automation. It may contribute to improved aircraft and system performance and overall efficiency of flight operations, and relieve the flight crew of certain tasks. Moreover, there are situations in which it is conditionally accepted that automation should perform tasks fully autonomously. To make this scenario complete, it can very well be applied to unmanned aircraft, which makes it a fully autonomous, robotic, non-human-centred system in which the human being has no critical role anymore.

In other words, autonomy is the ability to perform intended tasks in complex environments without input by a human. For autonomous flight, the necessary technological elements have proven to be capable of fully controlling an unmanned aircraft within its normal flight envelope and have demonstrated that automated aircraft control systems include relevant software being far more computationally competent than a human pilot.

But, if hazards or threats are detected, will the automation be able to cope with potentially unsafe situations? In any case, contingency management must be more than the so-called intelligent cockpit assistant or man-machine cooperation, in which the human will remain central. This automated support for cognitive human tasks such as problem solving and decision making under difficult conditions in an adverse environment has not been proven to rule out pilot error. It can even lead to overconfidence and complacency.

Taking robot inputs into account, the next question arises: can actions performed completely autonomously, such as in-flight planning, decision making, monitoring or studying trends, making predictions, recognizing complex emergency situations and problem solving by advanced computer technologies, entirely prevent (robotic) errors under similar harsh conditions at all times?

The difference between automation and various levels of autonomy must be clear. Modern aircraft rely increasingly on automation; however, this workload reducing feature can lead to an aircraft entering an undesirable state from which it is difficult or even impossible to recover from using traditional hand-flying techniques. The reason for this anomaly is that basic manual and cognitive flying skills can easily deteriorate due to a lack of practice and feel for the aircraft.

Automation means that the machine has no say in what happens to the aircraft. These aircraft perform by means of tools through human inputs, and are certified for autonomous flights, including take-off and landing. This type of machine has some control but mainly has an assistant role, while the pilot is in command. This is considered the intermediate level, mainly performed by only a single pilot. The human being as decision maker, *in casu* the aircraft commander, manages normal, abnormal and emergency flight situations, continuously backed up by a virtual assistant. An advanced derivative thereof is the remotely piloted aircraft operating in non-segregated airspace.

At full autonomy, the machine has full control, eliminating the need for a pilot. If an onboard or remote pilot is involved at all, the future smart machine can even override the aircraft commander's decision. For now, the question remains between the real and unreal on this topic. It should be noted that, in order to steer this seemingly precarious development in the right direction, the need for international regulations on AI application in general and its use in fully autonomous vehicles in particular is great. Eventually, due to adequate regulations, fully autonomous aircraft at this high level are quite capable of controlling and managing any cockpit functions at all times, including human decision making under any circumstances.

The functionality of fully autonomous aircraft control is implemented through machine-learning algorithms, the main underlying technology. To reach the level of capabilities analogous to that of the human brain, machine processing will have to match that of the human brain in memory, thinking speed, creativity and quality patterns of algorithms, taking into account the human capabilities and limitations.

In a full autonomy scenario, very powerful algorithms will be required to enable this technological achievement, together with the associated ultra-complex decision making processes, even under abnormal, unexpected aircraft operating conditions, to ensure safe flight and landing. But even in this setting, 100% flight safety cannot be guaranteed.

However, it is society that needs to be persuaded to accept and legitimate fully autonomous aircraft systems. Moreover, still of utmost importance, the predominant question remains: when will the aircraft commander with all the powers be made redundant, if ever? Sometime in the (far) future, there will be an answer to this pressing question.

Summary

The complex mechanism of the modern aviation system can only function through dedication, willpower, combined efforts and teamwork of countless individuals. Among those who are part of this collaborative strive, the aircraft commander occupies a rather exceptional position. During the flight, the aircraft commander shall have full authority and responsibility over the entire operation and safety of the aircraft, crew members, passengers and cargo, and shall maintain good order and discipline with regard to all occupants on board.

In the texts of ancient formal documents, legal instruments, reports and minutes on the subject of the legal status of the aircraft commander, the designation 'he' was for a long time dominant. This was prompted by the fact that in the early days of aviation, there was a typical man's bastion that restricted most women and allowed them to work only in support roles in the aviation industry. Especially in those days, the personification of the aircraft commander was a man, a tough but well-respected aviator.

However, as more women took up flying positions, particularly in the second half of the twentieth century, due to the inspiring effect of legendary female aviators, but also in a time characterized by societal changes and increasing educational and job opportunities for women, emancipation gained ground. Equality manifested also in aviation-related organizations and formal documents as the International Civil Aviation Organization (ICAO) Annexes.

While it is undoubtedly useful and necessary to study the authority and Legal Status of the Aircraft Commander from a theoretical, scholarly perspective, it is imperative to examine the issue from the practitioner's point of view as well. After all, the aircraft commander holds a key position in international air transportation and has rights and duties under public and private international law. Safety, efficiency and punctuality of the flight are largely dependent on his or her skills, experience, competence, alertness and judgement.

Although a large number of supranational (European Union) and national aviation laws and regulations contain provisions relating to the powers and duties of the aircraft commander, for example to maintain order and discipline on board, these legal provisions are characterized by a great variety in structure and content. No matter how substantively applicable national legislation may be, its effect in principle will stop at the national border. In relation to this fact, if rules governing the legal status of the aircraft commander are to have any broad practical value, they must be internationally effective. This precondition makes it intelligible that they must be uniform and functional on a global scale.

Since the aircraft commander cannot make beneficial use of the powers conferred by his or her national laws while operating under other jurisdictions, international regulation is considered necessary to remedy these deficiencies. For this reason, an international convention determining the legal status of the aircraft commander, in relation to the important and responsible role he or she fulfils in international air transportation, would seemingly be an obvious solution. History shows that many years of lengthy studies, discussions, reports, drafts and negotiations on this subject have so far unfortunately proved infeasible.

The 1919 Paris Convention, the principal international convention governing aerial navigation, initiated the birth of international air transportation, albeit on a modest scale. What seemed like a futuristic idea a few years earlier was now transformed into reality. But this emerging mode of transportation, the carriage of passengers and goods by air, requires a leading person on board the aircraft, a commanding officer, which would imply, among others, authority and responsibility, preferably enshrined in law.

However, whatever the exact role of the aircraft commander in international air transportation may have been in the past, generally speaking, his or her legal status in private and public international law, and to some extent in national legislations, has been largely neglected until the late 1920s. In those days, the situation of aircraft commanders became increasingly involved in legal issues such as an accurate definition of their status in the discharge of their duties.

In 1931, CITEJA (*Comité International Technique d'Experts Juridiques Aériens*), an international legal body, originated on the initiative of the French Government at the 1925 First International Conference on Private Air Law, provisionally adopted a proposed convention dealing with the legal status of the aircraft commander. From the establishment of CITEJA until its liquidation and subsequent inclusion into the ICAO in 1947, the Fourth Commission of CITEJA has long been concerned with the legal status of the aircraft commander in particular and of the other aircraft crew members in general.

Year after year, the subject of the legal status of the aircraft commander was placed on the agenda of the ICAO Assembly and the Work Programme of the ICAO Legal Committee. This Committee continued work on the subject until 1959 at which point it came to the practical conclusion that the powers of the aircraft commander should be included in the Draft Convention on the Legal Status of the Aircraft.

The eventual confluence resulted in the adoption of the 1963 Tokyo Convention on Offences and Certain Other Acts Committed on Board Aircraft. Chapter III – Powers of the Aircraft Commander – is devoted to the rights and duties of the aircraft commander with regard to offences against penal law and acts which, whether or not they are considered offences, may or do jeopardize the safety of the aircraft or of persons or property therein or which may jeopardize good order and discipline on board, while in flight.

Meanwhile, a number of Annexes to the 1944 Convention on International Civil Aviation (Chicago Convention) have been amended with rules on the powers, duties and responsibilities of the aircraft commander, also known as the pilot-in-command as defined by ICAO. The detailed technical rules embodied in the Annexes are of particular importance to the aircraft commander in the exercise of his or her profession. Considering that there is perhaps no other form of human activity characterized by such an international interconnection as commercial air transportation, it should be clear that the existence of internationally accepted and applied standards and procedures will be the first essential requirement for safe and efficient air navigation.

CITEJA and ICAO provided for international air transport agreements on highly important topics. However, the widely expected Convention on the Legal Status of the Aircraft Commander never saw the light of day. A majority of the delegations of the ICAO Legal Committee, after endless deliberations at subsequent sessions, believed that there was no practical need for regulation of the subject in the form of an international legal instrument.

A minority had emphasized the need to clarify and define the role of the aircraft commander in the applicable Annexes and other ICAO documents, in particular with regard to acts of unlawful interference, and assistance in search and rescue (SAR) operations to aircraft in distress. Some delegations were of the opinion that there were many legal and operational issues related to the subject that required adequate resolution, in particular the rights and duties of the aircraft commander during the pre- and post-flight phases, security and safety measures on board, and recalled again the significance of the Tokyo Convention which had been reinforced and modified for years by successive international legal instruments.

Finally, the ICAO Legal Committee established that unless problems of sufficient magnitude and practical importance emerged, further study on the subject was not warranted, especially as the exercise of certain functions by the aircraft commander in a foreign State would violate national sovereignty.

The ICAO Panel of Experts on the Legal Status of the Aircraft Commander came to the conclusion that existing regulations on the subject were scattered across several instruments that did not solve all the issues raised by the aircraft commander's status, in particular the authority and responsibility prior to, during and after the flight. The argument was that any possible solution for these issues would be closely related to matters of absolute national sovereignty, and would in fact most likely impede international air transportation.

International air transportation benefits most from equality of opportunities and sound, safe and efficient flight operations, based on internationally adopted agreements, not least with regard to the legal status of the aircraft commander. However, a majority of the ICAO Panel of Experts believed that the development of a new international convention on the subject would not provide the same flexibility for future amendments as the ICAO Annexes can provide.

Rationally, the Panel of Experts eventually determined that, given the flexibility of improvements or amendments to certain ICAO Annexes, no further study on the legal status of the aircraft commander was considered necessary at the time. Moreover, it was rightly assumed that the practical need for a ratified regulation was not really felt by the international community. This assumption was based on the factuality that an international Convention on the Legal Status of the Aircraft Commander would not have received the necessary ratification to enter into force.

Therefore, the destiny of the legal status of the aircraft commander would depend entirely on the SARPs in the ICAO Annexes, despite the fact that these Annexes do not constitute a solid lawful basis for international recognition of this particular legal status.

In the 1950s, a substantial growth in international air transportation was observed. A growing number of passenger aircraft were flying scheduled intercontinental routes, mainly but not only over the high seas, and many more intracontinental routes, frequently crossing different territories of contiguous sovereign States.

Therefore, there were many questions concerning the legal status of the aircraft and criminal aspects of matters related to this subject. From a legal point of view, a comprehensive research should be made into the case of criminal acts committed on board aircraft flying through the airspace of a particular State, as well as over the high seas.

Questions in this regard concerning the jurisdictions of the State of registry, the State of landing or the State having sovereignty over the territory flown over and the legal rules of the high seas were considered highly relevant.

The importance of the legal status of the aircraft would then take precedence over the legal status of the aircraft commander. However, the issue of authority and responsibility of the aircraft commander with respect to governmental agencies outside the aircraft was a sensitive one. A delicate balance needs to be struck between the powers of the aircraft commander and those of the sovereign State. In the years following this development, the need to prepare an international legal instrument against criminal acts committed on board aircraft including clear provisions concerning the powers of the aircraft commander became therefore extremely evident.

The Tokyo Convention has its origins in a 1950 study project by the ICAO Legal Committee and one of its Subcommittees. To this basic project, originally as conceptually wide as its name 'The Legal Status of the Aircraft', parts of a draft convention with the title

'Legal Status of the Aircraft Commander' were added. Both drafts were in fact superimposed documents. The connecting factor between the two topics of the study project, to eventually merge corresponding provisions into a single convention, was their relationship with crimes committed on board aircraft.

The changing global social landscape, the general increase in violence, in particular emerging criminal acts, unruly and disruptive behaviour of persons on board civil aircraft, caused the legal position of the aircraft commander to adapt to this 'new order'. The public law element in the cockpit could no longer be ignored because it is not surprising that the aircraft commander, as the competent authority on board the aircraft, carefully curbs these violations with the intention of attempting, often with the assistance from the crew and passengers, to remedy and de-escalate the situation on board so as not to jeopardize the safety of the aircraft, its crew and the passengers.

The aircraft commander, whether manipulating the aircraft controls or not, is responsible for the operation of that aircraft in accordance with the rules of the air, except that he or she may depart from these specific rules in circumstances that render such departure unconditionally necessary in the interest of the safety of the aircraft, crew and passengers. In exceptional situations, the aircraft commander is also entitled to invoke force majeure.

In case of unlawful interference or disruption during flight, the aircraft commander holds the powers, in particular but not only under national law, to use reasonable measures, including coercion such as stopping and arresting a suspect in the act, or in the absence of a law enforcement official on-site, to interrogate and search an alleged offender.

However, numerous public international law efforts have failed to reach consensus on a comprehensive codified Legal Status of the Aircraft Commander. While the Tokyo Convention has even included the powers of the aircraft commander in certain provisions, the question of his or her legal status is only partially settled.

The purpose of the Tokyo Convention is to protect the safety of the aircraft or of the persons or property therein and to maintain good order and discipline on board, while the aircraft is engaged in international air navigation. The activities regulated under the Convention fall into two categories: (a) offences against penal law and (b) acts which, whether they are not offences, may or do jeopardize the safety of the aircraft or of persons or property therein or which jeopardize good order and discipline on board.

The aircraft commander, other crew members and, under specific conditions, even passengers on board, are empowered to prevent the commission of acts, which in the opinion of the aircraft commander, would constitute serious offences under the penal law of the State of registry of the aircraft, and to restrain the alleged person (or persons) in question. The aircraft commander may also disembark that person or, if to his opinion (whom he has reasonable grounds to believe, according to the original 1963 text of the

Tokyo Convention), the offence in question is serious, deliver that person to the competent authorities of any Contracting State in the territory of which the aircraft has landed.

For actions taken in accordance with the Tokyo Convention, neither the aircraft commander, any other member of the crew, any (assisting) passenger, nor the person on whose behalf the flight was operated shall be held responsible in any proceeding on account of the treatment undergone by the person against whom the measures have been taken.

Whereas the Tokyo Convention in the first place applies to offences and other acts prejudicial to good order and discipline on board, the swift increase in unlawful seizure of aircraft by violence, sabotage and armed attacks on civil aviation targets in the sixties and seventies of the twentieth century called for a much wider range of security measures and provisions to be able to safeguard airline passengers, crew members, airport ground personnel and the general public in Contracting States.

Supplementary specialized international legal instruments to the Tokyo Convention such as the 1970 The Hague Convention for the Suppression of Unlawful Seizure of Aircraft (the so-called Anti-Hijacking Convention), the 1971 Montreal Convention for the Suppression of Unlawful Acts against the Safety of Civil Aviation (the so-called Sabotage Convention), the 1988 Montreal Protocol for the Suppression of Unlawful Acts of Violence at Airports Serving International Civil Aviation (the so-called Airport Protocol), the 2010 Beijing Convention on the Suppression of Unlawful Acts Relating to International Civil Aviation, the 2010 Beijing Protocol Supplementary to The Hague Convention, and the 2014 Montreal Protocol to Amend the Tokyo Convention (the so-called Unruly Passenger Protocol) have been adopted and entered into force over time to curb all kinds of threats against international civil aviation.

With regard to the decision making process during the flight operation, the aircraft commander, as the decisive authority on board is of crucial importance for the safe, efficient and regular conduct of this kind of operation. As the principal of a small but relatively isolated community, he or she occupies a determinant position when it comes to aeronautical decision making (ADM), in other words, the importance of good pilot judgement performed in a dynamic and complex environment. This type of decision making builds upon the foundation of conventional or traditional human decision making, but will enhance the process to mitigate the likelihood of pilot error.

Decision making in an aeronautical environment includes any pertinent decision a pilot must make while conducting the flight. This particular domain of aviation is considered a dynamic and complex, but above all safety-critical endeavour where making decisions can affect the lives of hundreds of people and have extraordinary economic and social impacts.

An apparently successful decision made in such an environment, characterized by, among other things, poorly structured problems, uncertainty, high stakes with high levels of risk and time constraints, might not necessarily be the optimal or most rational decision. It is the decision that the person in question understands and knows how to apply effectively.

The process of ADM consists of gathering and reviewing all available information, analyse and rate the applicable options, select a course of action and evaluate that course of action for correctness. It covers all aspects of decision making in the cockpit and identifies the steps involved in good decision making. ADM is strongly dependent on the flight crew's situational awareness which determines the solutions which will be considered and which available alternatives are known to the flight crew.

More specifically, situational awareness in complex operational environments is considered to be highly dependent on the flight crew's knowledge of specific task-related events and various phenomena. Maintaining situational awareness requires accurate perception and understanding of the relative significance of all flight-related factors and their future impact on the flight.

The decisive human element, in particular the aircraft commander, who explicitly makes crucial decisions in the interest of aviation safety, is the most compliant, flexible, interpretable and valuable individual in the entire aviation industry, but at the same time, the most vulnerable aviation professional to influences which can adversely affect his or her attitude and functioning in general, and decision making in particular. Coping well with different circumstances on board the aircraft mainly depends on acquired qualities such as leadership, knowledge, experience, skills and rational judgement of the aircraft commander.

The leadership role of the aircraft commander is essential with regard to optimal interaction between crew members, which means motivated crew coordination and teamwork resulting in more effective crew performance. Especially during high workloads, usually in demanding conditions, despite the aforementioned acquired qualities, the aircraft pilot, especially the aircraft commander with far-reaching responsibilities, is the most vulnerable to the risk of making (fatal) errors and, as a result, the rather controversial possibility of prosecution and punishment as well as civil liability (generally in the capacity of the employee).

Safety in international air transportation is at a significantly high level, *inter alia*, thanks to voluntary, though confidential, reporting of occurrences, including errors, unsafe situations or serious incidents. In the current thinking about civil aviation safety management, reporting of safety-related occurrences together with incident and accident investigation reports is extremely essential, in particular to further enhance protection against possible recurrence through adequate recommendations and subsequent actions.

The concept of just culture, a culture in which frontline operators or others are not punished for actions, omissions or decisions made by them in accordance with their experience and training, but in which gross negligence, wilful violations and destructive actions are not tolerated, has already become a commonly accepted, though not yet universally defined, phrase to express the intercourse with safety provisions that have become common usage within various domains such as civil aviation.

Most international air transportation incidents and accidents have resulted from significantly less than optimal performance, commonly classified as human errors. These human errors cannot be helpful in the prevention of civil aviation accidents. However, they may give an indication of where a fault in the system occurs although they do not provide any guidance why such a breakdown occurs. In civil aviation, human factors are meant to better understand how people can most safely and efficiently integrate with technology. Multiple human factors and external conditions may influence the manifestation of human error in any organization, but especially in the civil aviation industry.

Human factors in aviation is about people in their working situation, about their interaction on the human-machine interface or human-hardware interface, in which the human individual is the most important component, including ergonomics, displays and correct location and movement of cockpit controls, but also their interface with nonphysical features of aircraft systems (liveware-software) such as procedures, computer programmes, rules, manuals and symbology, and their relationship with environmental aspects, the liveware-environment interface. This interface means human-related biological, bodily rhythms, disturbances induced by external and internal environmental effects. Of utmost importance for humans is their mutual relationship, the liveware-liveware interface, which is all about the process of interaction between people affecting crew effectiveness and can be distinguished in people aspects related to physical knowledge, attitudes and cultures, and in team aspects dealing with crew teamwork, leadership and command, coordination and communication as well as personality interactions.

The term 'human factors' is defined as a multidisciplinary effort to generate and collect information about human capabilities and limitations and to apply that information to equipment, systems, facilities, manuals, procedures, environment, jobs, training, staffing and management of personnel for safe, comfortable and effective human performance. Factors such as workload, stress, vigilance, pressure, time constraints, situational awareness and sensory limitations can influence decision making, which in itself is a decisive factor.

Controlling, basically reducing human error on board an aircraft in flight, travelling at high speeds, cruising at high flight levels and over ultra-long distances, while exposed to ozone levels, radiation hazards and insidious performance reduction by circadian dysrhythmia or jet lag, sleep disturbance and deprivation, stress, fatigue, certain medication, tranquilizers, nutritional state and the potential use of narcotics or any other factors affecting physiological and psychological human well-being, human performance or fitness, is a huge and harsh challenge.

In human endeavours involving complicated enterprises, such as civil aviation, the vulnerability to making errors is considerably high, despite the ability to eliminate such errors by focusing on flight safety issues. Modern aircraft increasingly rely on automation, the single most important advancement in aviation technologies, but this innovative technique of controlling an aircraft in flight can unfortunately also cause serious incidents or even fatal accidents. Given that fact, there are concerns about the effect of automation on air transport pilots. Therefore, future cockpits should be designed to provide automation that is human-centred rather than technology driven. Regarding this vital safety aspect, it is stated that cockpits are designed to provide automation to assist, but not to replace members of the flight crew.

However, the pilot's involvement in the pure flying of the aircraft is more or less degraded to a monitoring role. To some extent, this seemingly passive role will generally make pilots more complacent. As a possible side effect, this automation-related complacency could easily lead to flight safety concerns such as the insidious neglect of knowledge of basic aerodynamics and flying skills, especially traditional hand-flying techniques. It is particularly the loss of these techniques that can lead to fatal human errors. Therefore, automation, basically the technology-oriented approach to automatic flight, can create a whole new set of pilot errors, unless human factors are skilfully identified and properly addressed. In addition, pilots should be aware of relationships between aircraft and environmental phenomena, in this case atmospheric features such as thunderstorms that can be associated with conditions conducive to icing and turbulence. In the sphere of influence of these phenomena, situational awareness is a crucial human factor in effective decision making.

Generally, effectiveness means identifying what needs to be done and the chosen criterion being the relevant one. With respect to situational awareness in aviation, researchers assumed that errors induced by a pilot's overall mental image can be classified into one of three major categories: level 1, failure to correctly perceive the information, level 2, failure to comprehend the correct situation, and level 3, failure to project the situation into the future.

The human factor has become increasingly popular as the aviation industry realized that human error, rather than mechanical failure, underlies the majority of aviation incidents and accidents. Yet, the level of flight safety, achieved by major airlines in most countries around the world, is one of the greatest success stories of today's digitized aviation industry. In the chain of the vital links such as design, testing, manufacturing, training, maintenance and operational use of commercial aircraft, humans are ultimately responsible for this success of the aviation industry.

To err is human, even or perhaps especially, in an automated digital environment such as modern aviation. Although very rarely, highly experienced professional pilots make errors; in the worst-case scenario, the errors are fatal to themselves, passengers and other crew members and third parties on the surface. Human errors during flight operations, *in casu* pilot errors, reflect that anybody acting in a flight support capacity can contribute to the error chain. Pilot error generally refers to an aircraft accident where an action or decision by the pilot, usually the aircraft commander, was the cause or contributing factor leading to the accident.

If human error in the cockpit is the cause of most aviation accidents, then should we not remove the human out of it? An interesting but at the same time controversial question. Modern time advanced automation is well capable of performing almost all of the functions needed to be done in the aircraft cockpit. However, even with the aid of highly advanced technologies, the human-centred automation principles will remain central to flight operations. These essential principles should ideally minimize the likelihood of errors. In practice, it is an overriding rule that people remain responsible for the safety of aircraft operations, whether the pilot is flying the aircraft remotely or is physically present and working in the cockpit.

While humans are far from being perfect sensors, it should be known that aircraft commanders in particular, as professional decision-makers, possess a number of invaluable qualities, the most important of which is the ability to reason effectively in the face of uncertainty and their capacities for abstract and conceptual analyses of an emergency. People, regarded as intelligent beings faced with an unexpected undefined situation, can provide a degree of flexibility that cannot now and may never be achieved by computational systems.

Except in predefined situations, automation should never assume command and it should be easy to be discontinued in those situations, which means that automation must remain subordinate to the human supervisor. On the other hand, it has been proven that fully autonomous flight operations of conventional manned aircraft and unmanned aircraft systems are feasible from a pure technological viewpoint. For contemporary conventional aircraft, a gradual transition trajectory to the concept of single-pilot operations (SiPO), which means that the entire flight will be carried out by one pilot on board using a virtual pilot assistant system. This new concept will be a viable though debatable scenario. In the context of reduced crew operations (RCO), this SiPO concept is preceded by extended minimum crew operations.

In this respect, the idea is to have two pilots in the cockpit for the more demanding parts of the flight, such as take-off and landing, but solo flying would be possible in the less demanding cruise phase of the flight. The assistant system performs a real-time assessment of the solo-pilot's cognitive state and provides useful and timely alerts based on predictions of that particular pilot's performance level.

Meanwhile, technological developments as an added value must aim to raise flight safety to an even higher level, although the single-pilot concept nullifies that safety step upwards. To the current state of affairs, technology is not a replacement for pilots. It undermines the level of flight safety when it comes to managing complex situations such as a not inconceivable sudden incapacitation of the only pilot on board where automation must be able to take full control of the aircraft, including decision making, thereby shifting the responsibility to the automation technology chain, a typical matter of shared responsibility.

With regard to the concept of single-pilot air transportation, according to various reports on flight safety, some parties within the aviation industry want to put profit before safety. In this way, however, the carefully established high level of safety will be uncompromisingly, not to say bluntly, eroded by short-term monetary gain. But above all, it will most likely lead to a dangerous increase in pilot responsibility and accountability.

A review about modern aircraft cockpits shows that various technical systems take over tasks previously performed by the flight crew. This new concept caused the pilot to move away from actually flying the aircraft to the tasks of programming and monitoring the aircraft automation. But the irony of automation is that the psychological effects, like diminished attention, boredom, automation complacency and overreliance, of the monitoring pilot due to the rather passive role, can create multiple safety problems.

However, if human factors-related issues, such as the rather limited performance of the human as monitor and effects on motivation, are properly addressed, there may as well be a justification for automation. But, if hazards or threats are detected, will automation be capable of coping with potentially unsafe conditions?

Somehow, contingency management has to be more than the so-called intelligent virtual pilot assistant or the human-centred human-machine collaboration. Indeed, it has been empirically established that this computerized assistance for cognitive human tasks such as troubleshooting and decision making under challenging conditions in an adverse environment has not been proven to exclude pilot error.

Taking robot input into account, the following question arises: can actions taken completely autonomously like flight planning, monitoring trends, decision making, making predictions, recognizing complex emergencies and troubleshooting by advanced computer technologies, entirely prevent (robotic) errors at all times in comparable harsh conditions? To achieve analogous capabilities to those of the human brain, machine processing will have to match that of the human brain in memory, thinking speed, creativity and algorithm patterns and quality, taken into account the human capabilities and limitations.

In a fully autonomous scenario, incidentally, a distant but not inconceivable future reality, most powerful algorithms will be required to enable these technological advancements together with associated complex decision making processes, even under abnormal, unexpected aircraft operating conditions, to be able to ensure safe flight and landing.

Full autonomy in aviation means that the machine has full control and can override the pilot's decision, if a pilot is involved at all. But even in this seemingly unusual setting, 100% flight safety cannot be guaranteed. However, the first priority is to convince the public to accept and legitimize fully autonomous air transportation systems. Secondly, the overriding question remains: when will pilots be superfluous? Moreover, will these conditions represent a real step forward in civil air transportation? Sometime in the distant future, answers to these pressing questions will come.

BIBLIOGRAPHY

ARTICLES AND BOOKS

Abeyratne, R.I.R., *Aviation Security: Legal and Regulatory Aspects* (Milton Park, Abingdon, Oxon: Routledge, 1998).

Abeyratne, R.I.R., *Legal Priorities in Air Transport* (Cham: Springer Nature, 2019).

Adams, R., "The Future of Flight," (2019) *Uniting Aviation – News and Features by ICAO*, 5 July 2019.

Amati, G., "Boeing's CEO Believes The 737 Max Will Get A Certification Extension," (2022) *Simply Flying News*, 26 September 2022.

Atkins, E., Director of U-M's Autonomous Aerospace Systems (A2SYS) Lab, "The Future of Autonomous Aircraft," (2020) *College of Engineering* (University of Michigan, 1 December 2020).

Baddeley, A.D., *Essentials of Human Memory*, Classic Edition (Hove, East Sussex: Psychology Press, 2014).

Bantekas, I., "Criminal Jurisdiction of States under International Law," (2011) *Max Planck Encyclopedias of Public International Law* [MPEPIL].

Barnhart, R.K., *et al*, *Introduction to Unmanned Aircraft Systems* (Boca Raton, FL: CRC Press, 2012).

Beaty, D., *The Human Factor in Aircraft Accidents* (New York: Stein and Day Publishers, 1969).

Bouvé, C.L., "Regulation of International Air Navigation under the Paris Convention," (1935) 6 *J. Air L. & Com.* 299.

Boyle, R.P., Pulsifer, R., "The Tokyo Convention on Offences and Certain Other Acts Committed on Board Aircraft," (1964) 30 *J. Air L. & Com.* 305.

Cohn, P., *et al*, "Commercial Drones Are Here: The Future of Unmanned Aerial Systems," (2017) *McKinsey & Company*, December 2017.

Cooper, J.C., "United States Participation in Drafting Paris Convention 1919," (1951) 18 *J. Air L. & Com.* 266.

Dannenberger, N., *et al*, "Traffic Solution or Technical Hype? Representative Population Survey on Delivery Drones and Air Taxis in Germany," Unpublished. doi: 10.13140/RG.2.2.17542.40003. Project: The Sky is the Limit: Future use of urban airspace (*Sky Limits*) by Kellermann, R., *et al* (01/19-12/20).

Dempsey, P.S., "Compliance & Enforcement in International Law: Achieving Global Uniformity in Aviation Safety," (2004) 30 *N. C. J. Int. L.*1.

Denaro, J.M., "In-Flight Crimes, the Tokyo Convention, and Federal Judicial Jurisdiction," (1969) 35 *J. Air L. & Com.* 171.

De Saussure, H., Fenston, J., "Conflicts in the Competence and Jurisdiction of Courts of Different States to Deal with Crimes Committed on Board Aircraft," (1952) I *McGill L. J.* 66, 69.

Dharani, K., *The Biology of Thought, a Neural Mechanism in the Generation of Thought – A New Molecular Model* (London: Academic Press, Elsevier, 2015).

Diederiks-Verschoor, I.H.Ph., Butler, M.A. (Legal advisor), *An Introduction to Air Law*, Eighth Revised Edition (Alphen aan den Rijn: Kluwer Law International, 2006).

Draper, R.A., "Transition from CITEJA to the Legal Committee of ICAO," (1948) 42(1) *Am. J. Int. L.* 155-157.

Earhart, A.M., *The Fun of It* (New York: Harcourt Brace and Company, 1932).

Flin, R., *et al*, Position Paper "Development of the NOTECHS (non-technical skills) System for Assessing Pilot's CRM Skills," in *Human Factors and Aerospace Safety, an International Journal*, Vol. 3, No. 2 (Harris, D., Muir, H.C., Editors-in-Chief) (Milton Park, Abingdon, Oxon: Routledge, 2018).

Gander, P., *et al*, "Fatigue Risk Management: Organizational Factors at the Regulatory and Industry/Company Level," (2011) 43(2) *Accid. Anal. Prev.* 573-590. doi:10.1016/j. aap.2009.11.007.

Gawron, V., "Nothing Can Go Wrong – A Review of Automation-Induced Complacency Research," (2019) *MITRE* Technical Report, January 2019.

Herber, B.P., "The Common Heritage Principle: Antarctica and the Developing Nations," (1991) 50(4) *Am. J. Econ. Soc.* 391-406.

Hodgkinson, D., Johnston, R., *Aviation Law and Drones: Unmanned Aircraft and the Future of Aviation* (Milton Park, Abingdon, Oxon: Routledge, 2018).

Honig, J.P., *The Legal Status of Aircraft* (The Hague: Martinus Nijhoff, 1956).

Hörmann, H.J., *FOR-DEC-A Prescriptive Model for Aeronautical Decision Making* in Fuller, R., Johnston, N. & McDonald, N. (Eds.) *Human factors in aviation operations. Proceedings of the 21ˢᵗ Conference of the European Association for Aviation Psychology (EAAP)*, (Andershot, UK: Avebury Aviation, 1995), Vol. 3, pp. 17-23.

Hufnagel, S., *Cross-Border Cooperation in Criminal Matters*, Oxford Bibliographies International Law, Transnational Criminal Law (New York: Oxford University Press, 2014).

Ide, J.J., "The History and Accomplishment of the International Technical Committee of Aerial Legal Experts (CITEJA)," (1932) 3 *J. Air L. & Com.* 27.

Jones, D.G., Endsley, M.R., "Sources of Situational Awareness Errors in Aviation." (1996) 67(6) *Aviat. Space Environ. Med.* 507-512.

Kamminga, M.S., *The Aircraft Commander in Commercial Air Transportation* (The Hague: Martinus Nijhoff, 1953).

Knauth, A.W., "The Citeja Meeting in Paris in January, 1939," (1939) 10 *J. Air L. & Com.* 167.

Knauth, A.W., "The Aircraft Commander in International Law," (1947) 14 *J. Air L. & Com.* 157.

Li, W-C., *et al*, "The Evaluation of Pilot's Situational Awareness During Mode Changes on Flight Mode Annunciators," (2016) *Safety and Accident Investigation Center, Cranfield University*, Bedfordshire, UK.

Loudon, R., Moriarty, D., "Rethinking the Briefing: Alaska Airlines Revamps Approach and Departure Briefings to Focus on Flight-Specific Threats," (2017) *Aero Safety World*, July-August 2017.

Mackenzie, D., *A History of the International Civil Aviation Organization* (Toronto: University of Toronto Press, 2010).

Mankiewicz, R.H., "The Legal Committee – Its Organization and Working Methods," (1966) 32 *J. Air L. & Com.* 94.

Mankiewicz, R.H. (Ed.), *Yearbook of Air and Space Law 1967, Institute of Air and Space Law McGill University* (Montreal: McGill-Queen's University Press, 1970).

Martinussen, M., Hunter, D.R., *Aviation Psychology and Human Factors*, Second Edition (Boca Raton, FL: CRC Press Taylor & Francis Group, 2018).

Mendes de Leon, P.M.J., "The Legal Force of ICAO SARPs in a Multilevel Jurisdictional Context," *Journaal Luchtrecht*, Special Edition No. 2-3 June 2013 (Schnitker, R.M., Ed.) The Hague: Sdu Publishers.

Mendes de Leon, P.M.J., *Introduction to Air Law*, Eleventh Edition (Alphen aan den Rijn: Kluwer Law International, 2022).

Milde, M., "News from International Organizations – ICAO Forthcoming Panel of Experts on the Legal Status of the Aircraft Commander, 9-22 April 1980," (1980) 5(1) *Air Space Law*.

Milde, M., "News from International Organizations – ICAO Report on the Meeting of the Panel of Experts – Legal Status of the Aircraft Commander, Montreal, 9-22 April, 1980," (1980) 5(3) *Air Space Law*.

Ostroumov, I.V., Kuzmenko, N.S., *Applications of Artificial Intelligence in Flight Management Systems*, and Sikirda, Y., Kasatkin, M., Tkachenko, D., *Intelligent Automated System for Supporting the Collaborative Decision Making by Operations of the Air Navigation System during Flight Emergencies* in Shmelova, T., Sikirda, Y., Sterenharz, A. (Eds.) *Handbook of Research on Artificial Intelligence Applications in the Aviation and Aerospace Industries* (Hersley, PA: IGI Global, 2020).

Pakush, C., Bossauer, P., "User Acceptance of Fully Autonomous Public Transport," *Department of Management Sciences, Bonn-Rhein-Sieg University*, Sankt Augustin, Germany, ICE-B 2017 14th International Conference on e-Bussiness.

Polkowska, M., "Unruly Passengers ICAO Cir. 288 Update," (2017) (34) *Revista Europea de Derecho de la Navegación Marítima y Aeronáutica*.

Reason, J.T., *Managing the Risk of Organizational Accidents* (Milton Park, Abingdon, Oxon: Routledge Taylor & Francis Group, 2016).

Rokutani, J., *Double Jeopardy, Self-Incrimination and Due Process of Law: The Fifth Amendment* (New York: Enslow Publishing, 2018).

Rosteck, T., "Robots Need More Human Skills: Connected and Equipped With Sensors and AI Capabilities, Machines Can Cooperatively Work With People. Together, They Can Increase Productivity and Sustainability," (2022) *IoT World Today*, 13 May 2022.

Salas, E., Maurino, D. (Eds.), *Human Factors in Aviation*, Second Edition (Burlington, MA: Academic Press, 2010).

Samuelson, N.B. (Lieutenant Colonel), "Equality in the Cockpit, a Brief History of Women in Aviation," (1984) 35 *Air Univ. Rev.* 4.

Sand, P.H., "The International Unification of Air Law," (1965) in *Law and Contemporary Problems*, Vol. 30, No. 2, Spring (Durham, NC: Duke University School of Law).

Schnitker, R.M., van het Kaar, D., *Aviation Accident and Incident Investigation, Concurrence of Technical and Judicial Inquiries in The Netherlands*, Essential Air and Space Law, Vol. 9 (Benkö, M.E., Series Editor) (The Hague: Eleven International Publishing, 2010).

Shubber, S., *Jurisdiction Over Crimes on Board Aircraft* (The Hague: Martinus Nijhoff, 1973).

Signal, T.L., *et al*, "Mitigating and Monitoring Flight Crew Fatigue on Westward Ultra-Long-Range Flights," (2014) 85 *Aviat. Space Environ. Med.* 1199-1208.

Soler, C., *The Global Prosecution of Core Crimes under International Law* (The Hague: T.M.C. Asser Press, 2019).

Sopilko, I. (National Aviation University, Kyiv, Ukraine), Shevechuk, Y. (University of Cambridge), "Jurisdiction over Crimes Committed on Board Aircraft in Flight under the Tokyo Convention 1963," (Proceedings of the National Aviation University, 2016), Vol. 69, No. 4. doi:10.18372/2306-1472.69.11064.

Tiewtrakul, T., Fletcher, S.R., "The Challenge of Regional Accents for Aviation English Language Proficiency Standards: A Study of Difficulties in Understanding in Air Traffic Control-Pilot Communications," (2010) 53(2) *Ergonomics* 229-239. doi:10.1080/00140130903470033.

Van Steenberghe, R., *Aut Dedere Aut Judicare*, Oxford Bibliographies. International Law (New York: Oxford University Press, 2013).

Van Wijk, A.A., "The Legal Status of the Aircraft Commander – Ups and Downs of a Controversial Personality in International Aviation" in *Essays in Air Law* (Kean, A., Ed.) (The Hague: Martinus Nijhoff Publishers, 1982).

Volpe, J.A., Stewart, J.T. Jr., "Aircraft Hijacking: Some Domestic and International Responses," (2017) 59(2) *Ky. J.* Article 3.

Wallis, R., *How Safe Are Our Skies? Assessing the Airlines' Response to Terrorism* (Westport, CT: Praeger Publishers, 2003).

Werfelman, L., "Intentionally Noncompliant: LOSA Data Show That Purposely Skipping a Checklist or Ducking Under a Glideslope Can Lead to Bigger Problems," (11 December 2013) *AeroSafety World*, Flight Safety Foundation, December 2013-January 2014.

Werfelman, L., "In It for the Ultra-Long-Haul," (2015) *AeroSafety World*, Flight Safety Foundation, April 2015.

Wollert, M., *Public Perception of Autonomous Aircraft*, A Thesis Presented in Partial Fulfillment of the Requirements for the Degree Master of Science in Technology (Arizona State University, May 2018).

Zsambok, C.E., Klein, G. (Eds.), *Naturalistic Decision Making* (New York: Psychology Press, 1997).

Documents

1936 U.S. Aviation Reports, Washington D.C., 15 June 1936 – CITEJA Report of the American Delegates, Paris meeting, February 1936.

1919 Paris Convention – *Convention Relating to the Regulation of Aerial Navigation*.

1928 Havana Convention – *Pan-American (or Inter-American) Convention on Commercial Aviation*.

1944 Chicago Convention – *Convention on International Civil Aviation*.

1963 Tokyo Convention – *Convention on Offences and Certain Other Acts Committed on Board Aircraft*.

1969 Vienna Convention on the Law of Treaties (VCLT).

1970 The Hague Convention – *Convention for the Suppression of Unlawful Seizure of Aircraft*.

1971 Montreal Convention – *Convention for the Suppression of Unlawful Acts against the Safety of Civil Aviation*.

1988 Montreal Protocol – *Protocol for the Suppression of Unlawful Acts of Violence at Airports Serving International Civil Aviation, Supplementary to the Convention for the Suppression of Unlawful Acts against the Safety of Civil Aviation*.

2010 Beijing Convention – *Convention on the Suppression of Unlawful Acts Relating to International Civil Aviation*.

2010 Beijing Protocol – *Protocol Supplementary to the Convention for the Suppression of Unlawful Seizure of Aircraft*.

2014 Montreal Protocol – *Protocol to Amend the Convention on Offences and Certain Other Acts Committed on Board Aircraft*.

Commission Implementing Regulation (EU) 2015/1018 of 29 June 2015 laying down a list classifying occurrences in civil aviation to be mandatorily reported according to

Regulation (EU) No. 376/2014 of the European Parliament and of the Council, L 163/1, 30.6.2015.

EASA Artificial Intelligence Roadmap: a human-centric approach to AI in aviation, February 2020, Version 1.0.

FAA Advisory Circular 60-22 Aeronautical Decision Making, 12/13/91.

FAA Pilot's Handbook of Aeronautical Knowledge FAA-H-8083-25B.

ICAO Circular 328-AN/190 Unmanned Aircraft Systems (UAS), 2011.

ICAO Doc. 9683-AN/950 Human Factors Training Manual, First Edition-1998.

ICAO Doc. 9966, Manual for the Oversight of Fatigue Management Approaches, Second Edition, 2016.

ICAO Doc. 9859-AN/474, Safety Management Manual (SMM), Third Edition-2013.

ICAO Doc. 9756-AN/965 Manual of Aircraft Accident Investigation, First Edition, 2011 – Part III Investigation and Second Edition, 2014 – Part IV Reporting.

ICAO Doc. A40-WP/268, EX/111, 1/8/19, Artificial Intelligence and Digitalization in Aviation.

ICAO Doc. 10117 Manual on the Legal Aspects of Unruly and Disruptive Passengers, First Edition, 2019.

ICAO Remotely Piloted Aircraft System (RPAS) Concept of Operations (CONOPS) for International IFR Operations.

Participation of the United States Government in International Conferences, 1 July 1946-30 June 1947, International Conferences: 1946-1947 Aviation. *United States Government Printing Office*, Washington: 1948.

Regulation (EU) 2018/1139 of the European Parliament and of the Council of 4 July 2018 on common rules in the field of civil aviation and establishing a European Union Aviation Safety Agency L 212/1, 22.8.2018.

Regulation (EU) No. 376/2014 of the European Parliament and of the Council of 3 April 2014 on the reporting, analysis and follow-up of occurrences in civil aviation, amending Regulation (EU) No. 996/2010 of the European Parliament and of the Council and repealing Directive 2003/42/EC of the European Parliament and of the Council and Commission Regulation (EC) No. 1321/2007 and (EC) No. 1330/2007, L 122/18, 24.4.2014.

Subcommittee on Resolution B of the Guadalajara Conference, (1963) 29 *J. Air L. & Com.* 241.

United Nations Juridical Yearbook 1964, U.N. New York.

About the Author

Dick van het Kaar LL.M. has been working in the aviation industry for more than 45 years. He started his flying career as a Royal Netherlands Air Force helicopter and jet fighter pilot and instructor. In 1977, he joined the world of commercial aviation and has logged more than 23,000 flying hours.

During his career as a Senior Captain on the Boeing 747 at KLM/Martinair, he studied public international law at the Open University of the Netherlands, where he earned his degree of Master of Laws.

Throughout much of his commercial aviation career, he was a member of the Appeal Council of the Dutch Airline Pilots Association. After serving an eight-year term as member of the Main Board as well as Chairman of the Legal Committee at the Royal Netherlands Aeronautical Association, he currently holds a position as senior adviser to the same organization in the field of Rules of the Air, Airspace Infrastructure and Environmental Affairs.

For several years, he was affiliated with the Aviation Academy of the Amsterdam University of Applied Sciences as an external examiner. In addition, he is the author of several aviation law-related research papers, books and treatises as well as articles in a large number of international air and space law journals.

Essential Air and Space Law (Series Editor: Marietta Benkö)

Volume 17: Tanveer Ahmad, Climate Change Governance in International Civil Aviation: Toward Regulating Emissions Relevant to Climate Change and Global Warming, ISBN 978-94-6236-692-3

Volume 18: Michael Milde, International Air Law and ICAO, third edition, ISBN 978-94-6236-619-0

Volume 19: Nataliia Malysheva, Space Law and Policy in the Post-Soviet States, ISBN 978-94-6236-847-7

Volume 20: Philippe Clerc, Space Law in the European Context, ISBN 978-94-6236-797-5

Volume 21: Benjamyn Scott, Aviation Cybersecurity: Regulatory Approach in the European Union, ISBN 978-94-6236-961-0

Volume 22: Dick van het Kaar, International Civil Aviation: Treaties, Institutions and Programmes, ISBN 978-94-6236-972-6

Volume 23: Lasantha Hettiarachchi, International Air Transport Association (IATA): Structure and Legitimacy of its Quasi-International Regulatory Power, ISBN 978-94-9094-758-3

Volume 24: Masataka Ogasawara & Joel Greer, Japan in Space, ISBN 978-94-6236-203-1

Volume 25: Ronald Schnitker & Dick van het Kaar, Drone Law and Policy, ISBN 978-94-6236-198-0

Volume 26: Marietta Benkö & Kai-Uwe Schrogl (eds.), Outer Space, Future for Humankind, ISBN 978-94-6236-225-3

Volume 27: Xiaodan Wu, China's Ambition in Space, ISBN 978-94-6236-277-2

Volume 28: Michael Milde, International Air Law and ICAO, revised and updated by Attila Sipos, fourth edition, ISBN 978-94-6236-622-0

Volume 29: Dick van het Kaar, The Aircraft Commander in International Air Transportation: Legal Powers, Duties and Decision Making, ISBN 978-90-4730-179-0